THE MEDIA
OF THE
REPUBLIC

Steele Wilson BOOKS

Steele Wilson Books
P.O. Box 372
Greensborough Victoria 3088
Email: stwilson@ozemail.com.au

First published 1999

Cover illustration and design Anna Wilson

Typeset in 11/13½ Plantin

Designed and typeset by
The Small Back Room
19 Sunset Avenue, Olinda 3788

Printed in Australia by
Openbook Publishers
205 Halifax Street, Adelaide 5000

National Library of Australia Cataloguing-in-Publication entry:

Charles, Gerard 1946 –
The Media of the Republic

ISBN 1 876262 06 0

1. Mass media criticism - Australia. 2. Mass media-Australia -
Moral and ethical aspects. I. Title.
070.430994

THE MEDIA
OF THE
REPUBLIC

Gerard Charles

Steele Wilson BOOKS

CONTENTS

IN COMMEMORATION

of the two hundred and first anniversary
of the death of Edmund Burke
at Beaconsfield, England,
9 July 1797

and

of the first anniversary of the death of
Diana, Princess of Wales,
killed in a car accident,
Paris, France,
31 August 1997

*T*here have been many internal revolutions in the government of countries, both as to persons and forms, in which neighbouring states have had little concern …

The present Revolution in France seems to me to be quite of another character and description, and to bear little resemblance or analogy to any of those which have been brought about in Europe, upon principles merely political. *It is a Revolution of doctrine and theoretic dogma.* It has a much greater resemblance to those changes which have been made upon religious grounds, in which a spirit of proselytism makes an essential part …

What direction the French spirit of proselytism is likely to take, and in what order it is likely to prevail in the several parts of Europe, it is not easy to determine. The seeds are sown almost everywhere, chiefly by newspaper circulation, infinitely more efficacious and extensive than they ever were. And they are a more important instrument than generally is imagined. They are part of the reading of all; they are the whole of the reading of the far greater number. There are thirty of them in Paris alone. The language diffuses them more widely than the English — though the English, too, are much read. The writers of these papers, indeed, for the greater part, are either unknown or in contempt, but they are like a battery, in which the stroke of any one ball produces no great effect, but the amount of continual repetition is decisive. *Let us only suffer any person to tell us his story, morning and evening, but for one twelve-month, and he will become our master.* [My emphasis.]

Edmund Burke, *Thoughts on French Affairs*, 1791

1

Sunday, 31 August 1997:
Diana is Killed

The death of Diana, Princess of Wales, is one of those events most people never forget — like the deaths of President Kennedy and Elvis Presley. You always remember precisely what you were doing at the very moment you heard the news. I still remember waking to hear the news of President Kennedy's death on the radio all those years ago. I still feel the atmosphere of our house, the solemn music playing on the radio, the grave voices of the news reports, and the apprehension and anxiety surrounding me. I would never have thought I would react in a similar way to the death of Princess Diana — even taking into account the terrible manner in which she met her death. A year later the impression of that tragic news and its aftermath had scarcely faded.

At around 10.20 a.m. on Sunday, 31 August, I walked into my sister's lounge room with my elderly parents. Most of the rest of my family were gathered in Sydney for a rare family get-together. My brother and his wife and another sister were looking intently at the TV as we were ushered in. 'Princess Diana's been in an accident,' my older brother said looking bewildered. Just then Jim Waley on the Channel 9 'SUNDAY' program was repeating a news flash. Diana and Dodi had been in an accident. Dodi was dead and Diana was seriously injured. We all stared in silence. Flicking from channel to channel we watched the news reports from still darkened European capitals until it was announced that Diana was dead. We were shocked. It was about 2.00 p.m. on a bright sunny Sunday afternoon in Sydney, Australia.

Later that afternoon I spoke to several people who had not had the radio or television on. I said immediately, 'Have you heard the news about Diana?' They reacted with stunned, silent shock. In the following days millions around the world from all countries and cultures would react in a similar way. But why were we all so shocked? There were a number of reasons, some more evident than others.

When I reflect on that Sunday I remember two thoughts continually turning around in my head. The first was about Prince Charles's feelings. How would he be reacting? I was sure he must have been feeling devastated. At the same time I was thinking of the persecution Charles and Diana had been forced to endure at the hands of the media through so many years. Many times I had exclaimed to family and friends that nobody could endure the spiteful hounding these two were facing. Nobody's life, not even the greatest saint's, could survive the constant scrutiny, the harassment, the gossip-mongering, the mockery, the ridicule, and the lies dogging their every move. Although Diana was in recent years far more hounded than Charles, Charles had been the most ridiculed, the most maligned and the most lied about public figure of any in my memory. There is now a Prince Charles mythology that has been built up over the years, a sort of magisterium of entertaining lies, distortions and misrepresentations that the media draw on when they turn their attention to him. I had always thought that the media would get both of them in the end. They got Diana. I suspect, one way or another, they'll get Prince Charles eventually.

One enduring image in the immediate aftermath of Diana's death was the television footage of Diana's brother, Earl Spencer, walking up the driveway to the front gates of his residence in South Africa and reading the following statement:

This is not a time for recrimination, but for sadness. However, I would say that I always believed the press would kill her in the end. Not even I could imagine that they would take such a direct hand in her death, as seems to be the case. It would appear that every proprietor and editor of every publication that has paid for intrusive and exploitative photographs of her, encouraging greedy and ruthless individuals to risk everything in pursuit of Diana's image, has blood on his hands today.

I could not find anybody who disagreed with this. The opposite. People enthusiastically agreed with it. The media were responsible at all levels. They had the choice of hounding or not hounding Diana.

They had the choice of paying or not paying for intrusive pictures. It was the photographers' decision to walk up and take the photos. It was their decision to ignore the pleading for respect, sympathy, and understanding. It was the copy editor and the picture editor's decision to run stories and pictures of an intrusive nature. It was their decision to ignore appeals to leave families in peace. What more can be said about the moral aspect of media hounding?[1] The media as a collective choose to ignore all moral prescriptions about privacy, sympathy, understanding, respect and goodwill. Most people think the media are a pack of hyenas who constantly gorge themselves on the lives of others in order to fill pages of newspapers and costly airtime on radio and television. And they are right. Money and power are the motivation — not an idealistic and relentless pursuit of the truth. The always serviceable 'free speech' arguments are the apparently impregnable shield for the media's money-grubbing actions. When truth appears it is merely coincidental. We need look no further than at what happened after the Mercedes carrying Diana, Dodi and their two security men crashed at high speed into a concrete pillar.[2]

Was that the occasion for the human breast to take over? Was that the time for the avenues to the heart to become unblocked? Was that the time for the human person to take pause, to drop the camera to the ground, to take stock of the human tragedy and to struggle to hold back the tears of remorse? No, it wasn't. Not even a bit. It was the time for the pack of media hyenas to go into a frenzy at the sight of the broken bodies in the Mercedes. Tourists and police have testified. The representatives of the media swarmed over the accident scene snarling at and savaging anybody who wanted to restrain them. In the midst of the scrambling around the smashed car two of the number clicked and snapped until their rolls of film were filled and then fled the scene.[3] Shortly after, at the Laurent Sola photo agency, three figures were almost beside themselves as their eyes dashed from photo to photo of the 30 to 40 snaps taken of the mangled crash scene. There were some clear shots of the fatally injured princess. The international bargaining over the princess's body started.

You control a pack of savaging hyenas by beating them back, leaving them cowed and seeking the first opportunity to break out all over again. And so it happened with the media who were frenziedly bargaining across continental Europe and the Atlantic. When the backlash against the media started in those countries bathing in the

full afternoon sun of 31 August, the media chiefs took fright and withdrew from the bargaining fearing for their livelihoods. Then coming
forward with hands over their breasts they said they would never entertain publishing such photos in the circumstances. Understandably,
Laurent Sola was indignant that only *his* greed and total lack of moral
feeling should be put on display. But mark my words, when they think
the opportunity is right, when they think there is no risk, like the hyenas they will be out again and hard at it. Those photos will be
published eventually.[4] The media will give reasons for publishing
them that will disgust the normal person.

It was this anger at the media that pervaded all my thinking for
the next few days. I was not the only one feeling angry. The number
of people around the world sharing my thoughts and feelings about
the treatment Diana received made me think for a while that perhaps
the media would back off. Perhaps the newspapers would at least, for
appearances sake, show some contrition. But there would be no such
display of contrition. Only a scrambling to justify their actions. I was
following the newspaper reports mainly in *The Australian* (from the
Murdoch stables) and by Wednesday, 3 September, my indignation at
what I was reading had reached a peak.[5] The collection of reports de-
flecting the blame from the media and attacking Prince Charles and
the royal family in this edition riled me so much that I sat down and
dashed off a letter to the editor. It was a fiery letter accusing the gentlemen of *The Australian* of hypocrisy and misrepresentation, of
self-serving ideology and self-aggrandisement, of using the death of
Princess Diana to promote a particular political agenda, and especially
to advance the material interests of their media empire. The editor of
The Australian may well run reports of the worldwide anger directed
at the paparazzi, but in reality the paparazzi were there to do the dirty
work for those on high. They and their media masters form a redoubt-
able team.

I did not send this letter. I thought (perhaps wrongly) that the letters editor would have had no time for a member of the public who
appeared unaware of the nature of fame and the media's relationship
with famous people. It was an angry letter but for all that it raised
substantial points that form the basis of what will follow in this work.
Indeed, I will be dealing extensively with the issue of the media's views
on fame and famous people. Outlined in a less emotive manner, these
are the main points raised:

- The media were entirely responsible for the death of the Princess of Wales.
- The actions of the media contradict traditional and instinctive moral thought and feeling.
- In our liberal-democratic system there is a ruling elite and their power, indeed their existence, depends on the continued ascendancy of republicanism *using the media as its mouthpiece*.
- The actions of the media are determined essentially by motives of power and greed. Ideology serves to buttress these motives.
- Traditional arrangements and traditional morality are the enemies of the ever-restless power-seeking ruling class. Their actions are indeed cloaked in moral rhetoric, but this does not reflect traditional morality but a set of ideas I shall call 'theoretic-republicanism'.
- By means of this set of ideas (theoretic-republicanism) traditional hierarchies have been gradually replaced by a ruling class with its own hammer-fisted hierarchy — right from a media aristocracy down through the ranks of media princes with their clerical support to the contemptible ideological flunkeys who do the (sometimes violent) dirty work.
- The media has seized on the death of Diana to promote the republican cause — as they understand republicanism. The killing of Diana has been a propaganda coup.

My object in this work will be to explain and justify these claims by providing evidence through an examination of the media reports following Princess Diana's death. An explanation of what I mean by 'theoretic-republicanism' will be crucial to this whole exercise.

The lapse of a year since Henri Paul lost control of the Mercedes has put a clarifying distance between the accident and our present reflection upon the event. The raw emotion of the time has been replaced by a more objective and closer examination of the event and its main players. Although I will be treating the reporting of the day in the context of the immediate time framework, the reader will not be able to avoid referring to the latest public information about the circumstances of the accident. But whatever the issues concerning the disputed details of the accident, I am concerned primarily with the media's treatment of the event. And it's not just an analysis of the actions of the media and of the theoretical backdrop to their reports that

I will embark upon. I will also be showing how the media typically respond to those who dissent from their assumptions about the world and who should govern it.

In this respect, I can already anticipate this latter task by pointing to a pattern of media behaviour that many will recognise immediately. If those whom I propose to attack are sufficiently disturbed by this work, their response through the media most likely will be to dismiss my claims as the ravings of the fanatic, of the ignorant, of the extreme right, of divisiveness, etc. It's a familiar litany of epithets.[6] Very often a balanced, reasoned response seems to have a low priority. On the other hand, if the media as the mouthpiece of the ruling elite is accused of bias, appeals are made to their innocence, to their idealism in going about their business of 'informing the public', of sacrificing themselves to bring 'the facts as they happen' to an unappreciative audience. The slogan about 'killing the messenger' will inevitably be trotted out, as if the media groups brought across the message *unchanged*.

The over-used media slogan about blaming the messenger for the content of an unpleasant message has it origins in ancient times when rulers or tribal chiefs communicated by special court envoys. Sometimes the message of one ruler to the other was so unacceptable that the messenger would become an innocent victim of the anger caused by the message. The feature that gives this saying its effective meaning is the passing on of the message *unchanged* by the messenger. But deliberately delivering the 'message' as received by a disinterested observer is not in the scheme of things for the media. We all know that. We all know that the message is modified to suit the objectives of the media organisation. We all know that we will never take a media report at face value — if we know what's good for us. When truth appears in the present media it is merely coincidental with predetermined aims. The task of the media consumer is to sort out what is coincidentally truthful.[7]

I am making the claim that the media is pervasively ideological and that ideology for the media has as its ultimate aim power and money, and class ascendancy. The coincidental appearance of truth in the media comes in two main forms. Firstly, facts may be embedded in a pervasively ideological piece. Any ideological apology has to incorporate factual information. It is the marshalling of the facts of any particular circumstance combined with ideological demonstration that reveals the skill of the ideological apologists. Secondly, facts may appear in an apparently neutral context but function ultimately in a tactical way. The clever propagandist is never so stupid as to beat his political drum in an even manner. The clever propagandist will know when to retreat and when to move forward. A propagandist bent on destroying the British royal house will have to determine how far he can go in his slander and mockery of an institution that is still admired and cherished the world over. He will know when to attack and when to retreat in mock obsequiousness. He will look for the breaches in the public's emotional make-up, those places where the heart can so easily be manipulated, and then will enter with all the tricks and stratagems at his disposal. Whatever the case, isolated fact is being manipulated for particular class aims.

If the media is looked at as a continuum both through time and across a particular time framework,[8] my claims will stand up. The evidence offered in this work aims to support these claims. But will I take the easy way out and seize on any old discredited rag for my purposes? No, let me take what is evidently considered one of Australia's most prestigious papers and a champion in the worldwide Murdoch stable: *The Australian*. We may take *The Australian* as representative of the Murdoch organisation worldwide and, in many respects, of the media as a whole. *The Australian* during the week following Diana's death drew on the instruments of the Murdoch empire around the world. In particular it drew on a number of important reports from *The Times*, London. For the purposes of this exercise I am going to examine the editions of *The Australian* covering Diana's death from 1 September to 9 September 1997. I will be referring to other media reports but will concentrate on the reports and articles in *The Australian* during this period.

The key to understanding the media's action in our 'liberal-democratic' system is understanding what theoretic-republicanism entails. Not all people who call themselves 'republicans' would accept the theoretical framework of theoretic-republicanism. What then is this 'world-vision' I am calling theoretic-republicanism?

2

Theoretic-Republicanism and Related Philosophical Issues

1. Theory and Theorising

The contents of this chapter may not seem directly related to an examination of particular media reports. I will ask the reader to bear with me because to understand the media's ideological assumptions is to understand the full scope of their actions. Very often the media is accused of a party political bias. This is not accurate. It's the ideological bias that's the key issue. Moreover, an understanding of the media's ideological assumptions may provide a greater insight into the way our society presently functions. A broader insight into the way the media conducts itself may also lead to a better understanding of how other institutions in our society are functioning — or not functioning.

The mention of 'theory' will arouse the interest of some readers. They will be curious to see how the arguments proceed and how well they stand up to their scrutiny. Feeling well acquainted with theory and theorising, they will feel equipped to pass judgement. The readers of this book will fall roughly into two groups, the first being a relatively small group in comparison with the other, and possessing power and influence in inverse proportion to their size.[1] The curious and confident theorist I just have mentioned belongs to the first group.

This group consists largely of graduates of our tertiary institutions. They are likely to have completed a major study in sociology, anthropology, or psychology, or to have been exposed to such disciplines in the course of their study or, less commonly, to have been provoked into such studies by the social 'inequities' they observe around them.

Their minds will have been trained in the 'scientific method'. They will have been trained to apply their reason rigorously and unrelentingly. The overlay of prejudice that had been built over the years prior to their selection for tertiary studies will have long been jettisoned as so much harmful baggage. The influences of their family, of their customs, of their national and historical traditions, and of their religion will have been dispensed with. They will proceed in their inquiries inductively and deductively and form beliefs that will continually attend the tribunal of their individual reason. Their constantly adjusted beliefs are brought together to form a theory about life that will guide them through the traps of prejudice and ignorance in the society around them.

Most readers trained in this manner may find their interest momentarily arrested by what they read here, but very quickly they will see not only the tenets of their own favourite theory implicitly challenged, they will see their very way of thinking coming under assault. Nevertheless, the strength of their training will not let them down. It will protect them from any doubt about their 'theoretical' position. They will find the flow of the argument unconvincing and even repugnant. They will deplore the absence of precise definition of terms, the lack of statistical and empirical evidence, and the neglect of case studies and favoured 'models'. They will be indignant that the 'latest' scientific research (i.e. the research they are familiar with) has not been mentioned let alone considered.

In addition, those that have refined the scientific method by advanced study and are familiar with the philosophical period I am covering may be appalled at the manner in which I attempt to abbreviate and combine philosophical works that are in some respects quite different. These readers may think at this stage the book worthy only of being ignored. At the risk of alienating some potential readers, I have to say that this book has not been written for them. I am writing for the second group. Even so, I would encourage the first group to persevere for they may find, despite the perceived theoretical and methodological failure, that they are to some extent in sympathy with the picture emerging of the Murdoch empire — however different their reasons are.

The second group consists of the intelligent reader who has most likely not been subjected to the rigours of the 'scientific method'. Or if he has, has managed to survive its influence. This person's thinking processes have been formed by the activity of daily existence. His logic is the logic of everyday life where purposes and values loom large in the thinking process and where family, customs and traditions and their prescriptive nature play a big role. If this person stops to reflect on his life and his daily activities, he rarely separates himself in complete abstraction; he is always part of actual events connected with his welfare and the welfare of others. He makes judgements about life in relation to the concrete circumstances. His judgements issue from a body of general principles which are abstracted from his concrete experiences but do not form a body of conclusive theory. Indeed, he would never think that the scope of his sometimes inexplicable life could be reduced to a series of theoretical propositions. He is the person who often looks upon the academic theorist as a 'wanker' and of little relevance to daily life. He is inclined, to the extent he thinks about it, to look upon the indulgent life of the universities as so much bludging.[2] It is this person that I am addressing and seeking to persuade.

In talking about theory in this chapter I am not aiming to outline yet another theory to counter the 'theorist' as I have described him above. I am aiming to show that theory is never just abstract theory, if it has any meaning at all. Its effective meaning takes it beyond a collection of words on paper; to be effective it leads to action. Thus I am attempting to indicate how 'theory' is used, how theory makes the transition from an *a priori* framework to concrete action, and that the action of theory is quite a different matter from the endless discussions provoked by the scientific method in tutorial rooms and lecture halls of universities.

2. The Age of Reason

The differences in reasoning I have just outlined are reflected in the present 'debate' in Australia about whether Australia should become a republic. Undoubtedly, many ordinary Australians are expressing a choice for a republic but I would claim there is a big gap between those ordinary Australian citizens who are wanting the change to a republic and those who are motivated by a theory of republicanism argued in an abstract manner. The gap in understanding is highlighted in two very different conceptions of what the constitution of a nation entails. One view holds that a constitution is a written document that is fixed *a priori* in the life of a nation, that the written document is self-contained and prescriptive, only waiting on changes deemed theoretically desirable.

The other holds that a country's constitution is far more than the written document. It can include a formal written statement but by far the most important part is what can be abstracted from the arrangements of a people as a 'people', that is, from their history, customs, traditions, laws and various other social arrangements. On this view, changing a country's constitution is not reducible to a theoretical analysis of the written instrument on the basis of the latest social theory after which alterations deemed theoretically necessary are recommended. If change is to be made then it arises from the social pressure created by developing tensions in the actual social arrangements. Change is implemented in such a way as to preserve the substantial character of the nation — which is the constitution in the broad sense. No change is allowable that does not presuppose the character of the nation. No theoretical right that does not presuppose the substance of the nation and its people can be claimed against it. A nation in the process of change and adjustment must make those changes to its constitution while conserving all that is good in its social and political arrangements. No *a priori* theory that proposes change willy nilly to the constitution can be legitimate. These different views, however briefly stated, correspond with the distinction I have made between the theorist's manner of reasoning and the social 'logic' of the ordinary person. What are the origins then of the modern theorist mentality? What are the motivations driving the theorist ever onwards?

The origins of this particular manner of thinking for the 'modern' mind can be found quite readily in the period now known as 'The Age of Reason'. This was the glorious time, they say, when 'the people' rose up against all superstition and arbitrary power, and took individual human reason as their sole guide and authority. The superstition they were fighting against was revealed religion. This meant Christianity and most particularly the Catholic Church. The arbitrary power they sought to overthrow was authority based on traditional social arrangements and vested in an inherited monarchy. At a higher and less obvious level was the effort to debunk the ancient Greek philosophies as reworked by St Augustine and St Thomas Aquinas, which formed the intellectual basis of European/Christian civilisation right through to the 18th century and at a constantly degenerating level to this very day. The most solid vestiges of Western civilisation are still largely based on this heritage. I don't want to burden the reader with a whole lot of academic jargon incomprehensible to those not initiated into the field, but it is useful to put the core of this intellectual heritage in brief terms.[3]

The intellectual heritage of European/Christian civilisation arose from an ongoing analysis by a number of great philosophers of the way the ordinary person conceives of reality and secures his knowledge of the world. It is often referred to as the 'common sense' philosophy. The school of thought resulting from this analysis is known as 'classical realism'.[4] Of all systems of thought classical realism has been the most enduring — however much it is now being ignored. Its opponents have sometimes disparaged it as 'glorified common sense'. Its adherents have not taken that to be an objection. Its starting point is the observations we make of the material world around us. If I look out the window while I write this, I see trees, cars, houses, clouds, dogs and cats, and many other things. These are particular things in our sensible world (i.e. the world of the senses). But if I take the neighbour's cat I just saw running by, I know it is a cat because it answers to the concept I have of a cat. A cat to be a cat possesses 'catness'. 'Catness' is that essence or substance that makes it a cat. I know if the cat died, 'catness' would not die with it. There can be other animals that answer to the concept of 'catness', animals that possess the essence of being a cat. An analysis of this simple thought process reveals that while we see the particular material cat with our eyes, our intellect 'sees' a supersensible quality, 'catness'. If we take all the other objects, we will arrive at the same analysis. In brief, we are aware of a material and an immaterial world. Not only that, this immaterial world has an intelligible structure. Cats and dogs and houses are not unconnected existences. They are in all sorts of relations to the world around them. One relation is that of causality.

The objects we see in the material world are in constant change. One thing becomes another, other things make another, some things move others, and so on. In all this we recognise what is one of the great principles of the world around us: the principle of causality. In the physical world causality can be defined by physical laws. The physical laws form a structure over and above the existence of physical objects. That is part of the immaterial order overseeing the world. There is also this enduring element of the principle of causality: the first cause, or the ultimate cause which is God. The great religions of the world rest on this basis, however differently their religious beliefs are expressed. I will come back to this shortly. Many people are satisfied that God exists because there had to be an original cause of all else that exists. We see an ordered world before us and God is conceived as the Author of that world. Realist philosophers (Plato, Aristotle, Plotinus, St Augustine, St Thomas Aquinas and many others) developed their analysis of these fundamental observations into an intricate philosophical system with its own specialised terminology (existence-essence, form-matter, substance-accident, act-potency, etc.).

Their analysis did not stop at the world of objects. They developed also the fundamental observations of social and moral behaviour. If God is the Author of the order of the physical world then he is also the Author of the social and moral worlds. In all cultures through all ages, we can find basic moral principles. Killing, stealing, adultery, for example, have been considered objectively wrong. It is true that a society may deviate in whole and in part from such moral principles. The explanation is that people and societies are fallible and can blind themselves to the objective nature of moral principles. But however much the unalterable moral principles are suppressed they rise again and again. Even non-believers find themselves trapped into talking about some moral principles as enduring regardless of the apparent exceptions they can think of. People recognise in the scheme of things what the philosophers have called the Natural Law.[5]

The Natural Law reflects God's moral order in the world and we human beings have been granted the ability through our God-given reason to recognise what we should do and should not do. This is the classical concept of natural law. Later philosophers would understand something quite different under 'natural law'. In the actual circumstances of a community the natural laws of social organisation and morality would be reflected in the particular traditions, customs, habits, and institutions. Indeed, in a healthy community the laws of God would inhere in these things. The basis, then, of the community's social and political laws would be the natural law which is the law of God. However differently the human law (or positive law) would be in its concrete expression from community to community, the natural law must be presupposed — if the laws and social arrangements are to be legitimate. These philosophers felt that this order of things could be observed through history, regardless of the human failure that is also abundantly evident. Whatever the differences in the expression of actual religious belief, the minimum requirement of any society, if it is to endure, is the recognition of God's order in the world.

This is a brief description of the great tradition of classical realism. Perhaps too brief. I have given the confident theorist of the first group much material to exercise his theoretical skills on. For my purposes, however, I want to stress that the realist school of philosophy resulted from an analysis of the manner in which the ordinary person thinks and acts in the world. Classical realism sought to explain what we do not doubt and take for granted in the world regardless of its sometimes inexplicable content. The ordinary person has no need of the works of Aristotle or Plato in order to live a full and happy life with work, community, family and friends. Indeed, the involved and specialised analysis would not be of benefit to him in most cases.

The philosophical speculation was best restricted to the academies where the professional philosopher could draw a connection between the philosophical system and the world of practical concerns, and pass that information onto those in the community who could mediate between the prescriptions of the speculative insights and society's ability to absorb them. The important point is that intellectual speculation in the realist school remained linked to the 'real' and actual world of the person.

The philosophers of 'The Age of Reason' broke this link. They turned the sequence of the actual world begetting theory around so that anything not reducible to a series of propositions would be put in question; theory would beget the world. Using words in a mathematical manner, their arguments took them out of the concrete conditions of human action into a rarefied, abstract world. They purposely stripped themselves of all the presuppositions of their lives, community and country. In their shivering metaphysical nakedness they embarked on a climb to power and set themselves adrift from the actual world that most of us live in. The three areas of traditional religion, authority, and philosophy came under unrelenting attack by theorists using what can be called the 'rationalistic method'. The rationalistic method would lead to an *a priori* vision of how the world should be. To know how society and people should behave would be known before the institution of a particular society on the basis of the prescriptions of the theory. Those societies already corruptly in existence could be altered and renewed on the basis of the same pre-scriptions. It would merely be a matter of checking the society off against the theoretical prescriptions.

There was great cleverness and variety in the many theories be-ing proposed in a crusading and proselytising spirit to bring down the realist heritage that had developed and formed over two thousand years. But there was always that one element they had in common: an unshakeable conviction that individual human reason must be the final judge in analysing the world. The judgements and prescriptions inherent in a body of traditions, customs, laws and religious beliefs would be disqualified. In due course a cluster of theories seemed to predominate in a period now referred to most often as the *Enlighten-ment* (but more accurately called the *French Enlightenment*). They were the theories of Hobbes, Locke, Hume, Rousseau, and Kant. Add Descartes to this group and just about all schools of modern thought following these philosophers can be traced back to their writings.

For our purposes here we can discard Kant whose most impor-tant work is totally incomprehensible to all but the initiated — that is, to those who have come under the tutelage of a superior, guiding intellect.[6] There is also great subtlety and cleverness in the theories of the other philosophers, but there are several core features that can be combined in a most seductive and comprehensible manner. To ex-plain how these core features are combined we can make our start a few centuries before in England.

Perhaps the first major attack on the tradition of ancient Greek philosophy came from a Dominican monk ensconced in that ancient English institution, Oxford University. William of Ockham (1290–1349) is known mainly these days for the philosophic device called Ockham's razor. Despite the present undeserved obscurity of William of Ockham his philosophic opus is impressive and influential. His de-velopment of nominalism would in my view qualify him for the title of 'father of modern philosophy' instead of Descartes. But that's an-other story. Of concern here is one of the most important features of his nominalism: the mind 'sees' only particular material things (men, dogs, cars, etc.). It does not 'see' natures or essences (catness, dogness, etc.), or non-material structures, or the like (the scheme of creation, God, heaven, goodness, evil). It does not perceive anything beyond the material. Now if one accepts this epistemological (knowledge) proposition that there is nothing beyond the world of particular material objects perceived by the senses, then the implications about the way one thinks about the world are enormous — especially in respect of moral, social and political matters. The Enlightenment philosophers accepted that Ockham was right in saying that the mind 'sees' only the particular. It does not discover an intelligible world of essences and the like over and above the particulars of sense perception.

To cut a tremendously long and complicated story short, if there are no universal natures or essences (e.g. dogness, catness), if there is no immaterial structure overseeing the activity of the human person (a system of unalterable moral rules), but only particular things, then we are faced with an endless appearance of particular material things with no perceptible (metaphysical) order.[7] If one finds order in the world then that order is the result of an *act of will*; there has been a decision to impose order on an intrinsically unordered realm. Taking this a few steps further with regard to the social and moral world, the individual in the natural state of this unordered world has no moral, social or political restrictions whatever. After all, there can be no such things in his natural world. *In essence*, he has a radical freedom and a radical equality with other individuals.

The establishment of any society then is essentially a decision to impose a stated order on a group of equal and free people agreeing to come together for their mutual advantage. This then is the manner of creating 'the republic'. The republic is created by an act of will by the citizens prior to its existence. No republic exists prior to the act of will. The particulars of government must be a decision by the whole body of free and equal individuals and that decision always results in a particular form of republic. The theory decides its form *a priori*. But the theory concerns far more than the establishment of the government. It prescribes the moral and social form of the republic. The moral principles, the laws and the institutions of a community are a matter for that community to make a decision about. No pre-ordained structure of the world is relevant. That's why I have given this global moral vision the term of 'theoretic-republicanism'.

One more important point about theoretic-republicanism: if the decision to set up government follows the agreement among free and equal individuals, then default of the agreement means that the individual is logically permitted to opt out of the agreement, that is, to return to the natural unordered moral-free realm and resume the 'unlimited rights' he enjoyed in his natural state. Given this essential individual freedom, it would be the gravest transgression of our individual status to have somebody lord it over us in a system of arbitrary human fabrication (especially that of monarchy). There can be nothing more serious than the transgression of the individual subjective rights flowing from the fact of our equality and freedom. Now, you may well ask, what is wrong with all that? That's surely to describe things as they really are? And who but the ignorant does not think like that these days?

Well, as beautiful as this picture is, it represents the cruellest fraud that has ever been foisted on the human race. The alleged superstition of Christianity is nothing compared to the fantasy of this 'rationalistic' scenario. To begin with, the theories from which this very recognisable conglomeration is drawn are full of holes, inconsistencies and flaws. In terms of their own method they are a complete failure. The most compelling philosophical position one is forced to via the rationalistic method is a thorough-going scepticism. If the adherents of rationalism claim to have definitively brought down the superstitious structure of belief in God and a revealed religion, they have brought everything else down. The 'definitive' rejection of belief in God, something that is peculiar to the epoch of rationalism (for in all traditionally formed societies belief in God is central), is merely one among the definitive rejection of all certain belief.

If scepticism is the most compelling position forced on us by the general method of rationalism, then in the end this restores belief in God to its pre-eminent position in the life of ordinary people who don't know about or want to know about a system which fails in its own method. The ordinary person who believes in God should remain completely unmoved by the university-educated smart alec who claims that belief in God has no foundation. The explanation he will give will be as confused as it sounds. Of course, it will not sound confused to those who have 'mastered' the relevant rhetoric. Nevertheless, I am not about to embark on yet another exposition of the key thoughts of Hume's *Treatise of Human Nature* or to try and wade through Hobbes's *Leviathan*. These books and their thousands of commentaries can be found taking up space in any university library. We will leave this enticing theoretical labyrinth to those selected to find their way through it. I am concerned not with development of theory but with the mentality and tactics that feed on this intellectual heroin.

In terms of understanding the arguments for radical freedom and equality, just how free and equal are we? Well, if anybody wants to understand the full scope of reasoning behind the assertions of radical individual equality and freedom then he will have to enrol in some sort of course given by somebody initiated into its mysteries. Believe me, it would be an extremely rare person who could pick up the works of these gurus of rationalism and understand the arguments without the patient guidance of a superior. The plain fact is that the tenets of theoretic freedom and equality are theoretic dogma that has to be taught and learnt dogmatically. The average person would not have the patience, interest, time and ability to arrive at a competent understanding of the theories — theories that would not aid them one jot in their daily lives.

The function of the university is to separate the initiates-elect from the ignorant masses. But in the long run many of those who have been chosen to be initiated will have learnt their lessons dogmatically from a directing superior intellect who will prepare them to regurgitate it all at the right moment, and to dismiss all those not trained in their rhetoric as stupid and ignorant.[8] Part of the gigantic rationalistic fraud is that the dogma, priests, bishops, theologians and hierarchy of the Catholic Church have been replaced by a different hierarchical structure and set of dogma. The rationalistic theories of freedom and equality served best to replace one system of authority with an opposing system of authority. The apostles of radical freedom and equality successfully laid the foundations for their power and ascendancy.

3. Authoriphobia and the Great Authoriphobic Paradox

What could be of more use to the power hungry than a dogmatic system of belief that asserts we have unlimited individual rights in a world where no *fixed* moral, social and political standards exist? Where all moral, social and political standards can only be the result of agreement and promulgated in written form — all of which can be at any moment overthrown? What presents a more conducive ground for self-aggrandisement and material accumulation than a society whose members accept dogmatically that it is continually in a reconstitutive condition — that all authority is in essence a transgression of the person's natural state? The answer is that nothing could be more useful and conducive to the power hungry. Those able to amass and wield power cleverly have open slather. All the obstacles presented by traditional morality, religion and traditional social arrangements have in principle been removed. Prevailing power will determine who is ruler and who is subject. Far from being a compelling 'theory', theoretic individual subjective rights sound rather like a pathological condition.

Few of us like being told what to do. But most of us agree it would be impractical to constantly challenge the designated authority in the many contexts in which we find ourselves. Indeed, we are more concerned with the people and the circumstances than with the presence of a co-ordinating authority. There are others, however, who suffer great pains under even the mildest authority — who feel acutely the transgression of their 'free nature'. These are those who have taken on most seriously the 'dictates of human reason'. Having reached by way of 'reason' the conclusion we are all equally free, they put aside without blush the fact that, in terms of their theory, maintenance of an agreement is essential if they want to keep society from falling apart at each moment. Each system of social management becomes immediately a challenge to their natural state of unlimited freedom. The more a system of social management becomes successful, and the more entrenched it becomes, the more embittered the resistance of the 'radically free and equal' subject. We are talking about a pathological condition we can call *authoriphobia.*

Authoriphobia is an obsessive/compulsive condition of varying degrees of seriousness. At its mildest it can cause disruption and nuisance in one's social environment. At its most serious it can devastate whole nations and periods in history. Its most intriguing feature is that it starts with the subject's mind giving 'reasoned' assent to what the subject sees as pre-eminently lucid propositions about the state of the human person. But the 'reasoned' position of radical freedom for the individual becomes, the more it is contemplated, the source of an upward-spiralling bitterness. The more the formulations of equality are implemented in a 'properly' constituted society, the more the established authority looms to torment the radically free subject. Thus the *Great Authorophobic Paradox.* Rather than give the full picture of this condition and its varying degrees of actual expression I will concern myself here only with describing its extremes. A discussion of its extremes will vividly convey the essential nature of authoriphobia and the way the authoriphobic person utilises the theory of freedom and equality just discussed. Of course, less serious degrees of the condition (which is readily identifiable in many nations of the so-called 'free world') will produce less serious outcomes. But they will be of the same nature and manifest the same features.

The idea of equality held by the authoriphobic subject is of a very particular sort. Other systems of belief hold also that people are essentially equal. Traditional Christian belief is that we are equal in that we all possess the same human nature with the same moral rights and duties. We are all called to a life of virtue. This concept of equality is not incompatible with the belief that the nature of the human person incorporates different levels of skill, ability, dignity and temporal rank. Indeed, the Christian concept of equality underpins the healthy functioning of the different ranks of skill and authority in the temporal sphere. It is emphasised in the key commandment 'to love God and thy neighbour as thyself'. The idea of equality subscribed to by the authoriphobic mind is of the *equalising* or *levelling* sort. According to this idea, there is and thus should be no temporal difference between individuals. Any manifested difference (that is, inequality) between individuals has been perniciously introduced by corrupt social and political systems. The task of the authoriphobic subject is to reconstitute a corrupt society by *levelling* measures. A most obvious levelling measure was the mandatory uniform of communist China. What more effective way of equalising society is there than making people wear exactly the same clothing? Levelling society is the great object of the authoriphobic mind. But levelling requires a leveller presiding over the systems of levelling.

Those that are most fanatical about equalising society crave the authority of the leveller. The reason is that the system of authority generated to level society produces a growing torment in the authoriphobic subject responsible for the systems of levelling. The more he is tormented by the authority he has generated the more he works to control the instruments of the levelling authority to escape his torment. He begins to identify himself with the levelling authority. Equality there must be, but it is for others. The effort to absorb the levelling authority brings an ever-greater power position which he does not hesitate to use to broaden the range and effectiveness of the levelling campaign. Success in his unrelenting efforts brings with it great power and an ever greater longing to rise above any situation of authority — even above the limits of his physical existence.

But if his efforts meet with failure, the results for society are potentially disastrous. The greater the failure, the closer he comes to opting out of society, that is, out of the agreement he sees himself trapped in. With total failure he finds himself back in his natural state where no moral standards exist to restrain him in his means of combating those who possess the great power he himself wanted to possess. But as an individual he must face the unpleasant reality that he holds no power over the prevailing authority. His only course of action is now to associate with like-minded radically free and equal subjects to combat in whatever way those who have limited his freedom and made him less equal than the possessors of power. Justified violence is now his mode of existence aimed especially at those who think in the same manner. In this way, an inevitable fragmentation in the body politic occurs with the various authoriphobic bodies agitating for the control of the society in the process of being levelled. Total war is declared against those falling outside the group's self-defined area of established freedom. This power struggle takes place above and out of reach of those being levelled and all tactics and weapons are allowable in bringing about the imposition of the group's particular idea of the 'free' order. Tactics and weapons are only condemned if they do not advance the 'right' authoriphobic faction. Bashings, stand-overs, vandalism, theft and calumny are all legitimate if they are committed on behalf of the faction.[9]

For the *successful* radically free and equal subject there are other issues. The amassing of great power and the necessity to hold both the levelled and the opposition in check present administrative, educational and policing problems. Two things happen in the extreme cases. An individual subject may decide to press on with his campaign to completely level society and to destroy the power position of his opponents. His object will be to continue to amass the necessary power but at the same time to introduce a limited hierarchy of servants who are guaranteed to wield his power in the way he wants. This limited body of servants will act as his executing arm. He has reached such heights that the only criterion for the means for maintaining and increasing power is the effectiveness of the means. All people and things have become expendable. All must bow to the decrees of a supreme leader possessing the power to control absolutely. The devastation wrought by this authoriphobic type is there in the history of the 20th century to see in all its gruesome detail.

In the second extreme case, the authoriphobic type recognises the risks of proceeding on his own. He sees the best manner of accumulating power as associating with like-minded subjects who have more or less reached the same level in the accumulation of power, prestige and property. These like-minded free and equal subjects form in a *virtual sense*[10] a ruling class who determine the means of levelling the rest of society and the administrative apparatus of securing what has been gained. Absolute formality in organising the class is not only unnecessary but also counter to its reconstitutive spirit. It's a framework of organisation with an acknowledged fluidity in its members' movements. In this ruling class a supreme directing body is chosen to oversee the most important functions of the levelling process and the securing of class hegemony. The supreme body presents no real threat in terms of power to the rest of the members of the class. This is really a necessary administrative matter and the membership of the supreme group is something of a reward for the services rendered to the ruling class as a whole. An essential feature of the ruling class is that the class members distribute their own offices. In this scenario, the authoriphobic's distaste of authority has not been diminished but mitigated by, firstly, the demands of practical politics and, secondly, by the knowledge that his position as oligarch presents him always with the means to limit the effects of the surrounding authority and the potential, always present, to amass a higher degree of power and thus reduce the torment of the forms of authority he himself is responsible for.

An important third reason for forming a ruling class is the administrative task of maintaining a levelled society. This is more easily undertaken in a class structure than in the absolutist position described above. The controlling functions are spread over more shoulders and a subservient hierarchy of sub-managers and theoretical flunkeys is more easily formed and supervised. The theoretical flunkey is an especially potent weapon in the hands of the ruling elite. The theoretical flunkey has accepted the principles of theoretic-republicanism not because he has been convinced by the arguments, for they are only half-understood. No, the flunkey has accepted the main principles enthusiastically as compelling dogma. This renders him ever ready to reel the main points off at a moment's notice with fluency and conviction. This is particularly useful in TV 'debates' where the allowable time-span for 'debating' admirably suits the flunkey's talents. The media boss has already fixed the terms and format, and the flunkey is able to enter the debate context immediately with his memorised dogma. Very often the debate is over before those who challenge the paradigm of theoretic-republicanism have managed to break even a small hole in the wall of assumptions that confronts them.

Furthermore, the administrative hierarchy generated by the ruling class is more acceptable to the levelled masses because it approaches more closely the ordinary person's idea of the structure of authority. The ordinary person feels instinctively the need for a constituted authority in society. Thus the masses are more compliant and this also renders the educational and policing tasks more manageable.

The educational task is of utmost importance because the reasons for levelling must be constantly promulgated and absorbed by the levelled masses. This issue of propaganda is not only one for educational institutions but, more importantly, for the instruments of public information dissemination, that is, the radio, TV and newspapers. Control of the media is maintained paradoxically by one of the great slogans of the authoriphobic mind: *A democratic and free society is dependent on the freedom of the press.* The media as mouthpiece of the ascendant class is crucial. When the ruling class of authoriphobic subjects has control of the media, it is able to disseminate in almost complete form its authoriphobic ideas and hold in check those elements in society who are its most detested enemies — those acting according to traditional ideas of society, morality and religion.[11] At all cost the authoriphobic mind must destroy any attempt to set up a system of standards that is *prior* to the free and equal subject instituting society by an act of will. A 'free' press is the necessary weapon in countering the insidious influences of traditional life. It is also the most effective weapon in projecting the idea that the ruling class is always working on behalf of the levelled masses. They project their form of rule as 'republicanism', a form of rule, they say, where all positions in society are open to all its free and equal members. In truth, the levelled masses are even less able than in a traditionally formed society to approach the ramparts of power. After all, they have been levelled by an all-powerful ruling elite.

Access to the ruling class is decided by its members, by a nomenclature, and the conditions of initiation are hardly less stringent than in any traditional society, traditional religion, or in an aristocracy decided by birth and state-appointment. One of the great hoaxes of the ruling elite is the claim that they are conserving a form of society in which everyone can aspire to be its president. Well, they can aspire, but that's all. The poor Aussie battler drinking his beer in Rooty Hill RSL can forget about ever being president. In an abstract sense, everything is possible except a contradiction. It's possible that the sun may rise tomorrow in the west. Indeed, that seems more likely to happen than any member of Rooty Hill RSL becoming president of Australia. The position of president in the republic is the property of the ruling class.

'Theoretic-republicanism' is the ideology of the authoriphobic mind. The discerning reader may think that it has other labels: left-wing, communist, Marxist, liberal, progressive, etc. I propose that theoretic-republicanism is the synthesis of not only all these denominations, but of denominations that seem in strict opposition, such as German National Socialism and Italian Fascism. Theoretic-republicanism is the umbrella under which all these movements shelter as subsets. They are in unrelenting and bitter opposition to traditionally formed societies who recognise the unchangeable laws of God. The dichotomy of political belief is usually understood as covering political belief from left-wing to right-wing. A great many people have recognised the close resemblance between the regimes of German National Socialism and the Soviet Union. The real political dichotomy is between those political systems based on theoretic-republican ideas and those based on realist metaphysics and the classical natural law. Two quite different societies evolve from these bases.

Now the ardent Marxist may howl in protest at his views being subsumed under the *bourgeois* theories of the Enlightenment — let alone being grouped with Nazism. It is not possible, nor necessary, to demonstrate in this space the affinity of Marxism with the core tenets of the Enlightenment. Let me observe only that Marxism is akin to a symphonic treatment of the essential Enlightenment themes. Regardless of its journey through the Hegelian dialectic, it ended up as a materialist dialectic with the same implications as the brotherly theories it squabbles with. Above all, the materialist dialectic of Marxism sanctified hatred as a legitimate weapon in bringing about the dissolution of inimical class structures and the advance of a state of insoluble freedom and equality.

Bernie Taft, former leader of the Communist Party of Australia, knew who his true brothers were. He said on the occasion of the death of B. A. Santamaria, Australia's foremost Catholic political leader, that while Santamaria supported Franco in the Spanish Civil War, he (Taft) 'was contemplating joining the International Brigades that fought on the side of the republic' (*The Age*, 26 February 1998).[12]

4. The Task of the Theoretic-Republican Media

The task of the theoretic-republican media is essentially to provide the propaganda of the ruling elite, not to disseminate information. In this task it must be particularly on guard to contain attempts to promote ideas that are incompatible with the authoriphobically formed society. As I have said, such ideas are those that are connected to systems *prior* to the free and equal subject's invention. The most dangerous onset of these ideas comes sometimes with the rise of a figure who has unexpected appeal to the masses. At other times it comes with the increasing admiration for somebody who either belongs to the vestiges of traditional arrangements or for somebody who projects a traditional 'decency'. In the first case, the sudden rise of a popular figure with unacceptable ideas is a danger precisely because that person has escaped the instruments of the ruling elite's authority — for the moment. It is even more dangerous if that person challenges aspects of the ruling class's ideology. The role of the media is to bring under control the influence of such a 'populist' figure.

In the second case, the figures of traditional power and traditional decency merely represent the ongoing task of the ruling elite to maintain a levelled society. Such figures are more easily controlled than those of the first. But the measures for containing both types of problems are the same.

Theoretic-republicanism is constantly promulgated as the face of the reasonable, moderate, compassionate human person. The organs of theoretic-republicanism are keen to project the image of reason as the sole guide in organising society. But when it comes to countering opposing voices, the last thing we find is an impartial reasoned response to those voices. The theoretic-republican media will fabricate its own version of the dissenting ideas and proceed to smear at every opportunity the dissenting person with the ideas it itself has manufactured. The aim is not to counter the opposition with argument for that would risk scrutiny of their own position and give collateral credibility to the other party. The aim is to discredit utterly any dissenting voices and to intimidate those who may be inclined to sympathy. In most cases the fabrication of a smear campaign is backed by mockery and ridicule, and the accusation that the dissenting voice is 'divisive' — one of the most serious crimes members of the levelled masses can commit. Anybody who deviates from the views of the ruling elite is 'divisive'. The 'debates' by members of the ruling elite are either their smear campaigns or the allowable discussions within their authoriphobic ideological range. Members of the permitted ideological range are allowed to disagree — even vehemently. In this event, the partakers of the 'debate' congratulate themselves on their balance, tolerance and commitment to democracy.

I am sure that many people will be able to put names to the image of the types of dissenting persons described here. However, in this brief work I am concerned with the second type of dangerous dissenter the theoretic-republican media moves against. The people I have in mind as continuing victims of such tactics are Prince Charles and Prime Minister John Howard. A full discussion of the media's treatment of John Howard must be left to another time. Let me just make some short comments by way of illustrating what I have already said.

John Howard's biggest problem is that he espouses traditional standards of decency. In other words, he has the fatal liability of openly proclaiming an order of morality *prior* to human devices — or more importantly prior to the fabrication of the ruling elite. John Howard's moral and political vision is different from the 'vision' of the ruling class — and that's equivalent to having no vision at all. At the end of 1997 and into 1998 we were witnessing the theoretic-republican media running this theme hard against John Howard. The image of John Howard as the weak, vacillating, visionless, bigoted figure was being promoted with all the vigour the ruling class could muster. If anybody looks reasonably at the course of John Howard's career as politician, one cannot escape the picture of a man with a high degree of tenacity, courage, and single-mindedness in pursuing a clear moral and political vision, however much one would disagree with that political vision.[13] Added to this is a real decency of character that is an obvious embarrassment to those who have the imposing title of National Political Editor of an authoriphobic media instrument.

Now some people may think, 'Hang on. John Howard is Prime Minister of Australia. He is head of the government therefore he must be head of the ruling class. This is just the sort of loony confusion to be expected from the paranoid, conspiracy-toting, extreme right-wing mind.' It should be very clear from what I have written that the vestiges of the traditional ruling authority are not to be identified with the structure of the ruling class in Australia. Let me be plain: our traditional parliamentary democracy was formed over a long period of time with many factors contributing. It is not analysable into a series of rationalistic propositions — even though that's the way the oligarchs like to present it. The written Australian Constitution is one side of the broader constitution of our social and political arrangements, much of it remaining unwritten but clear in the form of conventions, habits, customs, etc.

It is only the vestiges of Australia's parliamentary democracy that are still effective. The true rulers are those who have formed a *virtual* oligarchy subsisting in the vital organs of the Australian state and society and in the many new clubs, associations and especially 'government' bodies that have been generated like cancerous spots. It is these latter that have been formed outside the perimeters of our traditionally formed parliamentary democracy but fatally infect it. The pervasiveness of their presence and the extent of the implementation of their authoriphobic mentality are tragically evident in such matters as the Mabo Judgement and the many UN conventions that are being imposed upon us. The Mabo Judgement itself represents the most striking break from Australia's Constitution in the broad sense, shaking the Australian nation to its very foundations. The cracks opened up by this High Court judgement are widening to this day.

The virtual oligarchy prevailing over and structured within the Australian nation is not 'perfect'[14] and it's not meant to be. Again, the oligarchy's reconstitutive mode (i.e. the fluid ability to continually reconstitute inimical social and political forms, and deal with the inevitable recalcitrants) is of absolute importance. There will always be people resisting indoctrination or threatening to break out of the mould established for them. John Howard has been a great thorn in the side of the ruling class. He represents all they despise. Nevertheless, his rise to the pre-eminent position in our traditional form of government has not meant escaping their control. He is still their prisoner. The policies he is driving hard have been compromised in an attempt to escape the claws of the theoretic-republican media. But this was destined to be of no avail. I said when John Howard was elected Prime Minister that most likely he would not survive, that in the end the ruling class would have him. That looks to be the case at the time of writing.

As an illustration of the effectiveness of the media propaganda machine, I include the following letter which appeared in the letters section of *The Australian*, 17 February 1998. The writer was commenting on Prime Minister Howard's performance at the Constitutional Convention held in the old parliament house in Canberra. This is what he said:

> *Until the Constitutional Convention, most Australians thought of John Howard as a small-minded and mean-spirited little man, out of touch with the people. The convention has revealed to us a surprisingly attractive John Howard. It has revealed to him a passionate side of the Australian people.*
>
> *Mr Howard's performance in the closing hours of the convention showed us something of what he could really be. He demonstrated decisiveness, leadership and confidence such as we have never seen in him. He loves being Prime Minister. Now he has the chance to go down in history as a great one.*

I would say this to the author of this letter: you have been a typical victim of the propaganda run by the media. What you have learnt from observing John Howard at the Constitutional Convention is what many of us have observed through the years. One may not always agree with the position he takes on a particular political issue, but a fair-minded person observing him closely over a period of time would have to admit that his position is always based on an abiding set of moral and political principles. The great pity (and tragedy) about John Howard as Prime Minister is that the exercise of prudence has forced him to compromise or water down important political decisions. Without such compromises, however, he would have been dead in the water. The hunting packs of Canberra 'political' journalists at the behest of their media masters would have finished him off before his campaign for government started more than two years ago.

The recognition by many ordinary people that there exists a political and social elite in Australia who are ramming their particular 'vision' down their throats has well and truly broken into the open during the last two years in Australia. By the time this book is released, the 1998 federal election will have been over. It is to be hoped that the anti-theoretic-republican forces knew who the real enemy was. As much as there is dissatisfaction with some elements of John Howard's policy he is not the enemy. Indeed, he is the only leader at this time in Australia capable of bringing some unity and cohesion to the anti-theoretic-republican forces.

5. Prince Charles and Diana, Princess Of Wales

If Australia's oligarchic class despises John Howard and all he stands for, they can be consoled by the fact that they derive a lot of use and satisfaction from his dogged presence in the social and political life of Australia. He is not out of their control and, best of all, he serves as a sort of case study for their authoriphobic ideas — as a propaganda board on which to bounce off their most important principles. He may cause deep distaste but the oligarch's forbearance is rewarded with the propaganda value and the capacity especially for the theoretic-republican media to fill their pages with the necessary lessons for the masses. Prince Charles, however, is another problem entirely.

Everything about Prince Charles is the source of the greatest distress for the authoriphobic mind. It sees in Charles all it can never be. The authoriphobic subject stands stripped of all that makes him a person and a citizen of a particular time and place. All the riches of the human mind and spirit objectified in an array of art and tradition have been thrown aside to leave him grasping at a set of abstract propositions to hide his self-revolting nakedness. Whereas Prince Charles, without any choice whatever on his part, has been allotted a duty from the moment of his birth to the moment he departs this world. Without any choice at all he sits atop a vast cultural panorama stretching back through the centuries.

Even if the cultural panorama disappears out of the sight of the individual linked to a particular time and place, anybody who has not blinded himself, anybody who has not thrown off his heritage, can look to a figure that objectifies a rich and glorious past. The ordinary Australian not confused by a stay in the seminaries of theoretic-republicanism can look at the objectification that is Prince Charles and the royal family and feel the glories of a past that have contributed to make him and his nation what they are in a particular place and time. The poor denuded theoretic-republican has blocked the avenues to the heart and it is in the realm of the heart where man lives life to its richest. It is in the realm of the heart that the citizen can look over and beyond the person of Prince Charles at his own cultural heritage.[15]

The frustrated theoretic-republican armed with his abstract propositions about freedom and equality can only stand by and watch
uncomprehendingly as the masses display their unabated affection for
Britain's royal family despite all the mistakes and blunders some members of the royal family have made during the last two decades.

The theoretic-republican's obsessive efforts in the world's media
to re-educate the masses and rid them of their ignorance with regard
to royalty has been irritatingly ineffective. Why haven't the people
been turned off by the exposition of the individual weaknesses of the
members of the royal family? Surely the (highly illegal) taped phone
conversations of Prince Charles and Diana would have made them so
ridiculous that nobody could possibly believe that such royalty is
'above' the ordinary person. But the ordinary person intuitively makes
a distinction between the mere human person and the royal person
that symbolises and objectifies so much of what he feels about himself and his social environment. We know that Prince Charles in one
sense is merely a person with the same frail nature as ourselves, but
we place him in another sense above ourselves.

When the media bring to our attention what we did not want to
know, when they describe and exploit every little fault of the royal
person, they do not cause us to despise him. They arouse sympathy
and sorrow in the uncorrupted mind that the royal person has not been
able to uphold his duty, that his heavy load has caused him to falter.
Indeed, the sympathy overcomes the normal impulse to punish, and
what remains is the wish for the royal person to rise above his mistakes, to keep continually in mind that he is not just himself, but in a
transcendent manner he is 'the people'. He has the duty of raising not
only himself above his frailties but the people he embodies. To punish the king is in a sense to execute the social and cultural self. That
is why in past ages regicide was considered such a horrible crime.

The royal person who is there as a point in the cultural continuum
has achieved what the authoriphobic mind aspires to but can never
achieve: the royal person has in a figurative way transcended his physical limits. That also explains why the most 'ignorant' of ordinary folk
feel that kingship was instituted by God in the act of creating human
society. The act of cutting down the king and 'all the solemn plausi-
bilities' of life that surround him is ultimately the act of cutting off
the sources of life.

But even if we are constantly forced to think about the mere human person that is Prince Charles, what do we see really — I mean, really? Let's leave aside the magisterium of ridicule and slander built up by media over the years. I am a little older than Prince Charles and if I look back through the years there was always a Prince Charles 'there'. I remember the nuns at the local Sisters of Mercy convent talking about him with much affection. There was even a picture of him displayed at the back of one of the classrooms. That would have been in 1954. During those years my impressions were of a rather quiet, polite and well brought up boy. If this projects an unattractive picture in the 1990s, it was different in the 1950s. Quietness, good manners and respect were held to be good qualities. The worst types in society were the loud, ill-mannered and vulgar, because such people were intrinsically self-oriented and uncaring about their social environment. In other words, they were badly educated. To be well-mannered was to pay the respect due to your family, friends and those in necessary authority. To be quiet and well-mannered was not a sign of weakness or of subservience — quite the opposite. To remain well-mannered in the most trying situations was a sign of inner-strength. In terms of the turbulent male spirit, to remain in control of oneself in situations of extreme provocation and to take firm but appropriate action was considered *manly*.

As Prince Charles grew older, these seemed to be the qualities he most exemplified. The display of arrogance and superiority with which the vulgar theoretic-republican mind characterises the state of being royal was entirely absent in Prince Charles's case. We Australians had the opportunity to see him at close hand during his stay at Timbertop. Not only did Prince Charles display the admirable qualities of a bygone age but he seemed to be at pains to express his genuine admiration and affection for the Australian nation and its people. As he approached adulthood, I can remember a natural easiness of manner that became gradually evident in his conversations about and with Australian people.

Far from 'lording it' over us as a colony of Great Britain, Prince Charles seemed to have more than a genuine affection for Australia; he seemed to identify with the best qualities of the nation and its people. His contact with Australia was determining in his formation. He was to no small extent *Australianised*. The easy but polite manner with which he speaks has, I believe, its origins in his time in Australia. We have seen Prince Charles many times since those days and nobody who is capable of telling the truth could claim that a stuffy, arrogant, and superior manner characterised his behaviour. Even in the most trying circumstances, circumstances that have many celebrities throwing punches and tantrums, Prince Charles has maintained an open, easy and tolerating manner.

When it comes to Diana, Princess of Wales, most of us knew little about her and her background. All we saw on the TV reports was an attractive, unpretentious, but obviously well brought up young woman. There were already glimpses of that honesty of heart that came to characterise her behaviour through the years. But when Prince Charles chose her as his bride her royal background through him opened out before us. The courtship and the royal wedding were all that the natural understanding of the ordinary person could wish for. Many people spoke about the fairytale union of a prince and a princess. Diana seemed admirably to fill the needs of the crown prince of the Commonwealth — and eager to do so. Alas, none of us knew that it was the beginning not of a beautiful fairytale but of a Greek tragedy in which both the prince and the princess were sucked inexorably into the dark chasms that opened up before their every move. There was to be no escape.

Leaving aside the efforts of the theoretic-republican media to create a body of ridicule and slander about Prince Charles, there is still the question of how much the Prince and Princess, and how much the circumstances contributed to their problems. I have already said that no marriage could withstand the scrutiny that Charles and Diana's had to endure. To be constantly the object of attention, to have one's words and actions constantly analysed, to have one's image constantly relayed around the world, is a burden that nobody has ever had to endure and nobody could endure. But then to have the added foul and unscrupulous behaviour of the paparazzi, directed by the media bosses, this amounts to a new type of public execution where the observed pain is far more exquisite than any guillotine or slashing Islamic sword could deliver.

Given all this, I think that it is almost impossible to quantify the contribution of both individuals to their marriage breakdown. As individual people they both certainly had their faults. In particular, it now very clear that Diana brought to her marriage a set of severe unresolved emotional problems. Her disrupted emotional growth impeded a healthy discrimination of social obligation in the very different social contexts one finds oneself in. She seemed to want to apply the same rules of behaviour in all possible situations. Some people would call this immaturity. I will come back to this again and again in examining the way Diana behaved. The combination of Diana's problems with the necessary training for public life Prince Charles had to undergo was explosive. But in the absence of the unbearable pressures they were under, how likely is it that they would have successfully overcome the problems? Some couples manage to grow and rise above difficult incompatibilities.[16] We will never know. In what follows I will be looking more closely at the character and behaviour of Prince Charles and Diana as it relates to the media commentaries. For the moment I want to focus on Prince Charles.

All through the media coverage of the problems of Prince Charles and Diana, through all the mockery and lies levelled at Prince Charles, I have never observed him lose his composure to any significant degree. Of course, the more Prince Charles remained in control of himself, the more the media made him out to be stuffy, feelingless, emotionally crippled, and so on. What then would they prefer to see in Prince Charles? What role model should he have adopted? Would the media have preferred that Prince Charles behave like Rambo at the end of the film *Rambo (II)*? This is a scene where Rambo becomes so incensed at the 'injustice' he has had to endure that he goes completely off his rocker, screaming and firing his automatic rifle into the air, and finishes by plunging his huge bowie knife into the desk of the CIA officer he believes has wronged him! Or would they prefer him to be the aimless, weak, deceitful, self-indulgent male that parades through American sitcoms, such as George Costanza in *Seinfeld*. Or, as a colleague of mine has suggested, would they prefer as a role model for young boys 'the sensitive New Age types who favour self-indulgent *emotional openness* and LA psychobabble' over the self-restraint Prince Charles represents?

Those of us with traditional ideas of manliness think that Prince Charles, despite the great pressures upon him and the mistakes he has made, exemplifies to a great degree the inner fortitude and decency that largely constitutes manliness. This is a worthy model of manly behaviour to put before young males. The unrestrained and brutal behaviour of the Rambo type depicted in so many so-called action films is the 'macho' model that media feminists like to set up as the essence of maleness. This is the self-serving feminist stereotype that provides the basis for so much feminist 'theory' about the state of being male. Unfortunately, the model of the macho male is a model of male degeneration. Here we raise one of the most serious issues of the age: the degeneration of the male person. To lose control, to give in to one's passions, to hit out, to scream and rant and do violence to those who cross one is *macho* behaviour. It is one side of the picture of maleness in extreme degeneration. The other I will allude to shortly.

6. The Feral Male and the Inversion of Manliness

A recent survey on crime and violence in Australia revealed that overwhelmingly the violence committed against people is carried out by males. Of the males committing violence against others by far the biggest group is the 19 to 26 year old group. If you are to be murdered, you will most likely be murdered by a male in this age group at night and in one of the entertainment areas of a big city. But let's reduce the problem to more everyday terms. How many of us are subjected weekly to the aggressive, obstructive or abusive behaviour of young males on the loose? Moreover, the victim of male aggression and violence does not seem to be determined by gender. It seems to be decided by the circumstances. If anyone gets in the way of an abusive, violence-oriented male then they risk becoming the victim. While trying to do his duty a young constable, with a wife and two young children, is stabbed to death by an 18-year-old male drug dealer like any other person who would get in his way. It's only the self-serving ideologue who wants to depict all males as actually or potentially violent.[17]

Many men are appalled at the apparently out-of-control behaviour of young men as a group. They are frustrated that most people cannot walk down the street without running the risk of some arrogant young male standing in the middle of a pedestrian walkway, sitting on the steps blocking the entrance to a public place, sometimes spitting at your feet, other times offending the surroundings with loud drunken behaviour. And you know what will happen if you dare to say something. Most likely a complaint about the mere nuisance behaviour will provoke a stream of foul language. In the extreme, but not rare case, you might be pushed around and even bashed. I need not labour this point. There is nobody I know who would not agree with this brief account. Indeed, many people would say that the age range of the violent, abusive young male is 10 to 26 years.

I wonder how many adults have been told to get f—ed and piss off by 10-year-old boys who were being pulled up for bullying younger children or making a mess of a public place. How many teachers, if they dared, would own up to the number of times they have been told to 'get f—ed!' by a young male whose disruptive behaviour made the teaching process completely unworkable? How many teachers have been bashed or sexually harassed by some young male thug in the classroom? The particular ideological restraints on teachers are so great that the public will never know the complete details.

This is not the place to launch into a full-scale analysis of the problems of the modern male and the issue of educating males. That will be the subject of another work. I want only to say what is clear to many males who espouse traditional moral principles. Male and female are different in some critical aspects and one of the most important is what some people are calling what (for want of a better short description) I will call *male energy*. It's what seems to be the root cause of murder, rape and wars, but on the other hand it seems also responsible for much of the art, literature, law and philosophy that exists. What, in terms of male energy, makes the difference between causing a brutal war, and the unyielding, self-sacrificing courage that stands up to the tyrant who causes such a war? It is moral control. It is control of the passions.

The system of traditional morality[18] connected to traditional religion is one of imposing on oneself the principles and sanctions that have been prescribed in the scheme of things — whose author is God. Take this away, take away this inner system of constraint and you are only left with the arbitrary constraint that comes from outside. And who cares logically about that without being made to care? This is another irony of theoretic-republicanism. The truly 'free' person is *essentially* without reason for self-constraint. It is only self-interest determined by the environment and the imposed system of outer sanctions that will control. The great irony is that under the system of theoretic-republicanism male energy becomes an enslaving energy. The worst thing to have happened to the male this century is that he has been 'freed' from the inner moral restraints of traditional morality and religion and has been delivered over to his uncontrollable passions. How many males have been 'freed' to die in their drug-induced vomit, to live a greater part of their lives in the brutalising environment of jail, to die in the agonies of some sexually transmitted disease … These are the provinces mainly of the male. Need I go on?

Male energy as the distinguishing feature of the male has been let loose to torment us all and in the extreme cases to commit crimes of such horror that they must surely pierce the vaults of heaven and cry out for divine justice. And the body of thought that has laid the grounding for this horror is singularly unable and unwilling to deal with it. Much preferred is the desecration of innocence than the punishment of such horrible crimes. Indeed, in the depths of the theoretic-republican psyche is a sympathy for the perpetrator of horror. Because essentially the perpetrator of horror has exercised his freedom in the most dramatic manner possible. The results are merely unfortunate. Above all, the exercise of freedom must never be inhibited. The worst crime for the theoretic-republican mind is precisely what I am presently engaged in: an attack on the principles of theoretic-republicanism. The history of the 20th century is an account of the elimination of those resisting the ideologies of 'freedom'. No punishment is too bad for those resisting 'being freed'.

Male energy has been let loose by the theories of radical individual freedom to breed a generation of feral males. In the 1990s we are hedged in by the progeny of the baby-boomers, surely the most selfish generation in recorded history. If hearts bleed, they should bleed torrents of blood for those poor virgin soldiers who in 1939 set out from Australia's shores on the most honourable cause the manly mind can conceive of — never to return. They fought for a moral and manly freedom — freedom from the tyranny of an all-compassing ideology. Their hearts would break if they saw what the sons and daughters of their generation would do to that freedom. Their hearts would have broken in a thousand pieces if they had witnessed the rebellion of the post-war generation reach its apogee in the ridicule and desecration of the ANZAC tradition as it did in the mid-1970s. They would never have been able to conceive of the feral male of the 1990s in complete thrall to his basest passions. No honour. No respect. No backbone. It would never have entered their minds that so many males would so lose sight of the essence of their manliness that they would suffer a complete inversion of their male being and celebrate that inversion in the most foul and grotesque manner. The sacrifice of those virgin soldiers is crying out for vengeance.

In the face of all this do we need the arsonist to take a can of petrol to the fire? Do we need to congratulate ourselves that we allow the arsonist and the fire brigade to be one and the same? The last thing we need are the preachers of an unmanly freedom to continue their lessons in enslavement. We need men who know what manliness is and who will teach the lessons of courage, endurance, honour, self-sacrifice and self-control. We need men who will ensure that the truly weak and vulnerable in our society can *rely* on them for protection. Above all, we need men who will take responsibility for their families. Those men who exemplify inner courage, fairness, self-control and self-sacrifice in an honourable cause are worthy models to put before the young man of the 1990s. There are no males of perfect manly virtue. Prince Charles has his faults and weaknesses. He has made mistakes. Nevertheless, his strength of character (observable to those who want to look fairly) indicates that he belongs to this group.[19]

7. Applying the Tenets of Theoretic-Republicanism in the Media

I have sketched the fundamentals of theoretic-republicanism. I have discussed how these ideas rid human behaviour of any moral touchstone. The jettisoning in principle of any objective laws governing society and individual human behaviour leave the standards of behaviour to a public or state decision about what is to be implemented or imposed as standards. Standards of individual and public behaviour are ultimately imposed by the prevailing force — whether individual or corporate. The great modern paradox is that the imposed force is born of an uncompromising set of abstract propositions about radical individual freedom.

The object in examining the manner in which a member of the Murdoch empire dealt with the death of Diana, Princess of Wales, is to show how the fundamental principles of theoretic-republicanism are implemented in a particular case, how closely they are connected with the protection of hierarchy and power, and especially how they are manipulated to justify social and political discourse that is the very opposite of fair-minded reasoning. In this context I will examine how the articles, commentaries, editorials and reports are linked on each of the days immediately following Diana's death — and how they formed a campaign to reach certain predetermined objectives.

3

Monday, 1 September 1997:
The World Grieves While the Media Seek
Excuses

1. Grief Around the World for a Dead Princess

The day after the killing of Diana, Princess of Wales, *The Australian* produced a 10-page commemorative edition chock-a-block with expensive advertisements. The sales team at *The Australian* must have worked frantically to get everything in place. But the tightness of the deadline did not spoil the results. The front page of this commemorative edition is worthy of a skilful editorial team. It feeds straight into the general feeling that rose spontaneously from the hearts of millions of people around the world. The page is dominated by an exquisite full-colour photo of the Princess from the chest up. All the vulnerability, beauty, honesty and openness of heart is evident in this picture. Even now as I write these words with this picture of Diana in front of me I cannot help pausing to consider the eyes and the face in the picture. The millions of words spoken and the thousands of articles written about her would never succeed in conveying what this picture tells of the person and tragedy of Diana, Princess of Wales. The front-page headline supports the photo and appeals directly to the observed reaction worldwide to Diana's death.

1961 DIANA 1997
10-PAGE COMMEMORATIVE EDITION

The Queen and the Prince of Wales are deeply shocked and distressed by this terrible news.— *Buckingham Palace*

People's princess dead at 36

This is one of the few headlines appearing during the week of the accident that is true to the situation. Of course, any normal person would understand that the Queen and her family, like any other family, would be struck down with shock, grief and incomprehension. Any person with normal sensitivity would understand the distress immobilising the grieving family for a period of time.

The headline is followed by two front-page articles by the European correspondent of *The Australian*, Ean Higgins. The main article of the two gives a largely unembellished account of the accident that killed Diana, Dodi Fayed and Henri Paul, the driver of the car. Summing up the reaction around the world Higgins makes it evident that people high and low know who to blame for the tragedy. There is the full quotation from Earl Spencer already given (p.10 'Every proprietor and editor... has blood on his hands today ...'), the report that one of the photographers at the scene of the accident was beaten 'by angry witnesses', and the concern uttered by British Foreign Secretary, Robin Cook: '..."serious questions have to be asked" about the activities of the paparazzi'. Higgins ends this article by saying, 'Before yesterday's events, some angry commentators suggested that the media would hound Diana to death.'

Two other important points are mentioned in this article. Following from the headline quoting the Queen's and Prince Charles's shock and distress, Higgins reports that the 'Prince of Wales ... announced that he would fly from Balmoral Castle in Scotland to Paris to escort her [Diana's] body home.' Later we would learn how distressful this trip to Paris to pick up the body of his former wife was for Prince Charles (he emerged from viewing Diana's body red-eyed and visibly moved). The quiet dignified manner he maintained at the hospital and at the airport was to cover the intense grief he had shown in private. Apart from the media, his manner in dealing with his feelings and the situation was respected by those he came into contact with. Prince Charles's behaviour and distress at this time would be largely ignored or suppressed by most media instruments. Instead of the picture of a man grieving and distressed, a caricature of Prince Charles would be developed consistent with the media objectives. Higgins also previews the sympathy people around the world would express for the two young princes, William and Harry, who were so close to their mother. Secondly, the grief-stricken words of Tony Blair, Britain's Prime Minister, reflected the general feeling of the British people. Higgins reports

Tony Blair's announcement in this way:

Close to tears as he spoke last night, British Prime Minister Tony Blair said Diana would be remembered as 'the people's princess'.

'We are today a nation in a state of shock, in mourning, in grief which is so deeply painful for us,' Mr Blair said.

'She was a wonderful and warm human being ... her own life was sadly taken by tragedy. She touched the lives of many others, in Britain, through out the world.'

D. D. McNicoll (**Blair's Britain wakes to darkest day,** p. 2) follows this up with some further comment on how the people of Britain reacted to Diana's death. Tony Blair's emotional response is repeated in more detail but only as it represents the feeling of the nation: 'the country awoke to have its normally sleepy Sunday morning swamped with a wave of grief and mourning from people at all levels of society.' In response the media outlets gave over their programming to the news, flags flew at half-mast and people began giving material expression to their feelings by wearing black armbands and placing flowers at Kensington Palace. Tony Blair was open and heartfelt in his sympathy for the royal family: 'Our thoughts and prayers are with the Royal Family, in particular with the two sons, the two boys. Our hearts go out to them ...'

Nobody watching the television pictures of this speech could doubt the sincerity of feeling. There were comments from interviews with ordinary people each expressing their own feelings of grief. McNicoll also notes the reaction of people to the paparazzi: 'Angry members of the public shouted abuse at photographers waiting outside Buckingham Palace.' The statement from Buckingham Palace is mentioned (the Queen and Prince Charles are deeply distressed) and Mohammed Al Fayed is reported as saying the 'hounding [of] his eldest son and the princess contributed to the tragedy.'

Sarah Turnbull (**Mourning has broken all around the world,** p. 2) gives an account of the reactions from world figures to Diana's death. Included are President Chirac, President Clinton, President Mandela and Cardinal Basil Hume of the Catholic Church. They all express their grief and sorrow for the loss of such a warm, generous and beautiful person.

The Australian angle is provided on the final page of the commemorative edition. David Nason (**Leaders united in sorrow and sympathy for princes,** p. 9) gives an unembellished account of what some of Australia's political leaders said in response to Diana's death. All utter their shock and consternation at her sudden death and the trauma her sons will inevitably suffer because of the time and manner of her passing. John Howard sums up the feelings of the majority of ordinary Australians.

> *I extend my very deep sympathy, particularly to the two young sons (Prince William and Prince Henry), who have suffered the trauma of a marriage break-up and have now lost their mother at the very young age of 36.*

The second article from the Australian angle (**Australians helped in royal transition,** p. 9) is a straightforward commemorative piece. In many of the reports, as we shall see, there is a lot of sneer about the royal family, Diana's state of mind and her connection with the Al Fayed family.[1] There is none of that in this report. Indeed, we have an account of Princess Diana's connection with Australia that a lot of people could recognise. The report is actually more about how friendly and hospitable Australians are than about Diana herself. It mentions briefly the five visits Diana made to Australia highlighting in a very positive manner the affection the Australian people showed towards her, and the appreciation Diana expressed about the kind treatment given her in our friendly country.

We read that her first visit (February 1981, before the engagement to Charles was announced) was to escape the media harassment she was already being subjected to. One of her flat mates is quoted as saying: 'Things have got on top of Diana recently and she has gone away for a complete rest.' So already Diana was showing how burdensome the constant attention of the media was. She was showing what anybody could see right from the beginning: she was simply not emotionally equipped to handle the unrelenting pressure of the reporters and photographers pushing up against her every minute of the day. That did not matter for the reporters and others following her. We saw from the beginning that the media were totally devoid of the moral feeling most normal people have for the emotional state of others. In fact, it was all the better if Diana was pleading with them, shedding tears, showing herself unable to cope with their heartlessness, being led away discomposed, or breaking down and howling against her car while the cameras were brought close enough to capture the tears flowing down her cheeks. The last photos of Diana were taken from inches away as she lay crumpled and dying in the smashed Mercedes.

Higgins's second front-page article is brief and headed: **Shocked Royals attend church**. The report focuses precisely on the grief the royal family was experiencing. Within a few hours of Diana's death the nucleus of the royal family, as representatives of a Christian nation, arrived at the local church. In the Christian tradition they were there to express their grief and to pray for the repose of Diana's soul — although Higgins omits mentioning this obvious point. He concentrates on the appearance of the grief-stricken group of royal members as they assembled in public demonstrating that regardless of rank in this temporal sphere, we are all equal in the moral realm and must all submit to death and God's judgement. As I say, Higgins does not mention these Christian aspects of the royal attendance at the local church but if he knew anything about the religion that has been central to European culture he would be aware of the significance of the royal family assembling in prayer. As the royal family, they were not only there as private persons but also as representatives before God of the British people. At some stage in his reporting he should have mentioned it as information relevant to the occasion. He does not. Just how relevant this information is, will become apparent in the reports of days following. The royal family's attendance at Church would become a pivotal event in the media's reporting. But Higgins's account of the visible grief is appropriate and largely consistent with the TV pictures of the event.

> *Princes William and Harry were grief-stricken as they arrived at church with the Prince of Wales last night near the family's retreat at Balmoral Scotland ...*
> *The Queen mother was dressed in black, with a dark-suited Charles sitting between his sons, who looked heavy hearted and calm ...*

In fact, the television images show all members of the royal family looking heavy-hearted and solemn as they go about the traditional Christian manner of honouring the memory of a dearly departed one. Higgins goes on:

Flowers were piled high on the steps of the church as ordinary Britons joined world leaders at the outpouring of grief at the death of a 'people's princess'...

These flowers placed high on the steps were the first signs of communal grief, and the royal family in attending church and passing directly in front of the first demonstrations of communal grief were immediately acknowledging the grief of the nation. Floral tributes also appeared at the gates of Kensington Palace. They would grow to a thick expanse of colour covering the approaches to the palace. The spontaneous action of placing flowers at the local church in Balmoral and at the gates of Kensington Palace demonstrates what was evident to the unprejudiced mind. Ordinary people around the world felt deeply the loss of Diana and sympathised with the royal family. Nothing in Higgins's two articles gave any outward indication of how Diana's death would later be manipulated for political reasons. Alas, the picture of the royal family grieving in the appropriate manner would be re-edited and Ean Higgins would fall in obsequiously with the tone and direction prescribed by his masters at News Ltd.[2]

Much of the commemorative edition of *The Australian* was filled with reports and articles following up on different aspects of the two leading articles on the front page. But they were channelled in the direction indicated by the editorial board of *The Australian*. The summary reports of the worldwide grief in response to Diana's death reveal an undercurrent of the media's view of the British royal family. The underlying prejudice occasionally breaks the surface. For example, Sarah Turnbull in reporting the reaction of world leaders (**Mourning has broken all around the world**) could not leave off having a gratuitous sideswipe at Prince Charles and the royal family.

The Princess of Wales was adored in France and if anything her popularity increased after her divorce from Charles.

Whereas the rest of the British royals are regarded by the French as a dull, dowdy lot, Diana oozed glamour and chic. She became the unofficial patron of French couture and for fashion houses like Christian Dior, the beautiful much-photographed princess was the dream client.

Without hesitation, it seems, we are expected to accept this as an accurate report about the French people's poor opinion of the British royal family. No evidence appears necessary. When Turnbull talks about the 'French people' perhaps she really means that political or society faction in France that agrees with her particular views. The editorial masters at *The Australian* could have cut this simple-minded ridicule which had nothing at all to do with the comments of world leaders. In contrast, they could have seen on the Australian '60 minutes' program the night before that David Eads, BBC correspondent in Paris, said that the French people were 'great fans of the British royal family'. If I reflect on the reports of the French people's attitude to the British royal family during the years, this would seem closer to the truth.[3]

2. The Accident

Immediately following the accident, the TV networks gave a lot of time to reporting on the cause of the accident, Diana's injuries, and the ultimate cause of death. Although the issue of blame is covered at length, the Commemorative Edition devotes relatively little space to the circumstances surrounding the accident itself. In addition to the details in Higgins's report there is a brief and somewhat haphazard report (**Tourists first to witness mangled wreckage,** p. 2) about the first people to arrive at the accident. More detail about the scene of the crash was provided by TV interviews and coverage by CNN who are the main source for these details. Katherine Glascott (**Worst not known until surgery,** p. 2) gives an account of the injuries to Princess Diana and the inability of the French doctors to treat what was a fatal injury from the beginning. Diana died from a massive chest injury. The report is a small filler piece providing necessary factual information about the accident. A more substantial piece on the crash is provided by Michelle Gunn (**Police detain seven French photographers,** p. 3).

Gunn repeats much of the detail of the crash in Higgins's front-page report. There is the added information that the French police had detained seven press photographers who were chasing Diana and Dodi before the crash. These seven had apparently been among 'an estimated 30 photographers [who] had positioned themselves at the hotel entrance ...' and had prompted 'Diana and Fayed to flee via a rear exit ...' An important detail is given in this report which seemed to be ignored for a while but became a serious matter for investigation weeks later by the French police.

> *Fayed and the driver died instantly when the car, which was believed to have been overtaking another vehicle, swerved to avoid an oncoming car and smashed into a parapet at high speed.*

This is curious. Are the reporter and editor just being careless or was there substance to this early account of the accident? When, several days after the accident, it was found that Henri Paul's blood-alcohol levels were high, the line was taken that Henri Paul was heavily inebriated and simply lost control of a car he could never control at such a high speed. No one but a legally drunk driver was responsible for the accident. It was an unfortunate set of circumstances that led to a drunk driver being put in charge of the car that drove Diana and Dodi to their deaths. This appeared then (and still does) to be the main ploy by the media to escape blame for the accident. I will come back again to the events immediately prior to the accident and the issue of blame in the context of what we know a year later, but let me suggest a scenario that anybody at the time could have made up from the preliminary information — especially those who were familiar with the freeway that ran along the Seine to the Alma tunnel. I want to indicate how easily the media swung away from unpleasant implications in the detail of the accident.

How would Henri Paul be in a position to overtake one vehicle to find himself in the way of an *oncoming* vehicle on a freeway where there were two lanes on his side and concrete pillars separating his side from the two lanes running in the opposite direction? How can the obvious problem of the oncoming vehicle be resolved? Here's a possible explanation. The first vehicle Henri Paul had to 'overtake' was there to slow him down, and the second was travelling much more slowly in order to slow the car carrying the Princess and Dodi even further, while allowing the photographers to take good pictures. The slowness of the second vehicle may have given the confused impression to people glancing at it from a passing vehicle that it was *oncoming*, which was not possible in the circumstances. Slowing a target vehicle by manoeuvring a blocking vehicle at some point in front of the target vehicle is a common tactic employed by the paparazzi. The evidence gathered at the accident scene points to the existence of one vehicle, a white fiat UNO, which the Mercedes collided with just before the Alma tunnel.

Furthermore, we know that huge sums of money were being paid for exceptional photos of Diana. Such high fees increased the recklessness and daring of those pursuing her. We also know that the teams of paparazzi stationed strategically remain in contact with each other by mobile phone. Even in that early stage of reporting the accident, detail came to light that concurred with the later and clearer evidence. I will be dealing with the accident in detail in Chapter 11.

Gunn then comes up for the first time with one of the stock explanations for the accident run by the media. When the Princess and Dodi left the Ritz for the last time she comments:

Whether Diana and Dodi were encouraging the chauffeur to try and shake the pursuers, or whether they had any sense of what was about to happen, was unknown.

It will be fortunate for the media if it remains unknown for it can always be presented as causing or at least contributing to the accident. Dodi or Diana spurred the driver on to take unacceptable risks. It is up to Diana and Dodi's badly injured bodyguard, Trevor Rees-Jones, to clear this point up. At the moment of writing he has recalled seeing 'two cars and a motorbike' following the Mercedes, 'one [of which] seemed to be a white car with a boot which opened at the back and had two doors' (*The Age*, 7 March 1998). In the meantime, the speculation about the degree of blame Diana and Dodi may have to accept in urging on the driver seems to have waned. The evidence pointing to a white car playing a role in the accident could no longer be ignored.

Gunn mentions in passing the 'report' that one of the photographers was seen taking pictures of the crash and was 'beaten up by a witness who was appalled at his actions'. But what seemed of more importance to Gunn was the Princess's chance of happiness in her 'blossoming' relationship with 'her lover', Dodi Fayed. The true tragedy, according to Gunn, was that this final chance of happiness was denied Diana. She ends her report with this startling suggestion:

Admirers across the world had been fascinated by the blossoming relationship between Diana and the playboy heir. Had the queen of hearts at last found true love?

*It may be that it was **the efforts of over-zealous photographers hoping to help answer that question which ultimately cost the princess her life**.* [My emphasis.]

One doesn't know whether to laugh or throw up at this. Who is she kidding? Can you imagine it? All those well-disciplined paparazzi gathered outside the Ritz hotel politely musing on the chances of Diana's happiness with Dodi Fayed? Can you imagine they only broke off their quiet concerned conversations about this matter so dear to their hearts to chase Diana, all zeal, in order to solve this pressing problem? Only members of the media would have the gall to run with this explanation. But there's more to come in the efforts to exonerate the media from all blame in these events.

3. The Arab Connection

Some of the people at the centre of the story about Princess Diana's last hours were completely unknown to most of us around the world until the weeks before the accident. In fact, the name Al Fayed suddenly connected to Diana would have caused most of us to ask in surprise, 'Who is Al Fayed and where did he come from?' In fact, the appearance of the Al Fayed family on the scene was the reason the media wound up their 'activities' in following Diana to new levels. Now what does this Commemorative Edition on Diana's death have to say about the Arab connection? There are two short reports devoted to giving the reader some background information. The first starts off rather modestly.

Sian Powell (**Last loving rendez-vous at the Ritz**, p. 8) provides the reader with an account of the short history of the relationship between Diana and Dodi Fayed. We learn of Mohammed Al Fayed's business connection with the Spencer family. It was in this social context that Diana first met Dodi. We are also apprised of Mohammed Al Fayed's failed efforts to gain British citizenship which were surrounded by scandal. The Al Fayed name is thus lightly smeared leaving the way open for more concentrated attacks on the 'unsavoury' connection that Diana naively wandered into. In the second report (**Dodi lived the high life, on Daddy's leash**, p. 8), Powell gets down to business. The report appears in bold type next to the previous one. It provides more 'background' information on the Al Fayed family and on Dodi in particular. We are informed that although Australians would not know the name of Al Fayed it was well-known in Britain, 'almost infamous'.

> *Dodi Fayed is the son of the Egyptian millionaire Mohammed Fayed — the notorious entrepreneur who owns Harrods and the Paris Ritz, and who relaunched Punch magazine.*
>
> *Fayed senior, who became a household name when he was refused British citizenship for reasons that have never been thoroughly aired, was in recent years inextricably entangled in a cash-for-parliamentary questions affair.*

These two paragraphs ensure that the name 'Fayed' smells for the reader who has never heard of it before. Most people reading this would just assume it was deserved. But does the name 'Al Fayed' deserve the implicit smearing for the actual 'crimes' listed? If Al Fayed senior was refused British citizenship, should we automatically assume that it was due to his (implied) unsavoury character? In another context, if the British upper class were responsible for such views, they would be accused of discriminating against an Egyptian, that is, they would be accused of racism. And what about the crime of paying MPs for services? Surely this is just the sort of tactic the media use to gather information. The rest of this article amounts to a picture of Dodi Fayed as a spoilt, loose, self-indulged, rich brat whose aimless, contemptible activities were financed and controlled by an overbearing father. The reader will find that this caricature of the Al Fayed family is continually developed by the reports appearing in *The Australian*. It is all written in connection with Diana's character and behaviour. The reader will not be left to guess what he is meant to conclude from this connection.[4]

4. The Fairytale Princess, the Cruel Prince and the Wicked Royal Family

We now get on to the real meat of *The Australian's* Commemorative Edition. This is the time to air some key features of the media's magisterium of gossip and slander about Prince Charles and the British royal family. The 'reporting' task is left to Juliet Herd in London. She will be followed up by, among others, a practising psychoanalyst.

The title of Herd's first report (**And she lived happily never af-ter,** p. 6) indicates that its main theme would be the unhappy life of Diana. It is that, but it is also the occasion for yet another reporter to put the boot into Prince Charles by running through a list of the media's favourite tidbits about him. The impression is that Juliet Herd knows nothing for sure about Prince Charles but is content, for the benefit of the editorial masters of *The Australian,* to create her own fairytale based on the media-accepted dirt about him. It's the usual stuff. Diana, the beautiful, the warm, the compassionate, romantic, etc., was taken into 'the monarchy, an essentially stuffy, outdated institu-tion'. Charles, 'a sad man' according to Diana,[5] with the complicity of the wicked royal family, proceeded to squeeze this joyous, fragile, little bird to death. Concerned only with setting Diana up as breeder of a male heir, Charles continued on his hard-hearted way. Even on the honeymoon Camilla Parker Bowles, a former girlfriend of Prince Charles, 'haunted' Diana as an 'ever-growing spectre'. Herd writes as if the crunch in the marriage came on the honeymoon when Diana noticed Charles wearing a pair of cufflinks given to him by Camilla.

> *From that point on, the couple essentially began to live a lie, with Diana desperate still to believe in the fairytale and Charles determined to keep his mistress by his bedside …*

We are to believe that Diana put up with this for 12 years, and when things really started to go wrong 'the prince sorely tested her by becoming quite blatant in his meeting with Camilla'. As if keep-ing his mistress *by his bedside* would not be blatant! Then we have this wonderful quotation from Lord Beaverbrook (allegedly).

> *'It was Charles who ran to Camilla when things began to go wrong with Diana,' said Lord Beaverbrook, grandson of the Canadian newspaper tycoon. 'And once Camilla was ensconced, she started throwing her weight around. When she saw the romance was a runner, she simply took a proactive role. Of course, Diana was upset. She had every right to be.'*

If Lord Beaverbrook had really said this, then it sounds rather like late-night ramblings after a few hefty whiskies than a considered judgement. No, let's be fair to Lord Beaverbrook, the whole thing reads like a badly written fairytale. This last quotation does not fit in with the claim that Camilla never left the Prince's bedside, right from the beginning. Nor does it fit with what people like Lord Beaverbrook must have known about the relationship Prince Charles had with Camilla Parker Bowles over time. It was not a straightforward uninterrupted relationship between mistress and royal prince.[6] But anything will do, as long as it's some dirt on Prince Charles. Who cares how well it fits together and what evidence there is for the string of lurid charges about a public figure who in reality has no way of answering such childish gutter-gossip.

But in her effort to surround Diana with pathos and tragedy against the background of the wicked royal family, Herd does say some things coincidentally for which there is plenty of evidence.

> ... *Diana's royal progress was charted by the media with an obsessiveness and intrusiveness that bordered on the harmful — and was subsequently fatal.*

It does not seem to occur to Herd that she may be implicated in this sort of nasty media activity. Indeed, she seems oblivious to the fact that her present article represents just the sort of tabloid 'reporting' that was worrying Diana to death. She goes on:

> *She was to pay a terrible price for that short-lived happiness [with Dodi Fayed] ... As she and film producer Dodi, 41, cavorted in the cool blue of the Mediterranean ... the paparazzi engaged in a photographic feeding frenzy that continued unchecked until the couple's horrific deaths in a car crash in Paris.*

Herd seems to want to distance herself as a print journalist from the accident by describing the paparazzi as 'engaged in a *photographic* feeding frenzy ...' Sorry Ms Herd, you're part of the team. Those gentlemen are the shock troops to provide you with the material for a *writing* feeding frenzy so you can help your masters at *The Australian* fill the empty spaces on their newspaper pages with suitable propaganda.

Jane Fraser (**The fairy princess who lost her script**, p. 6) rescues Herd's tortured fairytale to some degree. She writes an interesting companion piece to Herd's report with the difference that Fraser writes well and entertains. Fraser appears often in *The Australian* so we know beforehand that the article will not pretend to be a deeply serious or factually accurate report. Her work is rather whimsical, flippant and amusingly satirical. Hers is an undisguised imaginative writing style intent on creating an impression not worrying too much about the facts. Here she writes in the style of a sad fairytale where all the mal-adjusted characters drag some sort of tragic affliction around with them. She repeats for the benefit of her prejudiced masters all the stock descriptions of Prince Charles and the class background of which he and Diana are products. Charles is old, stale, crusty and staid, having emerged from a background that is emotionally suppressed, oppressed, and twisted. But what does arise from this colourful picture of emotionally misshapen figures is a reasonably true picture of the emotional course of Diana's life.

Forget about the stereotypical theoretic-republican description of the English upper class and the influence this may have exerted on Diana emotionally. This is propaganda. A good lesson in 18th century English culture would show how ignorant this prejudiced picture is. What was evidently critical in Diana's emotional development was her abandonment by her mother. No matter what the social class, when a mother turns her back on her children and walks out she leaves behind not only the torment of her marriage. She also leaves behind a different sort of torment for the children to deal with. So it happened with Diana.

Equipped with deep insecurities, a poor education and little talent Diana was thrust into the world limelight where her beautiful person and open manner dazzled all but the very miserably minded.[7] If ever anybody's idea of a fairytale could come to life then surely it was on the occasion of the wedding of Diana with the crown prince of the British royal house. Diana said towards the end of her life that she had a lot of love to give, and that if she could give that love for a moment she would be satisfied she had done something worthwhile. This was both the great quality and liability of Diana. She ached to love, to be loved and to return love. She reduced the complex world around her to this simple equation. As a deeply wounded, fragile creature she seemed to have little chance in the world that lay ahead of her as she walked down the aisle of St Paul's on her wedding day.

Despite regurgitating the usual prejudice, Fraser's article highlights the tragedy of Diana in a world fundamentally inimical to her need of love. The over-used caricature of the vibrant, modern princess crushed by a maladjusted, heartless institution ignores the very grave problems of temperament, mind and emotional background that provided little support to Diana in dealing with the heartlessness of the world outside her private life. She could not comprehend the pitiless role played by a materialist media who hounded her unrelentingly and in the end were gearing up to savage her *en masse*.

On this subject, I have before me an article that appeared in *The Age*, 19 July 1997, just 42 days before Diana's death. It is entitled **Changing loyalties** by Judith Whelan.[8] If anybody doubts that the media were already turning violently against the person they had made so much money from, then they should read this. Diana had a big heart. The media have none. If she were still alive her heart would by now be breaking at the incomprehensible cruelty of those who had made an industry out of her. In whatever way, Diana was destined to be killed by the heartless, theoretic-republican, money-grubbing media.

Juliet Herd (**Heirs to the kingdom lose greatest love**, p. 7) gets another go at developing the fairytale started on p. 6. In consistent style she focuses on the terrible loss to the princes of the mother they would always have been close to. In particular, the loss to William must have been great and several stories are told to emphasise this — including some very personal detail that exemplify the close contact between Diana and William (as implicitly opposed to the wooden contact with Charles). Whether they are true or not nobody would know from just reading this piece. The main thing is they serve their purpose.

Herd again mentions the threatening and suffocating environment of the royal family from which the princes were 'protected' by Diana. She seems to want to develop this point but evidently runs out of steam. The trouble is that there is no concrete evidence she can offer to support the so often repeated claim that the princes would wither under the suffocating influence of the royal family. Quite the contrary. Any pictures of Prince Charles with the young princes suggest that they are more than comfortable with their father, and their grandparents. The picture chosen of the three by the river at Balmoral to head this article exemplifies this.[9] The TV reports on Prince Charles and Prince Harry in South Africa (late 1997) clearly show that the young prince has a close relationship with his father. Dare I suggest that

Charles's well-mannered, composed but relaxed behaviour appeals to his sons? That maintaining a composed and friendly manner is more dignified and mature than a selfish, loud, attention-seeking manner? And that this is more appealing to the princes as it is to a great many of us?

The unmentioned pertinent element in all these reports about the young princes' education is the 'Diana factor'. By this I mean the emotional instability that was being increasingly spoken about in Diana in the period before her death. This is conveniently ignored for it would not suit the particular propaganda objectives in this present affair. The reports previous to Diana's death about her emotional instability are studiously ignored. At another time when it suited their purposes, the media would be all over this question. You can picture the headlines: IS MENTAL INSTABILITY A SUITABLE BACK-GROUND FOR THE EDUCATION OF THE YOUNG PRINCES? This is an obvious example of the hypocrisy and double-dealing of the media for the usual purposes.

In the second place, it does not seem to occur to the ordinary media hack that Diana's overall intention was to give some balance, as she saw it, to the education of two princes born into quite a different cultural environment from that into which their father was born. Prince Charles's cultural environment was one that whole nations knew and were influenced by and not just the royal family. A further point is that Diana was part of the broader royal class by birth. Do people really think that she wanted to undermine what was left of the British monarchy? Do they think that she would want to rob her beloved sons of their birthright, of their patrimony?[10] Of course not. The media bosses know this. The honest, open side of Diana was simply used to attack the royal family, to promote the theoretic-republican cause, sell more papers, and acquire more power and position.

Murray Hedgecock (**Accepted by the public, but not church**, p. 7) backs up Herd's fairytale pieces with another propaganda piece disguised as journalistic comment. It's ostensibly about the technical problems that would arise in a union between Prince Charles and Camilla Parker Bowles. The problems encountered in such a union are superficially mentioned. It's basically this. Prince Charles as king would also be the Supreme Governor of the Church of England. But the Church of England still maintains the traditional Christian doctrine that divorced people cannot marry while their divorced partner is still alive. Murray refers to this doctrine as an 'old established' doctrine as (unfavourably) opposed to the 'more liberal approach'. Thus Charles could not marry Camilla and also be king.

The real issue of this disjointed article, however, is the future of the British monarchy and Hedgecock canvasses this with the usual tendentiousness. Diana was a great addition to the royal family as a 'charismatic, charming and popular figure'. Her demise, he says with disarming inconsistency, removes from the royal family the problems caused by Diana, the 'loose cannon'. Her behaviour together with that of the 'younger royals' caused people to lose confidence in the royal family. He cites 'recent opinion polls' as claiming most Britons believe 'Britain would be no worse off without a royal family'. In Hedgecock's mind these polls remain unanalysed and uncontended. The reader may think from the line of argument that with the removal of Diana and the rest of the royals smartening up their act, the enduring British monarchy would be on safer ground. But no, Hedgecock finishes his haphazard and contradictory piece with this observation.

> *But the abrupt loss of Diana, whose arrival as a member of the royal family on her wedding day of 21 July, 1981, was universally welcomed as injecting new life and excitement into the monarchy, can only leave the ancient institution appearing increasingly irrelevant to Britain's younger generation into the new millennium.*

Who cares about consistency and accuracy in detail? As long as Prince Charles and the royal family can be continually painted as 'dull', 'plodding', emotionally twisted, unresponsive, irrelevant, etc., then the job has been worthily done. As long as the reader, who has not time to examine the crassness of such articles, can glean the main message from skimming the surface, then the job has been more than worthily done.

In what seems an incomprehensible effort to put a seal on the contrast between Princess Diana and the royal family, *The Australian* has chosen to quote a person who has earned the contemptible title of 'Mr Paparazzo' (**Deaths an end to limits of good taste, says Mr Paparazzo**). Tazio Secchiarolli, 72, known as Mr Paparazzo, is reported as saying that 'there were no longer limits of good taste in his profession [*sic*].' This is like Pol Pot exclaiming that there was now too much genocide in the world. He also says that Diana and Dodi were wrong for fleeing from the press. Such people should stop and let themselves be photographed. Diana and Dodi were responsible for their accident! What else but such self-serving comments should we expect from Mr Paparazzo? He would not consider for a moment that if Diana had stopped for every photographer and reporter that wanted to bail her up she would have had absolutely no life at all. *The Australian* does not hesitate to leave in the choice media sentiment about the royal family coming from the lips of a chief figure among the paparazzi.

> *'I can't tell you how surprised and saddened I am. I liked her a lot,' Mr Secchiarolli said, referring to Diana. 'She was a real anti-conformist who made the royal family look like a bunch of pre-historic animals.'*

The reader should wonder why the *The Australian* chose not to balance Secchiarolli's sneer with some comment on Mr Paparazzo's status in the lowest level of media activity.

In all the accounts of the Diana accident there will be a constant refrain. Diana was lively, warm and open; the rest of the royal family are closed, cold, staid and emotionally crippled. But, as I have already indicated, it is questionable that Diana was really as radical and non-conformist in relation to the royal family as is made out by the theoretic-republicans. It is just as questionable that the other members of the royal family are cold and maladjusted. This media image of Diana and the royal family will be constantly tested in the course of this book. The next section gives us the chance to see how the media equivalent of the academic theologian functions in promoting the media contrast between Diana and the royal family.

5. The Psychoanalyst Earning Good Money on the Propaganda Circuit

Having provided an 'analysis' by 'professional' journalists of the issues of Diana's death, the editorial masters at *The Australian* now appeal to a big gun in the media arsenal, the *degreed* professional. This big gun has all the prestige and authority the academic theologian holds in any ecclesiastical hierarchy. In this case, psychoanalyst James Oliver is *The Australian's* man. Selections are adapted and presented from his book, *Britain on the Couch* (Century, London, 1997). The editor could not fiddle with the writing so it remained for him to arrange the selection in the most effective way possible. But, as it turns out, the selections could not always be bent to serve the right purposes. The author also points out that he is not offering 'proper clinical case histories', but is working up a picture based on what information is available.

The title that the editor has chosen for this 'article' (p. 4) tells us exactly what the objective is.

Tradition a tightrope in world without love

In the days before the death of the Princess of Wales,
OLIVER JAMES attempted a daring royal psychoanalysis

The attack is fully concentrated on (royal) tradition. This is an important propaganda piece. The theoretic-republican editor must constantly promote the picture of royal tradition as cold and loveless. A loveless structure is bound in the end to produce emotional and mental cripples, such as the members of the royal family. The contrast between the royal family and Diana is always to be kept in mind while reading James's analysis.

After reading the selections I would say that the most credible parts of his 'analysis' are based on information about the royal members that has surfaced over a period of time from many different sources. This information functions neutrally in propaganda terms. On the other hand, what may appear to be useful and effective reads too much like gossip. The most compelling information and argument would rather, in my view, run counter to the general theoretic-republican objectives of the News Ltd bosses. In particular, with regard to Diana, the evidence would seem to suggest that her troubles have their origins in our modern social environment and in particular in the tragic circumstances of her family life as a child, and not in the context of the royal marriage. A cool head is likely in the end to conclude that the disintegration of Diana's early family life (and its legacy of emotional instability) had perhaps the only chance of being remedied in an environment of stability and firm family tradition. Let's see whether I am correct.

The selections divide roughly into three parts. The first part is a brief comment on the state of modern existence for most people, men and women. It is worth quoting several paragraphs.

Many of us feel there is something missing from our lives today.

Despite unprecedented peace and prosperity, we are unhappier than we were.

There is an epidemic of irritability and aggression, of depression and paranoia, of obsessions, panics, addictions, compulsions, relationships that are not working, careers that dissatisfy, an outbreak of living in the future and pathological re-enactment of the past.

We feel like losers, even if our status would seem to make us winners.

At the same time, our attachments are falling apart.

Despite greatly improved opportunities, women are dissatisfied and men are confused.

The result is an unprecedented gender rancour and divorce rate.

The problem extends to some of the cleverest, wealthiest and most attractive people in the land — among them Princess Diana.

Who after honest consideration of our modern period could take issue with this general picture?[11] You do not have to be a trained psychoanalyst to come to these conclusions. The author does not use the word 'disintegration' but the picture painted is one of social disintegration — and few of us would escape one or more categories of this picture. Even the most stable family groups today witness in their close family context and in their social environment the failure of relationships, the seemingly inexplicable depression and despair of close ones, and the most abject failure in individual responsibility. How do we explain this?

Well, for those who regulate their lives according to traditional moral and religious principles, the explanation has been there since 1960,[12] the year the rot really set in. This was the time when those who wanted to analyse our society into elemental parts and rebuild on the basis of an *a priori* social structure started to have their way. All moral, religious, social, and political structures that were not compatible were to be hurled from the heights and those who would not go along would be dealt with. The guillotine was no longer acceptable, but the manner of liquidation was just as cruel and complete. In fact, the executioners, then and now, derive the greatest amusement and satisfaction from the lingering pain they are able to inflict on those declared theoretically *unacceptable*. Those who manage to push forward and break from the levelled masses to proclaim their traditional values have witnessed the lies, the distortions, the misrepresentations, the ridicule, the mockery, the abuse and the inevitable ostracism they have to cope with if they persist. Few of them have the courage to do so.

If your mind has not been formed by a stay in one of the seminaries of theoretic-republicanism, then you are likely to recognise in the length of your existence, a scheme of things in which there is a particular moral framework and all things reply to certain inherent structures. The social history of all peoples shows that up until the theoretic-republican period of the last two hundred years, people have believed that a man and a woman have different but complementary natures. They have believed that men and women are most happy and secure when these complementary natures are recognised and expressed in particular traditional arrangements, that wrong is done when these natures are denied or when either the man or the woman fails to fulfil the duty of the traditional arrangement that has been the authentic expression of their complementary natures.

In particular cases, unhappiness is the result of the failure of individual men and women to respond to the moral framework of their partnership. But when whole societies go about denying the moral fundamentals of our existence and embark on the destruction of their particular objectifications of moral duty then disintegration is the reward, and the individual degenerates into a morass of

> *irritability and aggression, of depression and paranoia, of obsessions, panics, addictions, compulsions, relationships that are not working, careers that dissatisfy, an outbreak of living in the future and pathological re-enactment of the past.*

The theoretic-republican mind will reject this as a lot of pernicious hogwash. In the traditional moral framework, a man who beats his wife does wrong for the very reason he transgresses the prescriptions of that moral framework. The theoretic-republican mind says that the 'structure' of traditional man/woman relationships is arbitrary, imposed and therefore evil. Such a dogmatic mind cannot admit of any other conclusion.[13] Thus the theoretic-republican editor reading this first passage from James's book will not for a moment recognise what the unaffected mind will recognise, but will think he is producing an analysis that indicts the traditional elements of society he has

not yet been able to destroy. Full of confidence he has gone on to se-
lect the passages about Diana's background he thinks will admirably
support his objective. But if we do what the 'rationalist' republican
exhorts us to do (that is, use our reasoning faculty) then we will come
to some conclusions that will not work for him.

Taking this a little further, and pre-empting what follows, if James
has drawn a true picture of the state of the modern person's emotional
health, then social commentators and those who control the apparatus of social organisation should surely look at the policies that
promote the social and moral trends leading to this unstable and dis-
satisfying condition. Surely one should find out why there was less
emotional instability and more happiness in society before the dramatic changes over the last thirty years. It would seem to be a death
wish to continually update society by applying more of the same social measures. There seems less explanation about this state affairs than
there is about the whales who insist upon beaching themselves when
the clear, open, life-giving sea lies just behind them.

In the second part, psychoanalyst James Oliver describes the tragic
circumstances of Diana's family life. It is an account of family breakdown, conflict, misery, desertion and a deprivation of the very thing
children need: love and security. Diana's own married life is compared
with her mother's, Frances Shand Kidd, and the comparison is revealing. There would be few of us who have not witnessed a similar
breakdown in family relationships. We know that this is essentially a
human problem. It is not restricted to any particular class, high or
low. The prince and the pauper are liable to be embroiled in the same
breakdown due to individual transgression in circumstances that are
universal and not due to the 'inherent' perniciousness of a particular
class structure. However much sympathy we hold for Diana, however
much admiration we have for her open, honest, affectionate nature,
we must recognise the tragic elements of her character which she
brought to her marriage with Prince Charles. Indeed, Oliver James
comments:

> *Given this disharmonious history, it is not surprising that Diana*
> *suffered from depression (for which she took the antidepressant Prozac*
> *and had psychotherapy), bulimia and suicidal thoughts. However, when*
> *she was interviewed on British television in 1995, she did not speak*
> *much of her childhood …*

She was so busy exposing Charles's inadequacies that she ignored her relationship with her own father ...

It's a pity that James does not put Charles's 'inadequacies' in parentheses. For it is clear that in the circumstances Charles's action would have to be viewed in the context of the accuser's emotional instability. James goes on to highlight Diana's great need to give love and receive love and how she was continually let down in this respect. This second selection ends with Diana's words about love and how she was terribly hurt by the betrayal of somebody she had loved very much. James's comment is surely appropriate.

'Yes, I adored him. Yes, I was in love with him [James Hewitt]. But I was very let down' — *as she has been by all the men in her life but perhaps most crucially of all by Earl Spencer [Diana's father], of whom there was not one mention [in the interview of 1995].*

If this analysis is true then it surely gets Prince Charles and the royal family off the hook. Diana came to her union with Prince Charles, and centuries of enduring national tradition with some severe emotional liabilities. She was certainly fragile, affectionate and innocent but she was not the innocent victim about to be crushed by a cold, heartless, inflexible system. She had already been crushed. The question arising from this is how well did Prince Charles handle the problems that followed Diana into their marriage. In fact, it is appropriate to ask whether the demands and duties of his institution (as with any other public institution) made it impossible for him to manage on his own. In a comparable public institution that is not the daily butt of an amoral media, there would be a range of assistance for those having to deal with such a severe personal problem.[14]

It is highly significant that a similar portrait of Prince Charles by Oliver James is not included in this selection. You would think that if James had anything to say about the crown prince he would have included some of it here, even briefly. But let me appeal to millions of men and women who have found themselves in a situation similar to that of Prince Charles: having to negotiate with a partner who is incapable of negotiating fruitfully in their close relationships, who refuses to respond to reasoned appeals. Those men and women know how soul-destroying it can be to try to accommodate and appease somebody who will not be accommodated or appeased, no matter what you do. Is this the situation Prince Charles was in? The evidence points this way. I have already sketched roughly what I think Prince Charles's character to be, and I have given reasons for thinking so. *The Australian* does not quote anything from Oliver James's analysis that contradicts this.

We should further consider that Prince Charles was not in the ordinary social context of having to deal with an emotionally damaged partner. He was born to be king of the United Kingdom of Britain and Ireland in the 21st century. Now the theoretic-republican mind likes to make out that being king is only a position of intolerable power, prestige and privilege. That may have occurred several centuries ago — circumstances which differ little from the power structure and its privileges generated by the 'republican' system as I have outlined. But it is not so today and Prince Charles is in the most unenviable situation with responsibilities and demands that no ordinary person would be capable of bearing. Truly in his case, a life's training is necessary for him to accept the burden of the position, and the unending slander emanating from the philosophers of *innovation, vanity and envy*[15] who now control the staff lists of the most important institutions in our parliamentary democracy. Thus for him to have to cope with an emotionally damaged wife would have been an intolerable load, as it apparently turned out to be.

Much is made of Prince Charles's relationship with Camilla Parker Bowles and how it allegedly endured from his single days into and through his marriage with Diana. But Prince Charles firmly rejects any such claim. He said publicly that he was only unfaithful to his marriage after it had 'irretrievably broken down'. There is no hard evidence to suggest otherwise, and nothing James says contradicts this. Indeed, the assumptions that form the background of the discipline of psychoanalysis would not only excuse Prince Charles's ultimate action but would justify it as the only reasonable way ahead. The traditional framework of morality does not excuse Charles's seeking consolation in someone he could love and trust, but acknowledges the desperate situation and the fallible nature of the human person. We who sympathise with the burden Prince Charles must bear wished that he could have managed in the circumstances. Regardless, let's keep in mind that Prince Charles's manner of dealing with this question is qualitatively different from that of the theoretic-republican who logically thinks nothing of following his sexual impulses no matter what the situation as long as there is no *perceivable* harm to the social environment.

One would expect that the third selection from James would be an analysis of Prince Charles, mixing his behaviour destructively with Diana's emotional liabilities. Not so. The News Ltd bosses have chosen passages from James's book that pretend to analyse the Queen Mother, the Queen herself and Sarah Ferguson, the Duchess of York. On the whole James's analysis is not only unconvincing, but it appears based on 'information' that is at the level of gossip.

James starts his 'analysis' of the Queen Mother in the ridiculing style of the tabloids. He refers to her 'watching over the royal family's calamities with gin and tonic in hand'. This is cheap and cowardly. We have more reason to refer gratuitously to a psychoanalyst like Oliver James as another wacky unstable shrink who turns up to his rooms with a sniff of cocaine to keep him settled. A psychiatrist once confided to me that the highest incidence of suicide was to be found among his colleagues. And who has not noticed that the people inclined to go into the psychotherapeutic professions sometimes seem badly in need of help themselves? Are these points less relevant to a discussion about a case of psychoanalysis than mentioning the Queen Mother's supposed preference for gin and tonic? Although I am assured by some people that the Queen Mother does like her gin and tonic and that this gives her an endearing quality, most readers have no way of knowing it. But it's not really the truth or otherwise of the Queen Mother's drinking preferences that is at issue here. It is the tactic in referring to it in the context of talking about emotional maladjustment, and the uses it can be put to in cementing a case against the royal family.

There's no doubt that James's intention is to argue that the Queen Mother is maladjusted. He relates a preamble of events in her life before he is ready to nail her particular maladjustment. It is not completely clear what the psychological malady is, but it seems to be a feeling of insecurity, a need to be loved, a need for attention and approbation. If this is indeed the malady then it is a malady that affects all of us. The selections from James's book are apparently meant to show that she is particularly afflicted by this malady. But what evidence does he provide? Well, he says, the Queen Mother was a 'gay young thing' in 'the jolly period'. 'She was already regal and charming by the age of four.' He especially attaches significance to the precocious greeting she gave to the Earl of Strathmore at this age: 'How do you do Mr Ralston? I have not seen you look so well for years and years.' From this he goes directly on to talk about the Queen Mother's 'desire to please and to charm, her love of acting ...' The fact that she was under the care of a 'strict disciplinarian' is also supposed to be a factor in creating behaviour that was designed to gain approbation and attention. There are a few other such vague details given that are meant to make the same point. They don't at all. If James is wanting to make the case that the Queen Mother is especially afflicted by some psychological disorder he has failed. Whatever evidence he has given would, as I say, apply to most people.

Many people would admit to the trifling insecurities he describes here. Many people would admit they like attention, even more so than the Queen Mother. Indeed, if the Queen Mother's supposed desire for attention amounts to a maladjustment then what are we to say of the entertainers we see on our TV screens each evening? In James's terms these are monsters of maladjustment. As for the highly significant greeting to Mr Ralston, let me remind Oliver James and the editorial staff of *The Australian* that just thirty years ago good manners, courtesy and respect were considered important. That exercising self-discipline in these matters was not a maladjustment. The maladjustment was the inability to be polite, courteous and respectful. The Queen Mother at the age of four was being educated in good manners in the way that was common up until the 1960s, with the difference that there were more demands on her because of her position. This hardly adds up to a malady. Indeed, we should ask what exactly is a psychological maladjustment. In the authoriphobic mind, those who do not reveal the same obsessive/compulsive attitude to authority in all its forms are maladjusted.

After what seems to be an attempt to demonstrate that the Queen Mother had a compulsive need of attention and approbation to cover her insecurities, James goes on to describe behaviour which would rather disprove the point. He raises a comparison with Diana which subtly puts the Queen Mother in the same emotional category as Diana. We are to ignore the fact that he produces no evidence to support this categorisation. He raises the very valid point of why the Queen Mother did not make her 'difficulties' more public, assuming that he has made a case for those 'difficulties'. The explanation he gives is more revealing about James than about the Queen Mother.

Firstly, he makes the distinction between the 'more circumspect, stiff-upper-lip generation' of the Queen and the more open generation of Diana. The term 'stiff-upper-lip' is a genuine case of unthinking stereotyping and is used as an argument by the political bigot. Most thinking people would think that the public flaunting of one's problems reflected a personal immaturity and that self-control in public indicated maturity rather than immaturity or maladjustment. I am sure that if James returned to some of his texts on psychotherapy he would find respected practitioners in the field agreeing with this. But let's face it. These passages are not really chosen for their professional acumen in psychotherapy or psychoanalysis. They are chosen for their political suitability.

James wonders whether the Queen Mother may have acted differently if she had been subjected to the same media attention as Diana. Indeed, how would most of us react if tormented in this way? James then relates some (unproven) detail about the Queen Mother that gives 'one clue'. He relates that she was 'offered up as a potential wife to the future king, Edward'. When Edward showed no interest 'she was punted in the direction of his younger brother Bertie'. (One must again note the ridiculing style of this account. One wonders whether James's consulting-room notes are written in the same manner. I am sure his patients would not like to be made fun of like this.) But Bertie had to propose three times before he was accepted by a woman who evidently wanted to be sure of his feelings and other possible 'entanglements'. Now most mature people would think, 'Well done. Here's a sensible person being appropriately prudent about her choice of a life-long partner.' We all know what a disaster a bad choice can turn out to be. But James thinks that these details demonstrate something else.

> *This scepticism may have resulted from a lifelong suspicion that nobody really loved her for herself, resulting from her childhood. But unlike Diana, whose childhood was considerably more disturbed, the Queen Mother did not take the hand of the first royal to present himself. Her need to be loved was tempered by caution and a desire to be the only leading lady in the drama of her husband's life.*

If Oliver James is looking to a career as a novelist then he should be encouraged to persist because he is not impressive as a psychoanalyst. Here he is trying to show the opposite of the conclusions the details most obviously point to. One of James's colleagues should take him aside and tell him that everybody likes and needs to be loved and when they finally come to choosing a partner they like to be the 'leading' person in that partner's life. But they also need to be cautious and prudent. A person's feelings for someone else can be so strong that caution is sometimes thrown aside, with disastrous results. It has been an important element in all traditional societies that older, experienced and mature people advise younger ones to be cautious and sensible in their pre-marital relationships. If more young people today approached their marriage with as much 'maladjustment' as the Queen Mother there would be far fewer divorces and far less misery for children. If James's arguments for a maladjusted Queen Mother fail, he has hardly more success with his analysis of the Queen. The difference is that he has some information that can be more easily exploited.

He wants to show that the Queen had symptoms of obsessive/compulsive disorder. He draws his information from a book written by the Queen's former governess. I have not read this book but I will bet London to a brick that the habits described by the governess (and exploited by James) were meant to convey an endearing picture of the child princess. Here's what James makes of the governess's remarks.

> ... [The Queen] had symptoms of obsessive compulsive disorder (OCD) as a small girl. In a sensational book published in 1953, her governess Marion Crawford ('Crawfie') unwittingly described these symptoms when she outlined Princess Elizabeth's 'obsessions'. These included a night ritual involving 30 toy horses, each a foot high, on wheels at the end of her bed. Crawfie wrote that the 'stable' routine was strictly observed.

When the governess used the word 'obsessions' it was obviously not in the context of a clinical report. In everyday use, this word refers most frequently to an abiding interest or to a habit pure and simple. In this context, it is entirely devoid of the connotations it has in a clinical sense. What were these habits that according to James point to the tormented condition of obsessive/compulsive disorder? Well, in addition to the ritual every night of lining up her toy horses the future queen put her shoes under her bed at a particular angle and she lined up the brown coffee sugar granules 'given to her as a treat after meals'. People should see this for the tabloid garbage it is. If such habits make a child obsessive/compulsive in clinical terms then most children suffer from the same problem. For what child does not exhibit some quaint, funny, endearing habit that disappears as they grow older? James has dishonestly taken what seems to be an endearing account of the child Elizabeth and used it for his own squalid purposes.[16]

I could continue to examine the rest of James's 'analysis' in the same manner but I would only be looking at similar 'information' trying to make the same points. James's object is to make the case that the Queen Mother and the Queen are maladjusted and this is a result of the 'repression' and 'denial' in their upbringing. But for the attentive, unprejudiced reader he must fail dismally. His writing and argument are at the level of gossip magazines and should end up as gossip magazines do: as pulp for more tabloid slander. If we review what we have seen of the Queen Mother and Queen through their years in the public spotlight, we cannot help but think that the opinion most people have of them is correct. Both show themselves to be stable, friendly, sympathetic and entirely committed to their duty of serving the subjects of Britain and the people of the Commonwealth. It is evident that James is not interested in the massive amount of information on public record that would contradict his political bigotry. His interest is apparently for the market his book is aimed at, and that includes the bosses of News Ltd who fortuitously could use selections from it in their Commemorative Edition of the life of Diana, Princess of Wales.

6. Stopping at Nothing to Shift Blame from the Media

We arrive now at the key concern of *The Australian* editorial committee in their Commemorative Edition of Diana's death. Before all else, News Ltd must work at destroying any suggestion, however minute, that the media were responsible for Diana's death. They will call on their most 'competent' writers to start a campaign that will be run hard through the following editions of *The Australian*. The first defence comes from D. D. McNicoll (**The pitfalls and pedestals of publicity**, p. 2). McNicoll's report represents the first commentary piece on the accident that killed Diana. It follows directly from the front-page accounts and is surrounded by further details of the accident and the worldwide reaction to Diana's death. The headline, its position and the subject of the article make it evident that this is the centrepiece article of this Commemorative Edition. It outlines for the first time the crucial 'you-asked-for-it' argument run by the media to defend themselves. Let me reproduce the first three paragraphs so the reader will understand its intent and its content.

> *The Princess of Wales had so woven the press and the paparazzi into her life over the last decade that, in recent months, it was almost as though neither could exist without the other.*
>
> *A photograph of Princess Diana's recent kiss with Dodi Fayed aboard his father's yacht in the Mediterranean sold around the world for more than $1 million. It may have been seen as intrusive, but Diana depended upon images captured by the same photographers to make her recent visit to Bosnia, to campaign against land mines, of world interest.*
>
> *A cover picture of Di could boost the circulation of a woman's magazine as surely as that cover could then boost her self image as the 'Queen of Hearts'.*

To reinforce the message the article is accompanied by a large photo of Diana surrounded by photographers and looking not only as though she were totally at home but, with hand raised, to be directing the proceedings. The theme that Princess Diana manipulated the press is expanded in the rest of the article. She manipulated the media firstly in her struggles with Prince Charles, 'royal in-laws' and the 'palace staff'. Later she 'used the eager media every step of the way' to promote her role as 'roving ambassador for Britain' and to promote the causes she espoused. McNicoll writes that Diana could not move without the attendance of a 'media-scrum' and that photographers would be 'regularly tipped off about events that would ensure Diana appeared on the front pages around the world.' Incredibly McNicoll claims that it 'was only when a photographer overstepped what she saw as her rules ... that Diana really objected to their presence.'

The clear thrust of the article is that Diana used the media for her own ends. Practically no attention is given to the manner and extent to which the media pursued Diana, from the beginning, as McNicoll acknowledges. They are merely painted as manipulated elements in a scenario which Diana had herself created. This is the all-important point. The object is to lead the reader to the conclusion that Diana was the victim of a scenario she herself was largely responsible for. And being responsible for the circumstances of media attention she was also responsible for its inevitable effects. Thus Diana was responsible ultimately for her own death! But apparently unconscious of the inconsistency in his report McNicoll himself offers evidence that contradicts his claims. He acknowledges that from the beginning of her relationship with Prince Charles, and through to her death, Diana had to endure constant media hounding. He quotes the British prime minister's office as saying in 1983 that 'they [the paparazzi] are making her life unbearable'. McNicoll speaks of attention from the paparazzi but no doubt the prime minister's office meant the media attention in general. This article is an attempt to clear the media of any blame in the death of Diana. I say 'attempt' because most decent minded people will reject it with the contempt it deserves.

Who cannot remember the frequent TV images of Diana distraught over the unrelenting hounding by the media? No fair-minded person could doubt who was really responsible for 'interweaving' Diana's life with the 'activity' of the media. That 'interweaving' took place from the beginning at the hands of the media and not, as McNicoll self-servingly claims, from a point ten years ago. In fact, it's an utter distortion to describe Diana's constant attempts to escape the media, her constant appeals to leave her in peace and her constant appeals for fair treatment as an 'interwoven' relationship. Earl Spencer was right in saying that Diana was the most hunted person of the modern era. And she was hunted by a media bereft of any moral feeling whatsoever. They hunted and she was hunted. And in the end they did not hesitate to distort the circumstances to escape, not blame so much, but any effort to restrict the activities of the theoretic-republican media. Rupert Murdoch, the great authoriphobic czar presiding over his *Disgusting Empire*, weeks later was warning his fellow media barons to resist any attempt at restricting 'freedom of speech' by any government's daring to introduce privacy laws. Privacy laws, he said, were to protect the privileged. What a joke! What a tragic joke that so many people would take him seriously and thereby help to add to the worldwide empire of one of the most privileged people in recorded history.

But still, some people would say, Diana did use the media for her own ends on occasions. And possibly they would point to some of the cases McNicoll has distorted. To acknowledge that Diana 'used' the media on 'occasions' is not at all to admit that Diana 'had interwoven' her life with the media 'almost as though neither could exist without the other'. To think so would be to be guilty of reasoning that would disgrace a sixth-grader. The simple truth is that Diana presented her side of the story with regard to her marriage breakdown through the channels that had already taken her apart and were being used against her. Whatever the truth about the palace staff's attacks on Diana, her perception was that it was so. She logically had no other recourse than to go through the same channels that people were using (in her view) to attack and discredit her. Now this hardly amounts to manipulation as one normally understands it. If it is manipulation it is so in a very tenuous sense. It makes everybody regularly guilty of manipulation. No, a clear case of manipulation is the very piece I am now examining.

This so-called Commemorative Edition presented to the public by *The Australian* is an outstanding example of the media's manipulation of events for their own ends. Diana, who is presented as a clever manipulator of the media, was in fact in media terms an innocent — she was foolishly innocent. She was continually done like a dinner by the media experts at distortion, misrepresentation and manipulation such as sit behind the editorial desks at News Ltd. Diana at times was obviously trying to deal with her tormentors in a conciliatory manner. She trusted that as fellow human beings they would respond in like manner. Those of us who see the media for what it is, know how tragically misplaced her trust was. We will have further occasion to discuss Diana's naive and ultimately self-destructive manner of dealing with the people in the media.

At the end of his article McNicoll says that Diana told reporters she would leave England if it weren't for her sons, so burdensome did she find the media treatment of her. He also quotes from Diana's interview with *Le Monde* in Paris.

The press is ferocious. It forgives nothing. It only hunts for mistakes. Every intention is twisted, every gesture criticised.

Are these the words of someone who cannot exist without the attention of the media? Why does McNicoll include this in his article with such brazen inconsistency, almost as if he is mocking those who wish to remain rational, feeling human beings? If this article were to be judged from a moral and (true) journalistic point of view, it would be judged very badly. But it is not to be judged in this way; it is to be judged solely from a propagandist view. From that point of view it succeeds admirably.

Robert Lusetich (**Celebrity chases a game: paparazzi,** p. 2) is called on to provide a supporting piece for the previous article. Its importance is indicated by the fact that it is printed in bold type. Now imagine if John Howard or Tony Blair were accused of some grave political crime. Firstly, the News Ltd papers would gush self-righteous outrage. But imagine how much worse it would be if John Howard or Tony Blair insisted on *pleading* and *judging* their cause in such a serious case through the officers of their own political machine. Imagine the 'scandal' if they refused all attempts to set up independent bodies of enquiry or to resort to the proper judicial instruments. Let's not doubt it, the full might of Murdoch's *Disgusting Empire* would be brought to bear and the political days of John Howard and Tony Blair would be numbered. Well, in the best tradition of forelock-tugging for his masters at *The Australian*, this is exactly what Lusetich does in this piece. He has a point to make and to make his point he draws on the 'testimony' of two paparazzi.

Lusetich starts off his article by quoting from interviews with Tom Cruise and Nicole Kidman directly after the accident. Anybody who saw or heard the interviews with these two knows that both are highly critical of the behaviour of the paparazzi. They join with other celebrities like George Clooney in condemning behaviour that is (they say) essentially without principle. George Clooney is especially vocal in this respect. Lusetich quotes Tom Cruise as saying that he and his wife had been harassed in just such a way as Diana in the very same tunnel in Paris. Big money paid by newspapers made the paparazzi persistent. What Tom and Nicole meant, of course, was that big money paid by editors without principle to reporters without principle amounted to misery and a highly deadly pursuit in all places around the world. There was no place where Tom and Nicole could escape such people. Little did Tom realise that his words would be used to throw it all back at him and make him look like a hypocrite. Here's how Lusetich starts the move to shift the blame back to the celebrity.

[Cruise said] 'You look at the kind of money that is generated for the

newspapers and for these paparazzi — that's why paparazzi are so persistent.'

Cruise called for laws to control photographers but one paparazzo told The Australian *yesterday celebrities and their bodyguards enjoyed the chases.*

Kevin Smith, a former Fleet Street reporter who created the tabloid-minded Splash news agency in Los Angeles, said Diana, who spoke last week of how the paparazzi had 'blighted' her life, initiated the often high-speed chases.

It's amazing, isn't it? This sort of thing just goes to show that the amoral media mind will not recoil from any manner of offending truth and decency if there is a chance they will get away with it. I ask the reader if he can remember or think of any evidence that would convince one that Diana 'initiated' and 'enjoyed' the high-speed chases which had 'blighted' her life. All the sound evidence that can be diluted from the many media reports points convincingly in the opposite direction. It's hardly worth arguing a case for which there is so much evidence. Diana felt her life crushed by the harassment of the media. If Diana was in a high-speed chase it was because she was being chased. Apart from the concrete evidence, there is the evidence of reason. A chaser can only logically initiate a chase. A chase becomes a chase when a chaser comes into action. Otherwise Diana in a car at speed is no more than that: Diana driving in a car at high speed. Only the hunters of Diana could possibly initiate a chase. A chase ceases to be a chase when the chaser stops or when the one chased is caught. I won't labour such an obvious point anymore. But none of this stops Lusetich from quoting at length Smith's attempts to demonstrate in yet another manner that Diana was responsible for causing her own death.

Smith's recommendation for such people as Diana is not to 'initiate' high-speed chases for their pleasure because they are 'highly dangerous and completely unnecessary'. He means of course that the chased and hunted should simply submit to the wishes of the reporters. That is like asking the rape victim to be done with the struggle and submit to being violated. Or like asking the hunted rabbit to stand still and be shot and not waste the hunter's time and energy for in the end the result will be the same.

Not satisfied with the testimony of the well-credentialled

paparazzo, Smith, Lusetich goes on to draw on the 'testimony' of Alan Zanger, 'a photographer who has been stalking celebrities the world over for the past seven years'. We must congratulate Lusetich for his corrupt connections. Of course, paparazzo Zanger supports the 'views' of Smith but adds another angle to the argument Smith has adduced to clear the media of blame.

> *Zanger ... also blamed celebrities for not co-operating more with photographers.*
> '*The more elusive they are, the more valuable the photos become, the more relentless we become,*' *he said.*

Are we really to believe that the paparazzi want celebrities to act in a way that will lower the price of the photos? Not a bit. This is sheer hypocrisy. The last thing the media want is a posed photo of a famous person or couple. The evidence is that the paparazzi use all tactics possible to provoke an incident that will raise the price of their photos. It's no holds barred. Abuse, insults, pushing, shoving, cornering in a confined space, are all part of the arsenal of tactics. Kes Wingfield, one of Diana's and Dodi's bodyguards on the day of the accident, testifies that two paparazzi vehicles on the way into Paris from Le Bourget airport were working in tandem to block and harass the car carrying Diana and Dodi.[17] This is a common tactic: paparazzi vehicles connected by radio or mobile phone working in teams to provoke incidents. If the reader thinks the paparazzi are a disorganised bunch of photographers crowding around the celebrity-victim he should think again. The most successful paparazzi are highly organised, use the most modern electronic equipment, plan team tactics that know no moral boundaries and are in close contact with the media bosses whom they serve and who pay their fat fees. I have no doubts that two vehicles belonging to one of the media teams were responsible in this manner for the crash of the car carrying Diana and Dodi. But more of that later.

The more revealing point, however, in the above words of Zanger, is the implicit admission that he and his colleagues place no moral limits on their actions. He is saying the actions of the paparazzi are governed solely by the actions of the celebrities. There are no moral limits he and his colleagues recognise. All he sees is an object of value that has to be treated in a certain manner in order to maximise its value. To hell with any other consideration.

Lusetich returns to Smith to provide another argument to clear the media of blame in Diana's death. This is one that in the following days will receive attention from the academic commentators. It is significant that its first appearance in *The Australian* should be from the mouth of a paparazzo. Here's what Lusetich quotes Smith as saying.

> *Smith said if anyone had the last shots of Diana, lying next to her dead boyfriend, Fleet Street tabloids would 'start bidding at one million US dollars and go from there.' He would not blame the photographers entirely.*
>
> *'Obviously, if some paps have caused this accident, then it's terrible and indefensible, but remember that it's the public that has this fascination with Diana,' he said.*

Firstly, Smith supports my view that the photos the Laurent Sola agency is holding of the dying Diana are worth a fortune. Every newspaper or TV station around the world has their eye on them. As soon as the media mind is convinced that no ideological or material harm will be caused by their appearance, they will appear in their entirety.

Secondly, we have the argument that the vicious appetite of the public is responsible for the paparazzi activity that led to the death of Diana.[18] The media are simply blameless people doing their job in providing for the public taste. We have again at the same time the admission that the media know no moral boundaries. In satisfying the alleged vicious appetite of the public for photos of Diana, they are simply responding mechanically to the demand for an object of value. Let the amoral, impersonal forces of the marketplace work themselves out. Or, let the public impose restraints on themselves that the paparazzi free themselves from. One does not know whether to be more disgusted by the amoral attitude or by the hypocrisy. I will come back to the discussion of the public's 'vicious' appetite for sensational news.

All in all, Lusetich should be rewarded for presenting uncritically in such clear form, and put into the mouths of the paparazzi, the main arguments used by the general media to free them and their usual activities from any blame in Diana's death — or any such death arising from their usual 'journalistic' activity.

This brings me to the end of my examination of the content of *The Australian's* 10-Page Commemorative Edition produced on the occasion of the death of the Princess of Wales. What sort of preliminary evaluation would we make of the reports and articles? What are the major themes? Well, if we want to evaluate them from a journalistic point of view they are for the most part slapdash, unresearched, badly edited and badly written. But *The Australian's* editorial bosses evidently couldn't care about the quality of the writing. They are only concerned with the propaganda and material objectives the reports and articles serve. The rest doesn't matter. As long as the British royal family, and Prince Charles in particular, can be smeared, mocked, and lied about, then all propaganda and business objectives are on safe ground. As long as the media can be defended successfully from any blame in the death of Diana then it's business as usual.

The reader is left to reflect on the manner in which the editorial staff of *The Australian* have gone about 'celebrating' the life of a person for whom millions around the world showed such shock and grief at her passing. What sort of minds are so quick to spring into action to provide such a lot of ill will, misrepresentations, prejudice and political bigotry? What is our society like that it should produce such people to head up powerful media organisations?

Towards the end of my examination of the Commemorative Edition I referred to Rupert Murdoch's business empire as the *Disgusting Empire*. This is no mere name-calling; it is an apt description for a worldwide empire that is being built on the amoral foundations of theoretic-republicanism. The *Disgusting Empire* has many enemies. But the reader should be discriminating about the extent of the opposition. Many of Rupert Murdoch's declared enemies subscribe precisely to the same theoretic-republican principles. They simply cannot stand the fact that Rupert is at the head of such an empire and they are not. They will use the same arguments and the same manoeuvrings to topple him if they can.

The Commemorative Edition was released on the morning of the first day following the death of Diana. The full extent of public affection and grief was not yet clear. Neither was the extent of the culpability everybody but the media attributed to the media. The content of the Commemorative Edition revealed clearly the nature of the spontaneous reaction of News Ltd's editorial staff to the event. From now on we will observe the change in the attack and defence as events unfold, as events appear gradually more favourable to the media's cause. In the end we will observe how the media thinks it has the opportunity to deliver a *coup de grace* to the royal family and the establishment of the constitutional monarchy.

As an example of how most of us responded to the news of Diana's death I will include David Nason's report (**Fergie's sister appeals for sanity, respect from media**, p. 7) on the reaction of the Duchess of York's sister, Jane Luedecke. Jane Luedecke appeals for decency and respect for personal privacy. These are her words:

> *Should the cause of this tragic loss be attributed in some way to the media relentlessly pursuing yet another story, I pray that some sanity and civility may prevail.*
>
> *As a result a greater right to privacy of the individual will be upheld ...*
>
> *My heart goes out to her sons, Prince William and Prince Harry, and to her family and friends at this time of great tragedy.*

Jane Luedecke shows herself to be well-mannered and civilised, expressing moral sentiments that many of us wholeheartedly agree with. Her appeal to the media for decency and respect will have fallen on deaf ears for one of the great commandments of the media is:

Thou shalt at no time, in whatever manner, make distinctions between any places, persons or things with regard to harvesting profit and ideological advantage from information-bearing situations.

4

Tuesday, 2 September 1997:
The Shifting of Blame

1. The Princess Is Carried Home to Rest

The Australian chooses a subdued headline for the beginning of the
second day following the death of Princess Diana.

DIANA
THE WORLD MOURNS
Princess home for final honour

Under the headline there is a striking colour photo of the pall-bear-
ers from the RAF's Queen's Colour squadron approaching the waiting
hearse with Diana's casket. The casket had been brought by plane from
Paris. To the right and in a solemn line, Prince Charles, Diana's sisters and Tony Blair with other functionaries look on while the
servicemen seem about to set the casket in the hearse. Charles's
demeanour is distracted. He is standing at the far right of the line.
He had gone to Paris with Diana's sisters to arrange the transfer of
Diana's body, and he and Diana's sisters had sat there in the RAF
transport plane as it carried Diana back to England. The picture
matches the mood of the grieving millions worldwide. Two reports by
Ean Higgins appear under the front-page picture.

In accordance with the mood of the headline, the first report
('**Unique funeral for a unique person**') concentrates on two issues:
the preparation for Diana's funeral and the uproar worldwide about
the intrusive activities of the media. In suitably subdued terms Higgins
gives an account of the decision taken by the British Government and

the royal family for the type of funeral that would be appropriate for Diana, Princess of Wales. It would be 'one of the most elaborate public tributes of modern times'. In the words of Buckingham Palace, it would be a 'unique funeral for a unique person'. Notice that *The Australian* has used the words of the Palace as the headline for this front-page article. The following description of the funeral by Higgins (connecting Church, State and royal family) is also pertinent to what comes later.

> *In a ceremony designed to bind* **Church, State and family** *together in a spectacular but* **dignified** *event, Diana's casket will be trooped from St James Palace to the abbey in a procession past some of Britain's most august institutions including Whitehall and Parliament Square.* [My emphasis.]

Higgins goes on to say that the funeral arrangements struck a 'delicate balance' between what the grieving public would like and

> *... the concern of Diana's family and Prince William and Prince Harry that they should retain* **dignity and privacy**. [My emphasis.]

It was evident both from Higgins's article and the constant TV images at the time that the British government, the royal family and the Spencer family had discussed the arrangements with the young princes especially in mind. It reflected the sympathy and concern worldwide for the princes William and Harry. Now their mother was dead their welfare was of the first concern. Higgins reports that the royal family had gathered around and were comforting the princes who were 'deeply shaken and in grief over the loss of their mother'. What person of normal human sympathies and clear-mindedness could disagree with the arrangements as they are described here? The public demonstration, the role of Church and State, and the respect for the dignity and privacy of the family of the departed one seemed admirably and appropriately combined. But scarcely had the arrangements been made and hardly had the printing ink dried when they and the actions of the royal family were completely misrepresented in such a way as to launch a violent and unremitting attack on them and the institution of the monarchy. The following days would reveal the full extent of the attack.

In this present report, Higgins devotes about a third to the debate over whether 'new laws or codes of practice should be enacted to curb boundless media intrusion into the lives of royals and other public figures'. He specifically mentions the outrage and bitterness worldwide directed not only at the paparazzi but equally against editors and media proprietors: 'Tirades against the paparazzi and the editors and media proprietors who bought their pictures continued'. It is something indeed that *The Australian* allowed such an accurate report on the worldwide feeling about the behaviour of the media. But it would make up for this allowance. A sign of what is to come is in Higgins's quoting Richard Stott, 'a prominent media commentator'. This 'prominent media commentator' says that covering the romance of Diana and Dodi was 'legitimate'. Nobody of right mind would seriously dispute the legitimacy of covering the story of Diana and Dodi. That's not the issue. The issue is about *the way* the story is covered; it's about *moral behaviour*. The theoretic-republican media does not recognise the word 'moral' in the sense the ordinary person does. Higgins should use the proper term for Richard Stott's status: 'media apologist'. Higgins also mentions briefly the funeral of Dodi Fayed within 24 hours of his death, in accordance with Muslim custom. Mohammed Al Fayed is reported as having shed tears at the death of his son. There is no dispute here about the private nature of the burial ceremonies.

Higgins's second report (**Dodi's father demands manslaughter enquiry**) is about the detention of the photographers arrested at the scene of the accident, the legal issues in France, and Dodi Fayed's father calling for a full manslaughter investigation. Again, a significant detail about the accident is alleged:

> 'A lawyer for Mohammed Fayed said a motorcycle was seen zig-zagging in front of the car, which a witness said was surrounded by so many bikes he thought it was an official cortege.'

It is reasonable to ask why the allegation of the motorbike zig-zagging in front of the Mercedes was dropped at the time when apparently more than one witness made a similar claim?

Higgins includes the following without further comment:

> Adding to outrage over the paparazzi's actions, newspapers confirmed a French photographer had offered at a price of more than $1 million for

photographs of Diana apparently conscious before she was pulled out of the car wreck.

One wonders whether Richard Stott includes this action in the 'legitimate coverage' of the Diana and Dodi affair. If not, he should explain why.

2. The World Continues to Grieve

Much of page 2 of the 2 September edition of *The Australian* is an account of the outpouring of grief, affection and admiration from people the world over for Princess Diana. Various people, high and low, express their shock and sorrow at the princess's parting. All agree on the princess's open, warm, and sympathetic nature. She showed her best side above all to the suffering, the dispossessed and disadvantaged. Few Australians will forget the images of Diana embracing schoolgirl, Emma Jones, after Emma had asked for a hug during Diana's visit to Australia in 1996. This scene exemplified the best side of Diana's character. These details are provided in **Sense of humanity strikes national chord** by Kristine Gough, Kate Meikle and Ben Hutchings. In **Parliament pours out its sorry heart**, Michael Gordon and Don Greenlees give an account of what Prime Minister John Howard, Deputy Prime Minister Tim Fischer and Opposition Leader Kim Beazley said. Their words reflected the views of most Australians. John Howard said Diana was a beautiful woman who appealed to the imagination of Australians.

> *The outpouring of emotion and sadness from so many people within the mainstream of our society and other societies is a testament to that ...*
>
> *It was not only her style and beauty but her spontaneity, her friendliness, her warmth and her capacity to evoke — particularly in the young in our community — the image of a warm and modern woman ...*
>
> *She was a person who, in her relatively short life, experienced what many would regard as both the highs and lows of the ultimate as far as public life is concerned ...*

Kim Beazley said:

I think it was probably a surprise to many of us that we missed her. It was a surprise to me ...
all of a sudden you realise that all that service of hers, all those images of her in those circumstances in which she chose to place herself, all came home ...
She did all of these things with great daring, great joy, great spontaneous affection.
There were pictures of her walking down the roads in not yet cleared mined areas. Nevertheless, she was prepared to put an image of herself alongside a terrible problem — likewise, sitting for a long time holding hands with lepers; likewise, sitting for a long time holding an HIV-AIDS-affected baby ...

It is an irony that the most vilified professionals in our community (politicians) reflected the true feelings of the Australian people towards Diana. D. D. McNicoll should note that images of Diana holding hands with a leper or holding an HIV-AIDS infected baby in her arms are hardly the equivalent action of a bunch of amoral media representatives chasing and hounding Diana relentlessly. The only people in the world who cannot see this for themselves are evidently respected media figures like McNicoll and those who write the editorials for *The Australian* (I will be coming to the 2 September editorial shortly).

The final article at the bottom of page 2 is by Ean Higgins (**On-lookers fall silent as Charles returns home with casket**) who gives more detail on the arrival of the plane bringing Diana back to England. He describes the group of media people on the tarmac getting on with their work of reporting the arrival of the plane, some expressing regret about the accident others making inappropriate jokes about the 'baggage' on the plane. On the outside of the gates to the air base was a crowd of Diana's admirers 'who largely blamed the media for Diana's death'. While some of the reporters were trying to distance themselves from the activity of the paparazzi one of Princess Diana's admirers outside the gates said: 'They [the media] more or less drove her to death, really, it's not a nice thing.' The three articles by Ean Higgins so far in this 2 September edition have been dispassionate, moderate, and emphatic about the public's view of where the blame for Princess Diana's death lay. He reports the public's view with little attempt to contradict it at this stage. That is the task of others for the moment.

3. Prince William Employed to Torment His Father

Juliet Herd returns to her fairytale account of the effect of Diana's death on the two young princes (**Prince taught to rule from the street**). Again, we must congratulate the headline-writing ability of the editor, for once more this headline gives just the right notion of the opposition Herd had been harping on in her stories about Diana and Charles (between staid and relaxed, stiff and friendly, etc., with Charles being staid and Diana being relaxed). Herd speaks of Diana's attempt to give the young princes a broad education, providing them with a view of life from the perspective of the ordinary person. Their 'more staid [and] formal upbringing' of the royal environment was to be balanced by outings among the ordinary people.

Herd herself provides no firm information or credible argument to support this continual opposition. There is plenty of evidence to suggest that not only did Prince Charles himself escape the 'formal' environment of royal protocol in his youth but that his manner and character reflect this; that he himself would have in no way objected to Diana's care of the princes but most likely fully supported the princes' routine of 'external visitations' to the ordinary folk; and that Prince Charles, the princes and the royal family enjoy a warm relationship. The many photos in the papers and the TV images of the royal family together in the days and weeks following the death of Diana support this.[1]

Did Herd and her colleagues miss the pictures of twelve-year-old Prince Harry holding Prince Charles's hand while looking at the floral tributes to Diana left by ordinary people? How many boys of this age would continue to hold their father's hand? Only an affectionate boy with much regard for his father would do such a thing in public. Or perhaps it was a deliberate act by young Harry. Perhaps he has the spirit of young Prince Hal[2] and deliberately engaged in a gesture that defied and held in contempt the great media barons who want his father dead and buried. Prince Harry's behaviour during his mother's funeral seemed also a challenge (see Chapter 10). Such occasions contradict all the nonsense Herd and other self-serving theoretic-republican reporters regurgitate at the drop of a hat.

Herd admits herself that Charles is 'as devoted to his sons as Diana was' but this does not stop her from making inconsistent claims about their royal environment. Indeed, she seems to have little idea of the distinction between royal protocol and the warm family life the princes obviously share with the members of the broader royal family. That same distinction between formal protocol and more relaxed private occasions can be found also in the business, political, administrative and educational areas, where plenty of ordinary people are to be found. Juliet Herd should take herself off to a graduation ceremony at any university. She will find that the graduands and the families love the formality of the occasion. It would be laughable to suggest that because a graduand and her family love the formal occasion that they are stiff, staid and unfriendly in their private lives. All the prejudice, bigotry and inconsistency of argument the media show towards to the royal family is expressed in the following passage from Herd's article.

> *Already, the royal family can be seen to have closed ranks around the boys, taking them to church at Balmoral on the morning of their mother's death — showing them that duty is the royal way of overcoming grief.*
>
> *But the boys will also need to be given the chance to express their loss through tears and talk and Charles, despite his stiff reserve at times, is likely to encourage them to release their anger in private.*

Suddenly Prince Charles is reserved 'at times'. And what is the staid, emotional cripple in the rest of the reports doing encouraging the princes to 'release their anger'? Of course, such inconsistency is of no account. As long as the media's myth of the 'royal family' can be perpetuated in whatever way is to hand. With regard to church-going as a demonstration of duty, let me point out the obvious to Herd and her colleagues. Those who are still believing Christians go to church not only on a Sunday morning but especially on the occasion of the death of a member of the family. You see, Christians believe in the after-life and the efficacy of prayer as a claim on God's mercy for the repose of the soul of the departed one. The attendance at church to plead with the Almighty for everlasting happiness for Diana shows the deepest emotion and feeling towards Diana and the cleansing surrender of the individual to the decrees of Providence. This may be language that the media mind finds incomprehensible, but it is contemptible that some reporter should turn this into the only way the royal family has of overcoming grief, and call it 'duty'.

Herd finishes her report by agitating for a move particularly favoured by the bored, unconscionable media at this point: Prince

William skipping over Prince Charles to ascend the throne of England. This is to ensure that the monarchy *modernises*. In theoretic-republican language *modernise* means *disappear*. Who can forget Premier Carr's efforts to *modernise* the office of Governor in New South Wales? Carr removed the Governor from his imposing vice-regal residence in the centre of Sydney, and banished him to some obscure spot in the suburbs. Applauding theoretic-republicans had no doubt what he was about — neither did anyone else.

Accompanying Juliet Herd's piece is an article entitled, **William holds key to House without Di**. The media's fantasy about the royal family is continued. William as the true follower of Diana must ascend the throne over Prince Charles to ensure the existence of the withering British royal family. So-called 'royal biographer', Anthony Holden, is appealed to for his views. It seems that most of the people who call themselves royal watchers or royal biographers are the worst offenders at perpetuating the media garbage about the royal family. Holden shows himself willing to go on with the same distinctions Herd harps on: warm, 'relevant' Diana vs. the lifeless, irrelevant royal family. Diana, we are to understand, was in the process of 'reinventing' the role of the monarchy when she died. The royal family must do without her and, according to Holden, the future looks bleak for them. Their bad 'handling' of Diana has turned public feeling against them. Media driven polls were cited in support. We will have occasion to mention Holden and his bigotry later on.

Another royal biographer, Professor Ben Pimlott, is quoted as saying that Diana's death would shift the spotlight to William and he wonders whether the media 'can avoid destroying him in the way it contributed to [Diana's] death.' The report also acknowledges William's resentment and anger towards the media for its treatment of his mother. If the spotlight falls on him then I think that inevitably he will express that anger with the full knowledge that people the world over supported him and his brother with their warm, heartfelt sympathy at the time of their mother's death. When that happens we will all see that the present frenzied media agitation for Prince William's ascending the throne will change dramatically.

Really, people should not be under any misapprehension about the media's support for William. He is only supported because it is a way of attacking Prince Charles and the establishment of the monarchy. When Prince William turns out to be his mother and father's son, a true defender of the monarchy in accordance with the education he has received from both Diana and Charles, the theoretic-republican media will descend on him unmercifully.

4. A Glimpse at the Real Charles

At the bottom left-hand corner of the same page 3, we find for a change a balanced article (**Charles free to marry, but not Camilla**) by Ray Moseley in London. But the question of *if and who* Charles can marry is not the only matter brought up. In fact, it is surprising the sort of information included here because it goes against so much of the media bigotry the reader has been subjected to so far.

Firstly, as the title indicates, the author canvasses the chances Charles has of marrying Camilla Parker Bowles. Anybody, including Charles, who knows anything about the Church of England will know that this is not possible as long as Charles professes himself a member and future head of the Church of England. Moseley says there are recent hints that Charles is preparing the public for marriage to Camilla, but this must be dismissed as the usual media agitation. Charles is reported frequently as being determined to ascend the throne. He knows he cannot have both.

More interesting in this report is the information about Prince Charles and his relationship with his sons and their mother. Moseley says that Prince Charles in the days following the death of Diana would concentrate on his role as father and comfort his sons. He would leave the public mourning for the Spencer family. This is the way it happened. And isn't it just the way it should be? What normal compassionate person could disagree with this? Here the 'emotional cripple' of the media mind chooses to play the natural emotional role and not exhibit the 'staid, stiff reserve' of 'royalty'. In this case, he has placed his private family responsibilities over *protocol and public duty*. In reality, Prince Charles is playing his natural self and not the role the media have fabricated to fill their pages with propaganda.

Moseley also surmises that 'the public feeling' (he means the views propagated by the media) against Charles because of his role in the destruction of his marriage to Diana may be exacerbated by Diana's death. After all, according to this view, Charles's infidelity with Camilla Parker Bowles was the cause of the marriage failure.

Moseley generously reports that Charles was very definite about re-jecting this claim: '... he insisted that [the infidelity] happened only after the marriage had irretrievably broken down.' All the evidence that can be reviewed in terms of media reports and a review of Charles's behaviour would support this. I ask the reader whether the media would have missed gathering the evidence if Charles really had conducted an affair with Camilla from the beginning of his marriage with Diana. Remember the highly illegal taping of Charles's phone calls? Do you imagine that the vultures of the media would not have been able to get any information at all to prove the infidelity if it had been a continuing relationship? Well, there has not been one skerrick of hard evidence that Charles was having an affair before the marriage had irretrievably broken down.

Moseley, in a similar generous gesture, goes on to relate what ap-pears to be the true state of affairs emerging from all the media reports and TV footage. It is important to reproduce the full passage as it re-lates to what will be reported in the following days. Moseley reports that Charles and Diana wanted to put the bitterness of their marriage break-up behind them.

> *But in recent months both indicated that they wanted to put the bitter-ness behind them and devote themselves to the well-being of their sons, who had had to bear the strain of the public warfare between their parents.*
>
> *Charles and Diana told British court correspondents **they had never had any disagreement concerning their children**, and they shared time with them when the boys were not in school.*
>
> *The two boys were said to adore their mother and also **to have a close, loving relationship with Charles**.* [My emphasis.]

This is completely in line with the TV footage we saw in the year or so before Diana's death.[3] I remember several occasions when both par-ents attended their sons to some function or other and, on at least one occasion, Diana kissed Charles on both cheeks as she said goodbye. These passages also undermine a great deal of the malicious nonsense that has so far appeared in *The Australian* since Diana's death. Despite all this, Moseley has to ask 'whether Prince Charles, never very popu-lar with the British public, will be able to rehabilitate his image ...' Again, I say this 'image' should be regarded as the 'image' fabricated by the theoretic-republican media and successfully promoted through most media channels. It does not fit the evidence and is not that of the thousands who turn out to greet Prince Charles wherever he goes.

5. William Groomed by 'Republican' Diana

Moseley's article seems destined to remain an oasis in the midst of the pervading media bigotry, for we turn the page to find a report drawing on all the assumptions of the media fantasy about the royal family. The article comes from a reporter writing for Britain's most illustrious newspaper, *The Times*, an eminent instrument of the Murdoch empire. The writer goes by the impressive name of William Rees-Mogg and one must admit that his writing is of the appropriate standard for *The Times*.[4] By this I mean that what Rees-Mogg has to say is well expressed. It's a pity about the content which, not surprisingly, does not match the standard of expression. The editor at *The Australian* has been able to give the right title and introduction:

If not a saint, a saviour of the monarchy
Diana, Princess of Wales, saw that the monarchy must adapt to
survive. Thwarted in life, she may succeed in death —
if Prince William continues her work,
writes William Rees-Mogg in London.

The article is based on the contrast I have been refuting. In this respect, I can add little more to what I have said. There are, however, a few remarks that can be made about a new dimension Rees-Mogg brings to the issue. Rees-Mogg claims that Diana 'always hated pomposity, distrusted the excessive ceremony of the court, and had a gift for ordinary friendships'. It's not exactly clear what he means when he says that Diana 'distrusted excessive ceremony'. Why would one *distrust* excessive ceremony? Is excessive ceremony in itself deceptive? Does he mean that the royal family, supposing they wanted to deceive or bully Diana, mounted an excessive ceremony to get away with it? This is either journalistic waffle, or an expression of paranoia on the part of Rees-Mogg, or the attribution of paranoia to Diana with regard to the royal family. This last point, if true, would undermine the whole media fantasy about Diana and the royal family.

The second point is that if Diana hated pomposity, should we automatically assume that Prince Charles and the royal family love pomposity? There is no evidence to suggest that the royal family are pompous or lovers of 'excessive ceremony'. Or does Rees-Mogg betray his prejudices and mean that all tradition and all ceremony, especially if it is connected to the royal house, is pompous and excessive? Is it that any occasion which historically takes precedence over the members of the media is pompous? This is another display of media hypocrisy. There are no greater displays of pomposity and self-importance than are to be witnessed in the daily media. We are unable to escape the preening media stars who are certainly not there for their journalistic ability. Some are very definitely there for their youth and nubile appearance.

The thrust of Rees-Mogg's article is, however, not the repetition of the assumptions of the media fantasy about the royal family. He aims, as I say, at giving a new angle to the view. He introduces this new angle with the following comment about Diana:

> *Diana had great gifts. She was largely unacademic; indeed she rather distrusted intellectual interests in case they got in the way of her strong intuitive sense.*

I would agree with this description as far as it goes. Diana said herself on occasions that she thought with her heart and that sometimes got her into trouble. One occasion, especially, I can think of when that description was justified. It was during her visit to Bosnia where landmines had been laid. A reporter bailed her up in her rounds and asked her how she reacted to the accusation that she was being politically irresponsible or naive — at least something to that effect. Diana looked immediately as if someone had struck her in the face. She replied that she was just trying to help. Later in the car with her minders and while the cameras were still on her she said that she felt like weeping. This occasion exemplified her nature exactly. Diana had no interest in politics, political philosophy or any other 'intellectual' question that keeps many of the media busy. She thought with her heart and was concerned only with the concrete situation individuals found themselves in. She felt for the disadvantaged and suffering because someone was suffering, not because some philosophical or intellectual system was being transgressed.

Having acknowledged Diana's non-academic and non-intellectual temperament, Rees-Mogg with brazen inconsistency goes on to connect Diana with the policies of New Labour and to outline three distinct phases in Diana's reflection on the present state of the monarchy. The picture is painted of a reflective Diana with an abiding concern for the nature and standing of the British monarchy in the modern world. According to Rees-Mogg, Diana's reflective view of the monarchy was incisive, progressive, and accurate in the remedies that were needed to 'modernise' a moribund institution full of staid, conservative, unimaginative family and supportive staff. Naturally, this bunch of unimaginative royal troglodytes thwarted Diana at every turn. But while Diana was alive, there was still hope that she would negotiate the walls of royal ignorance by grooming William precisely for the role that was needed to save the British monarchy. William was the only one in the royal family, besides herself, who 'under her influence', understood the precarious state of the monarchy and its need to 'modernise'. Now, woe is us, all seems lost with Diana's death! The only hope is in the son of Diana, that son who, it is hoped, has absorbed all Diana's redemptive philosophy with regard to the system of monarchy in the modern world.

One would think that a self-respecting journalist would be embarrassed to propagate such evident nonsense. There is no compelling evidence that Diana thought in this manner about the British monarchy. As Rees-Mogg himself admits, Diana was not an intellectual and showed no inclination to analyse her position in the British monarchy in such terms. All the evidence points to Diana's examining her situation only in terms of personal relationships relating to her need to love and be loved. If she thought that Charles was hard-hearted, then what she was calling for was a conversion of heart — not of the system or structure of the 'modern' monarchy. Diana would have been the last person to have wanted royal ceremony and tradition fundamentally changed. Diana was not in denial of her considerable aristocratic background.[5] And as is already abundantly clear, Diana's own burdensome problems contributed greatly to the conflict she had with Charles and to her *perception* that established royal protocol was *sometimes* without feeling.

There is much immaturity in the thought that life can be reduced to hugs and kisses and that there is no place for solemn ceremony in a life of joy, contentment and warm relationships. Most people, in fact, show their appreciation for the ceremony on a solemn occasion when they think it appropriate (for weddings, initiations, inductions, awards, and so on). But let's finish with this article for I will start repeating the evidence and arguments I have already offered to contradict views such as those of Rees-Mogg. It is simply an attempt to advance a particular political agenda. Agitating to force Charles to abdicate his role as king on the pretext that William is more suitable king material, is just another tactic of the theoretic-republican mind to undermine the monarchy to the point where prevailing elites will be able to get rid of the institution altogether.

6. The Media Sneers at the Response of Ordinary People to Diana's Death

The Rees-Mogg article is accompanied by a short piece in bold type entitled, **Hagiography the enemy of history**. It is presented by Jane Shilling in London and is taken from an edition of *The Times*. This is a worthy piece of hypocritical, journalistic sneer. Shilling says that the mythology of Diana, or her deification has escaped 'the control of ordinary historical record'. What she means, of course, is that the ordinary person's feelings about Diana have forced themselves on the media. *For the moment* they have escaped the supervision of the theoretic-republican media's control. The last thing the theoretic-republican mind could bear would be to have a princess mythologised. It might seem, heaven forbid, that there is something intrinsically worthy in being a princess. So while some of her colleagues are forced to report the public's outpouring of grief and admiration for Diana, such as Jane Shilling will take it upon themselves to entertain with some suitable ridicule.

Within hours of Diana's death, Shilling sneers, '... touching, ugly bunches of garage flowers began to arrive with scribbled notes ...' She goes on to report a couple who had travelled from 'Blackburn, near Manchester' to pay homage to Diana and express their grief. Shilling comments that 'it seemed a long way to come for a dead princess with whom they had never had any dealings'. If it had been some sleazy, amoral rock star who had departed this world drowned in his own vomit, it would have been the valid expression of the 'people's' innate goodness, no doubt. But as it concerns a princess, such an expression of grief has to be the 'populist', vulgar expression of the unsupervisable masses. When 'the people' act in accordance with the promulgated tenets of theoretic-republicanism they are 'the people'; when they act contrary to those tenets, they become the victims of 'undemocratic populism'. Note again the appropriate heading the editor at *The Australian* has put above this piece. *Hagiography* has to do with the writings about the saints. In this case, the hagiography is the wrong one for the editorial bosses at *The Australian*.

7. At Last the Charitable Works of the Princess

Amidst all the discussion about the problems of Diana and Charles, and who is to blame for the accident, there is some occasional mention of Diana's charitable work. A brief Reuters report from Washington (**Impetus for treaty ban on landmines**) introduces the subject thus: 'The death of the Princess of Wales may provide fresh impetus for her favourite international cause — a global campaign to ban anti-personnel landmines.' US senator, Patrick Leahy, is quoted as crediting Diana with very effective efforts to bring the seriousness of the problem before the international public. He says:

> In life [Diana] made major changes in landmine policy and I think in death she will continue to, because people will realise what she stood for … As terrible as the death is, it will bring home what it is that she did and what it is that she cared so passionately about.
>
> I don't think her efforts are going to be ignored. I think much of what she did will live on … She put very much a human face on the tragedy of landmines.

Senator Leahy's words are a well-founded tribute to the great qualities of Diana, Princess of Wales. It is just the sort of report that should be included in commemorating the death of such a world figure as Diana. Even more, it is the sort of matter that should be discussed and enlarged upon at this point. But for the editorial bosses at *The Australian* the matter is only worth a few lines at the bottom of page 4, out of the way of the necessary propaganda pieces. In fact, it is situated next to a trivial report about 'Kanga's' opinions of Camilla Parker Bowles's chances in marrying Prince Charles. 'Kanga' is the late Lady Dale Tryon whom Prince Charles in his younger days nicknamed 'Kanga', apparently because she was Australian. She is reported as being a close friend of Prince Charles.

The report is headed, **Camilla no chance says Kanga**. The opening paragraph reports Kanga as saying that 'Camilla Parker Bowles will never be married to Prince Charles, let alone be Queen ...' The rest of the report, except for the final paragraph, is about Kanga's great admiration and sympathy for Diana ... But the final paragraph is the clincher; it reports the ailing Kanga's obvious dislike of Camilla Parker Bowles in terms favoured by the tabloid mentality.

> *She (Camilla) knew Charles before she married Parker Bowles, and she didn't come near Charles until the very minute he married Diana, the perfect English rose, and then she came along and wrecked the marriage. She is not at all a nice person. She may think otherwise, but I know Charles will never marry her.*

At least we have here someone else wrecking Diana's marriage besides the cruel Prince Charles. But it won't do. The TV reports on the emotional and physical problems Lady Tryon was suffering at the time made it clear that Prince Charles's 'Kanga' was not at her best or fittest when asked for her views about Camilla Parker Bowles. It is a matter of record that Charles considered Camilla a long-term dear friend. It is a matter of record that his relationship with her was far more profound and complex than that of the prince/mistress relationship with which the media smear both of them. It would be a matter of some investigation to reveal the length and the nature of Prince Charles's changing relationship with Camilla Parker Bowles — and exactly when it blossomed into the full romantic attachment it is today.[6] But this is not the time for any reporter or media organisation to contemplate such an investigation; it is just the time for the media to focus in on what may spill from the lips of an unwell person. This little piece about Kanga has something for everybody, especially for those who accept the image of Camilla Parker Bowles as the marriage wrecker.

8. Shifting the Blame — A Pang of Conscience

The report on page 4 by Kate Legge brings us back to the issue of blame. The distinguishing feature of this report is that it comes as the first, frank, personal admission of guilt by a journalist appearing in *The Australian* following the death of Princess Diana. But the guilt is qualified in that it concerns Kate Legge the person, the member of society, and not Kate Legge the reporter. The report is surprisingly entitled, **Wakeup call for us to mend our ways**.

Legge starts by admitting that many people, high and low, were drawn to the 'celebrity mush and royal family gossip'. But the death of Diana prompted one to consider whether 'the peddlers of dope on Di and Dodi were in fact merchants of death'. This is, indeed, an admission. But then comes a revealing passage.

We all nurse a flicker of guilt swept along in a current of social and technological change no legislative reforms to entrench privacy could possibly halt.

Legge then wonders whether the death of Diana resulting from the pursuit of the paparazzi could prompt *us* 'to mend our ways'. Then she goes on to add,

However, I doubt even this has the power to fence off territory we now trample over without thinking twice.

The death of shame was mourned by British columnist Christopher Hitchens in an important essay last year which looked at the disappearance of corporate and personal propriety.

Why is this revealing? It's revealing because Kate Legge is confirming the 'moral' analysis I offered to the reader under the explanation of the philosophical foundations of theoretic-republicanism. Notice first of all that 'technological change' has been our master and that the only means of controlling our behaviour within this change is by legislative action. And legislative action was not able to keep pace. There is absolutely no hint of the moral vision of our forefathers — that personal behaviour belonged in the first place to the domain of our own innate powers of moral judgement, that we possess a rational nature that is able to recognise the standards of right and wrong written by God in the scheme of nature.

Of course, we know the theoretic-republican thinks this is baloney and that's just the point. The descent into our basest animal passions can only be controlled by an act of will, that is, the decision to impose an external order on the otherwise non-moral chaos of those passions. The inability of the acts of will (or the imposition of order) to keep pace with events exonerates us all, especially the media, from any moral guilt in the disgusting behaviour of the media. In an unreflective exhibition of moral naivety, Kate Legge quotes a colleague as recognising that the society of economic leaders has given itself over body and soul to the amoral tenets of theoretic-republicanism. This is the explanation for 'the death of shame'.

Despite showing some willingness to own up to being corrupted by the 'moral' vision of the ruling elite, ultimately Legge shows how much she is in thrall to the editorial masters at the *Disgusting Empire*. She comes up with an argument to excuse the behaviour of the media that should have revolted her as she wrote it. The preamble to the argument is the demonstration by examples that people, especially famous people, have become increasingly open about their private lives in a way undreamt of a generation ago. This has whetted the appetite of the public who have become increasingly hungry for such information. And the intrusive media has been willing to attempt to satisfy this insatiable appetite at the cost of privacy rights. Then we have the argument:

> *If frustrations with the paparazzi represents the downside of privacy's demise, then last week's Wood royal commission report on paedophilia is one example of the good which flows from the rise of disclosure.*

Legge is using a form of argument that is a favourite weapon of the media. It is the tactic to take two sets of circumstances, seek a common factor in the two sets (it doesn't matter how tenuous) and then proceed to equate the circumstances on the basis of an alleged substantial commonality. In the above sets, Legge is taking 'disclosure' as the common factor. ('Disclosure' or 'openness of society' is the substance of both sets of activity with the 'downside' of the paparazzi activity being an 'accidental' quality.) This form of argument is also to be found in the following: an apple is a fruit, an orange is a fruit, therefore an apple is an orange. It is the same fallacy that explains the inability of some social commentators to distinguish between a smack and a bashing. It is obvious nonsense but the level of nonsense is no greater than Legge's argument. She realises she has come up with a whopper and tries to qualify it.

> *While the incentive to report sexual abuse is far removed from the desire*

*to gawk at shots of Di and Dodi, both developments reflect the openness
of modern society.*

Come off it, Kate Legge! You can do better than this. You are not the
usual run of the self-justifying gutter reporter. You have already
pointed to the reasons for the behaviour of the out-of-control media
— and the rise of people who do not think twice about desecrating
children's bodies. It's also the reason that the untouchables in our society do not think twice about corrupting our children's minds. And
what is worse: desecrating a child's body or a child's soul?

You see, it's the loss of shame. It's the acceptance of the key theoretic-republican principle that there is no objective moral order to be
found in nature, that 'morality' has to be imposed by written human
law — to the extent that it can be imposed. The paedophile standing
before Justice Wood is no more morally guilty in your terms than the
paparazzi. The paedophile is no more morally guilty than the homo-
sexual or those who get their kicks from bestiality. The argument to
defend these states is the same. Public morality and its attendant sanctions come by way of the imposition of a written legislative order
decided on by the *prevailing* human legislators. Otherwise 'moral' decision is a matter for the private subjective sphere. Moral decision in
this context is a matter of individual preference. The reason the
paedophile is now being hunted is because of the outcry from ordinary people who are instinctively revolted by the idea of an adult
having sex with a child. It is the public mood that is driving the instruments of the elite who in reality have no feeling for the *essential*
moral transgression. The process is happening with the death of Diana.
The ordinary person's innate moral sense has come into operation and
the outrage has put the theoretic-republican media on the defensive
forcing them to bring out their big guns and to trim their defences.

There is a world of difference between the properly constituted
legal authority of the political order investigating a grave moral problem in society, and the out-of-control media who are on the loose for
material gain and for no other reason. The media do not give a damn
about the human person. The media's action does not come under the
heading of 'disclosure' even less so than a royal commission investigating a moral problem in our society. Legge should know that the
latter form of 'disclosure' has been in the traditional political system
for centuries and has to do essentially with justice, and whatever 'dis-

closure' is involved has to do with the presentation of evidence. It's such an obvious point. It's just as tragic that it needs to be explained to such as Kate Legge.

She finishes her report by repeating one of the main arguments to excuse the media's role in the death of Diana. She says that it is not the chequebooks of the editors that need to be put away. Ensuring the protection of the individual from the media vultures 'will require a massive shift in public taste and restraint'. But what motive can she put forward in theoretic-republican terms that will bring about internal, individual moral restraint? In the terms she has chosen to argue in, she is whistling in the wind. The full discussion of the culpability of the 'vicious' public appetite is yet to come. It is a measure of the prevailing moral blindness that so many commentators cannot get their heads around the fundamental proposition that media persecution of an individual is wrong in itself — however much other factors create the occasion for moral failure.

9. Shifting Blame — Technical Escape

D. D. McNicoll (**Witnesses condemn paparazzi over close-ups**, p. 5) turns his attention to the actions and subsequent arrest of the photographers who were in pursuit of Diana and Dodi on the day of the accident. He reports the outrage of witnesses who said the photographers were taking photos centimetres away from the bodies while police were trying to prevent them. Witnesses also reported 'photographers, riding motorcycles, had swarmed around the sedan before it entered the tunnel …' But this report is not about the outrage of witnesses. It is an effort to shift the blame from the media to the driver of the powerful Mercedes S-280. Unfortunately, in doing so, McNicoll provides information that ultimately works against him. This is how he introduces the matter.

> But as calls for international legal restraints on paparazzi mounted yesterday, motoring experts suggested the action of the driver may have been a factor in the horrific crash which killed Diana and Dodi.

The main thrust of the evidence and argument that follow is that Henri Paul was 'not a professional chauffeur' and was thus incapable of handling a powerful car trying to escape the motorcycles of the paparazzi. We now know that Henri Paul did have training in defensive driving and occasionally drove for the Ritz hotel. We also know that his defensive driving skills were tested annually. He was in fact the driver of the car that accompanied the car carrying Diana and Dodi from Le Bourget airport to the Ritz on the day of the accident. But if McNicoll wants to provide evidence that the driver was 'a factor' in the crash because he could not handle a powerful car trying to escape the motorbikes of the paparazzi, he also provides evidence against the paparazzi who said Henri Paul outsped them and they were too far behind the car when it entered the tunnel to have been a cause in the accident. Surely experienced motorcyclists could have kept up with an 'untrained' driver of a powerful Mercedes trying to negotiate the narrow twisting streets of central Paris. McNicoll is giving further credibility to those witnesses who said motorbikes were swarming around the car. In all he provides support for the contention that the accident was directly the result of the paparazzi carrying out the obstructive tactics they utilise in team mode to stop their quarry.

10. The Office of the Republican Inquisition

As we move from this report to the accompanying one we meet one of the 'exulted ones' presiding over the theoretic-republican empire worldwide. He is the cardinal-theologian of the ruling elite, the Prefect of the Congregation for Authoriphobic Doctrine, the Chief of the Office of the Republican Inquisition that ensures the fidelity of the levelled masses to the dogma of theoretic-republicanism. In Australia, he is Terry O'Gorman who goes under the truly *newspeak* title of *President of the Australian Council of Civil Liberties*. O'Gorman has branches of the Republican Inquisition in every state of Australia. What citizen of Australia has not been confronted with the appearance on television of one of the Inquisition's officers pontificating on this or that 'human right'? It's usually the 'right' of the individual not to have to subject himself to the ordinary norms of good sense, decency, good taste and morality — the right of the individual to legislate for himself on the 'standards' he will choose to obey. We can name the paparazzi as one of the great beneficiaries of such a 'right'.

In **World Media blacklists any photos of dying Princess**, Richard Yallop embarks on a self-righteous account of how most media organisations had rejected the photos of the fatally injured princess being hawked around the world. (We know that the possible effect on newspaper sales and subsequent loss of power were the reasons the media organisations rejected the photos — and certainly not any sense of decency.) But Terry O'Gorman is quickly introduced as saying that 'he was seeking a ban on photographs of media subjects on private property ... He said the circumstances of Diana's death reinforced the need for stricter media controls in Australia.' Didn't somebody tell O'Gorman that Princess Diana was hounded to death in public places, that the Alma tunnel was actually a public place? It was surely more appropriate in these circumstances to talk of controls of the media in *public* places.

O blasphemy! What wickedness to suggest that the media should have restraints put on them in public places! Australian Press Council vice-chairman, Lange Powell, is reported as responding in just this way to O'Gorman's seizing the opportunity to protect and highlight 'the rights' of the individual in private. Powell said that the 'gross invasiveness on a public street' 'leading' to Diana's death should be reviewed. Powell is to be congratulated on making such a rare admission, although he says 'leading' and not 'causing'.

O'Gorman would be frowning from the heights on such a rash, unreflective comment. A quiet word in Powell's ear later by some theoretic-republican flunkey would inform Powell that the imposition of 'moral' order on the public realm was a very delicate matter and should not be canvassed in the public forum. That was better left to those whose doctrinal understanding was equipped to handle such matters. Any clumsy handling of the imposed moral order may inhibit the dissemination of the 'right' information for public consumption and broadcast ideas that undermine the theoretic-republican gains. Above all, the 'freedom of the press' must be protected. Any restraint here would be a thrust at the vital parts of the Empire.

No, O'Gorman has made the *appropriate* response in the matter. It is legitimate to express concern about the 'deplorable conduct' of the 'mainstream media' but only in terms that focus on renegade elements exceeding the boundaries of the established 'moral order'. It is right to highlight the harmful actions of individuals intruding into the non-public space. The public order has no business here, whatever the nature of the act. It also deflects pressure from the public realm which must always remain under the control of the Republican Inquisition.

Mark Ryan, assistant secretary of the Media, Entertainment and Arts Alliance, supports the distinction between the public and private realms. He is reported as saying that 'he did not think greater controls were necessary because the Australian media could distinguish between covering someone's public duty and their private life'. Who's he trying to kid? Most people would choke on their coffee reading that sanctimonious statement. Ryan goes on to say that if there are any controls they should be 'in the boardrooms of the media organisations who pay for photos'. But this comment reflects a quarrel over power among brothers. Ryan is reflecting the view that the media boardroom has the power he thinks his union should possess. They both espouse the same broad theoretic-republican principles. Any talk of controls is in the terms of an imposed order. Ryan is not talking about the moral restraints the individual recognises within the natural order of things, and which should be obeyed apart from any human law.

And what happened to the question of the media's harassing Diana to death in a public place? Well, that is of little concern. After all, the theoretic-republican knows that Diana is not at all the representative of the 'democratic', republican order she can be made out to support. In the end, she was a member of an order of things the world can do without.

11. The Public's Vicious Appetite is Responsible for Diana's Death

Tracy Sutherland (**Celebrities point finger but some say we all must share the blame**) takes over from Kate Legge in shifting the blame from the media to the public appetite for gossip. Sutherland's report is brilliantly supported by a close-up picture of flowers and a message placed outside Britain's consulate in New York. It is a very odd-looking card and message. The message is clear and appealing, neatly printed in rich blue ink. Its composition and design would be worthy of a writer and a graphic artist in one of the great advertising agencies of New York. In contrast to most messages seen in news reports this message was unsigned. It reads:

DIANA,
We all share a small piece of
responsibility for your death. I am
very sorry. May you rest in peace.
You'll be dearly missed.

Sutherland pursues the intent of the message in her report by saying that in the face of calls for legislation to control the media, 'some observers have questioned to what extent society in general is also culpable'. ('Some' in this context refers to members or flunkeys of the ruling elite). She quotes David Marshall, the author of *Celebrity and Power*, as saying that we are all 'complicit' in reading the stories about Diana. Complicit in what? Does the act of reading a report *in itself* make the reader complicit in an act that others have committed? If I pick up a magazine in the doctor's waiting room and happen across an article on Diana, what does that effectively or logically make me complicit in? Brief reflection on the formulation of this question will tell the rational mind that the mere reading about an act already completed cannot in any sense make the reader complicit in that act — certainly not in a necessary logical sense. Are we to think on this argument that the avid reader of crime reports becomes necessarily complicit in those crimes? It is a nonsense only the propagandist would dare to propose.

Some may object that the analogical argument of the crime reader is faulty because the case of the reader of crime is not the same as the case of the reader of reports about celebrities. Well, it is and it isn't. The analogy of the crime reader is relevant in demonstrating that the mere reading about an immoral act cannot make one complicit in the immoral act already completed. That's the nonsense. It is right, however, to point out that the crime reporter does not commit an immoral act in writing about crime. He is simply writing about the criminal acts of others. But let's change the example to bring it more in line with the celebrity/paparazzi case.

Say the crime reporter who saw a substantial and growing market in crime writing arranged a series of gruesome murders so that he could exploit the existing market. Does that make the reader of crime reporting who eventually comes across the reports, complicit in those murders? Hardly. The crucial point is that the market for celebrity gossip and crime reports presents an occasion for someone to exploit that market. The exploiting agent, without the prior agreement, knowledge, and actual and explicit support of the market consumer, carries out a series of independent steps to produce the product that will appeal to and satisfy the perceived demand. Let's take a second example.

Is the reader of child pornography complicit in the production of child pornography? Is he (partly) responsible for the degradation of the child victim? If he is, on both accounts, then is the reader of celebrity gossip by analogy complicit in its production? This is a more complex case, but the analogy still does not hold up. Firstly, the consumer of child pornography, as much as his independent act of obtaining such reading is depraved, is again merely providing the market or the occasion for the producer of child pornography. The act of the producer in acquiring innocent children and setting them up for the taking of pornographic pictures must count as an individual act of extreme moral depravity for which he is entirely responsible. The exploiting of the occasion does not involve anybody else in his individual act.

Does that mean that the consumer of child pornography is not responsible for the degradation of the child? If not directly responsible for the individual child in a particular case of child pornography, then he is responsible for the degradation of children in a communal sense. His depraved proclivities are both harmful to the moral fabric of society and render the children who come into contact with him potential or actual victims. He presents such a threat to the life of the community that the state can legitimately declare his activities criminal and punishable. Because the producer of child pornography acts to excite his depravity even further, he (the producer) is by far the greater threat to the community and should be dealt with accordingly.

Secondly, the analogy does not work because the consumer of celebrity gossip can hardly be compared to the consumer of child pornography. The worst that can be said of the avid reader of celebrity gossip is that he is giving rein to his baser inclinations, meaning his inclination to be amused and distracted by gossip and glitter. One can talk about the vicious appetite of the public for news about celebrities but that is hardly in the same class as the depravity connected with child pornography. Furthermore, the interest in celebrity news that creates the market to be exploited is very uneven. The most 'vicious' of consumers may buy as many magazines and newspapers as possible to satisfy their curiosity. But a large number would buy a magazine only occasionally about their favourite celebrity. Others would pick up a magazine in a waiting room of a doctor, dentist, and many other professionals. The occasional purchase and the subscriptions by businesses are enough to create a sizeable market for the gossip magazines and their advertisers. When we consider that a lucrative market for a gossip magazine would be 500,000 units per issue, we can see that not many people with a 'vicious appetite' need be attracted. Thus the 'public' that is allegedly complicit in the immoral acts of the media does not extend comprehensively over the population we generally call 'the public'.

I will take a third analogical argument that aims to demonstrate the complicity of 'the public' in the immoral acts of the media. This is one that was presented to me in writing. Its author put it like this: the claim that holding the 'vicious appetite' of the public partly responsible for Diana's death is 'merely media-motivated attempts to shift the blame from the media ... is quite wrong. It's like suggesting that to reproach users for the prevalence of child prostitution is just an excuse to get pimps off the hook.' But the comparison is way off beam. The reading of a gossip magazine is not an immoral act in itself, no matter how trivial and mindless it may appear to superior minds; whereas the act of an adult having sex with a child is among the most repugnant of immoral acts. Secondly, the purchase of a gossip magazine implies a loose relationship between the media and the reader quite different from that of the pimp, the child victim, and the sex offender. In the latter case, the three parties are closely connected materially and temporally in a victim-abuser relationship.

The crucial point in the argument against the complicity of the public in the hounding of Diana is that the occasion of the market for gossip magazines and newspapers does not involve a causal relationship. It is true to say that if the market was not there for gossip magazines there would be no gossip magazines. But that does not imply a causal link between the reader and the manner in which gossip magazines gain or create their information. The removal of the demand merely removes the occasion for action that may be moral or immoral depending on the people who commit the acts of gathering or creating information. The act of gathering information is not wrong in itself. It is HOW the information is gathered. The moral content of those acts depends solely on the doer of the act and not on any party whose attention may be excited by the final product.

In the end, the media bosses are consciously and deliberately exploiting our fallible human nature and not the depraved habits and inclinations of a small section of the community, as in the case of child pornography and child sexual exploitation. The user of child pornography can be under no illusions about how the product he is reading came into being. The reader of gossip has no way of knowing how a particular report was made that ends up being situated between a great deal of other inoffensive information. All the analogies thus far presented fail in their object.

Unembarrassed by the nonsense she is reporting, Sutherland goes on to invoke the authority of 'British commentators' who 'have noted the love/hate relationship enjoyed by the princess and the media.' This is essentially the same argument propounded by McNicoll and just as self-serving and unconvincing. The authoritative figures quoted by Sutherland do nevertheless provide some new angles. Firstly, Lord McGregor of Durris, chairman of the Press Complaints Commission in 1993,

> *was forced to conclude 'that the princess had, in practice, invaded her own privacy' by briefing journalists about her private life.*

We stagger from one nonsense to the other. Apart from the incoherent formulation of the charge, this is simply offending basic moral reasoning. If Diana revealed aspects of her private life to journalists, what does that mean? Surely no more than that the Princess is authorising the public use of specific information that, in accordance with the theoretic-republican idea of privacy, she has personal control over. A love-hate relationship cannot be concluded logically from this action in any way. Neither does the act of authorising use of particular private information logically give licence to any other unconnected activity. Does the act of lending somebody my car give that person licence to do whatever he wants with it? Such an act of trust entails a moral responsibility. This is the core moral point in my refuting the contention that the public's 'vicious appetites' are complicit in *causing* Diana's death.

A member of the media has a moral responsibility not to harm or controvert the normal rights of the individual no matter how many people are interested in what is reported. The act of media harassment is wrong in itself. The argument that McGregor and other such confused thinkers propose is the necessary connection between Diana's co-operating with or utilising media channels, and the licence by the media to do whatever they want with regard to harvesting information about such people as Diana. Quite apart from the moral aspect of such activity, the logic of such a proposal is not worthy of the reasoning of a school child. Indeed, I may be insulting the school child.

To reinforce McGregor's wonky reasoning Sutherland appeals to a 'media-theologian' in one of Australia's theoretic-republican seminaries. He is Associate Professor Nash of the Department of Journalism at Sydney's University of Technology. Nash is quoted as saying that Diana was a 'virtuoso' in media manipulation. She was not. The evidence suggests just the opposite. She was lax, impetuous and naive when it came to the media. She trusted too much in the good intentions of her fellow-citizens and ended up miscalculating badly on the few occasions she chose to give a substantial account of her views through media channels.

Secondly, what degree of manipulation was involved in Diana's telling a bunch of media hyenas who were following her around that she would be in a particular place at a particular time to promote a particular *charitable* cause? What sort of minds equate this activity with the behaviour we witness daily from the media? Unconcerned by the evidential problems in his assertion (he knows he won't be challenged in the media), Nash gives an extra dimension to the blame arguments. Sutherland reports his argument thus:

> *Saying other European royal families do not suffer the same media spotlight, he [Nash] argues Buckingham Palace must also take some responsibility for setting up the Diana 'fairytale' to help resurrect the monarchy.*

Nash may well have been peeved at the mangled manner in which Sutherland reports his argument, for what is the meaningful connection between the first part and the second part of the argument? Unless, of course, Nash is accustomed to putting his views in this mangled way. Nevertheless, the meaning does not escape us. We'll skirt quickly around the typical theoretic-republican paranoia in the claim that the palace 'set up' Charles's marriage with Diana (and thus the 'fairytale') in order 'to resurrect the monarchy'. Many parents would do far more than the Palace obviously did to ensure the connection of their children to the right partner. The theoretic-republican mind could never allow that the wicked royal family, just like republican families, could want their son well married. It is so easy for the republican ideologue to twist something so ordinary in life to suit their ideological agenda. Let me also add that the **Obituary** provided by *The Times* on page 17 of this same edition states that Diana 'fell in love with the Prince, was keen to be Princess of Wales and saw in him a challenge'.

Even if we admit the Palace did have a hand in arranging the marriage of Diana and Charles (the core element of the alleged 'Diana fairytale'), does that logically entail a responsibility for whatever happens thereafter? Of course not. This argument looks like the *post hoc ergo propter hoc* fallacy, which is simply the fallacy of claiming that because B followed A in time, A caused B. We might as well say that Diana's mother and father were responsible for the accident because in their selfish love act they brought Diana into the world. Nash must be aware of the nonsensical argument he is offering. I suspect he is having a gratuitous swipe at the royal family to amuse and excite his like-minded colleagues.

12. *The Australian* Editorial Board Decides Who's to Blame

Having softened the reader up with the attempts thus far to shift the blame of Diana's death from the media collectively to anybody or anything else at all, *The Australian* editorial committee weighs in with a centrepiece editorial (p. 14) to highlight the main arguments to defend the *Disgusting Empire*. I think the reader should pause over what this editorial says and the manner in which it is presented, and consider the function of the supporting reports. I will consider the editorial paragraph by paragraph. The editorial starts off, as it usually does in *The Australian*, by projecting a pseudo-balance in its presentation.

> *There is a natural desire to blame someone for the tragic death of Princess Diana but it is too easy simply to blame the media. At one level, the Princess of Wales's death was the result of a terrible accident. The driver of the car in which she was a passenger lost control while moving at speed through a Paris traffic tunnel. It is also true, though, that the media — specifically the paparazzi — contributed to the circumstances which put her in that place at that time. The courts will presumably decide whether any individuals acted to endanger the lives of those in the car. But the photographers were there because people all over the world are fascinated by the kind of pictures they were trying to take. To that extent, Princess Diana's death can be blamed partly on the desire of millions of people to know more about her than she was sometimes prepared to reveal.*

Here we have all the sanctimony, self-interest, and slippery verbal manoeuvring the media is famous for. No media group is more talented in this area than the *Disgusting Empire*.

It is natural to apportion blame in seeking the 'cause' of a tragic event, private or public. Our society has set up institutions and rules to seek out the cause and apportion blame in important or suspected criminal circumstances. The editorial writer's oblique meaning here, though, is that the 'people' are being ruled by their ignorant passions in attributing blame and he is cloaking this underhanded meaning in the unexceptionable reasoning about cause and blame.

Remember, for the theoretic-republican overseer the people are 'the people' when they behave in line with the tenets and prescriptions of the prevailing theoretic-republican order. When they go against these prescriptions in their irremediable ignorance they become the ignorant masses. One chief purpose of this editorial is to gently remind the 'educated reader' (the host of theoretic-republican flunkeys scattered throughout the organs of the state) that the media has the thankless task of dealing with the emotions of the masses who are often difficult to supervise. The heading of the editorial says it all.

Paparazzi serve a fickle mob

The editorial goes on to distinguish between the 'terrible accident' and the issue of apportioning blame. For the editorial writer the essence of the event is its accidental nature. The rest is disputable. It is disputable mostly in a legal sense, and not in a moral sense. Let's consider this line of argument more closely. If you are walking along the path of a busy main-road shopping centre and without thinking suddenly take a step onto the road in front of a car driving at a safe speed and are run over, it is clear you have caused an accident. If you are killed, the police and your relations would no doubt accept that you had been involved in a 'terrible accident' and that no legal or moral blame could be reasonably apportioned in this case. It was an accident as this word is generally understood.

But if you are a young woman rushing along that same street late in the evening, terrified because for the last 30 minutes you have been closely stalked by two powerful-looking men, and if in your terror you step off the footpath in front of a car travelling at a safe speed and are killed, would we call that a 'terrible accident' in the same sense?

Legally, there may be some dispute about the culpability of the stalkers. A clever lawyer without moral scruples can work wonders with the legal system. But morally, nobody would dare to say that the stalkers were not the cause of the accident and must bear the full responsibility — morally and legally, if our legal system is to reflect moral principle. Few would dare to say that the young woman was partly to blame because she was young and attractive, and thus contradictingly invited the unwanted attention of the males who were simply responding to the demands of their nature and the social environment that condones the pursuit of young females by males. No one would ask how a young woman can set herself up as a centre of attraction and then refuse what she herself implicitly sanctions.

The uncorrupted mind would have no hesitation in rejecting this manner of thinking. It would have no difficulty in recognising that stalking a young woman in this way is not a case of the male naturally responding to the attractions of a young female and wanting to come into contact with her. Stalking has a completely different moral character. It falls outside the natural moral context of female and male relations. It is aberrant moral behaviour which, in this case, directly brought about the death of the young woman. If a group of hunters chased a kangaroo around a field and in the end it ran out onto the road to be run over and killed, we would laugh if anybody tried to tell us the kangaroo died by accident. No, the hunters would be under no such misapprehension, they would carry home the kangaroo and display it as a kill. The example of a young woman being stalked to her death in a suburban street is a simple case of the male transgressing the moral imperatives of his social nature. For the purposes of illustrating the essential point about responsibility I will take this scenario a little further.

Although the pursuit of females by males is part of our general human nature, there are clear limits to male and female interaction. In a healthy *traditional* society the moral prescriptions of female-male interaction are reflected in the very traditions of that society. For example, 18th century English society generated a set of rules and manners to enable male and female to meet in *decency, safety, self-respect* and *enjoyment*. A male might follow a female at a discreet distance along the paths of a well-known public place; he was not permitted to do more unless introduced in the permissible social context and unless the female acknowledged the attention. And if the attention were acknowledged, the male was expected to act with honour and not seize the occasion to use every possible subterfuge to seduce the female. This sometimes happened, but there was public and private censure for such transgressions. In the last years of the 20th century there remain but a few vestiges of those codes of conduct in our *regressing* Australian society. A brief consideration of those codes would reveal not something arbitrary or oppressive, as is often claimed, but a proven manner of social intercourse that was anchored in our moral nature. The moral framework of our nature in the established order of the world oversees society's formulation of viable concrete rules of behaviour.[7]

Now the 'moral' mentality that discarded that system of social interaction as arbitrary and a limitation on our radical free nature also ushered in the degenerate male who thinks nothing of harassing and stalking whatever female as long as he can escape consequent action that is harmful to himself. Any female is thus fair game. It is the same moral mentality that is operating in this editorial in an equivalent set of circumstances. We can apply the same thinking to the issue of media intrusiveness.

It is part of our nature to be inquisitive about the lives of our fellow man. We are curious to know the good and the bad. We are especially keen to know about the lives of the famous, and news about such people will attract most of us. But our moral nature (to which we can blind ourselves) tells us that there should be limits to the access of that information, and that there are also limits to the means of acquiring that information. As much as we feel curious about the lives of our next-door neighbour, our moral nature will not allow us to install listening devices, tap telephones, hire a detective service and open the neighbour's mail in the attempt to satisfy our curiosity. This is clear enough for the ordinary person who is not running a media empire.

Our everyday society has accepted rules respecting the private lives of its members. We call people who transgress those rules busybodies, gossipmongers and calumniators, and other things besides. And when the intrusion is serious it becomes a matter of grave moral concern that is reflected in differing ways in common and statute law. As I say, this is clear enough to the ordinary uncorrupted mind. Society's viable rules for respecting the privacy of others are rooted in our moral nature; they are not the result of the efforts of some 'democratically' elected legislator who wishes to impose a particular order on an un-ordered mass of self-seeking individuals. Now let's return to the editorial writer's defence of his claim that the curious public is 'partly to blame' for the death of Diana.

> *The public has a fascination for celebrities — royalty, presidents, film stars, media moguls. This is recognised by radio and television stations, magazines and newspapers which respond to the fascination to boost their audiences. The role the subjects play in this equation may be willing or unwilling. For instance, publicity improves earning power for film stars but may not be welcomed by a presidential candidate caught out in an extra-marital affair. The media's interest depends on there being a market. If people did not buy magazines or view the videotapes, then the interest would die. Ironically, many who provide the market would argue pruriently[8] against the paparazzi securing the images which prompt them to buy the products.*

Nobody would dispute the public fascination for entertainers. The more admired the entertainer, the greater the interest. It is entirely legitimate for the 'media' to provide information about that enter-tainer. That is, legitimate within the framework of our moral nature. When the individual who is the actor is functioning temporally and spatially within the bounds of the entertainment role it is legitimate to consider *in principle* that time and space available for public inter-est. Exceptions in *particular* circumstances cannot be ruled out. For example, if a famous actor on stage is suddenly called to the side be-cause his wife has just been killed in a car accident outside the theatre, the ordinary moral human being present would be overcome with feel-ings of sympathy and sorrow at the tragedy rather than responding to a morbid interest in the actor as actor responding to a tragedy. Or, if that same actor suddenly took sick at a press conference and lost control of his bowels, what decent-minded person would consider that media had a right to keep the cameras rolling? But, these particular exceptional instances aside, the function of entertainer implies a lim-ited, willing availability to the instruments that satisfy public interest.

If it happens that the entertainer through ability and physical at-tractiveness excites a massive interest in the public it is hard to see how an increase in fame would entail logically a change to the ele-ments of the commitment an entertainer takes on by virtue of his choosing to be an entertainer. The entertainer, famous or not, has merely committed himself to a limited availability of his person to public interest. The essential point is the *prior* status of the entertainer as a *person*.

If we accept that we all possess the same human nature and thus the same status of personhood we would not dare to assert that the entertainer by virtue of his choosing the entertainment profession suddenly has given up his essential personhood, and the rights attached to personhood. On the other hand, the choice of the person to be an entertainer also entails the choice about the limits of availability to public interest. The extent of availability depends on the way the person chooses to function as an entertainer. If the person as an entertainer chooses to do one film, or one performance, or one play during the year, then he has committed himself to public scrutiny commensurate with the extent of the performance. Outside the boundaries of this commitment the entertainer possesses the same rights as all other persons. He has the right to enjoy his privacy, his family, his friends, his interests without the intrusion of other people, whoever they are. If the entertainer wants to appear 'in public' in addition to one performance then that is solely his choice. The scrutiny he has committed himself to, is limited to the extent of that chosen performance, temporally and spatially. The choice of the person to be an entertainer does not *in itself* create a moral obligation to any media empire. And it certainly does not suspend his rights as a person and citizen.

The editorial writer is pulling a moral swifty, equating the function of the politician with the function of an entertainer to justify the intrusion of the media in the lives of famous people. Although increasingly people are saying that the private activities (mostly this means sexual activity) of politicians should not be a consideration in judging their performance as politicians, there are still a great many of us who think that the marital infidelity of a politician is of serious moral import and should be brought to the attention of the public. Now the editorial writer pretends that he cannot see the distinction between the unwanted attention of the media in the case of the politician and that of the entertainer. The conflating and distorting of examples and functions such as these is a common tactic of media organisations to justify their morally repugnant activities. How close, then, are the two functions of being an entertainer and a politician?

The politician also enjoys the essential and prior status of the person, but his choice to function as a politician entails a very particular set of commitments, in many respects entirely different from that of the entertainer. Whereas the entertainer has undertaken to amuse, entertain and distract the public, the politician has committed himself essentially to a public moral role. He has put himself forward as a person who is both competent and morally able to take on the grave responsibility of caring for the common good of the people of the society in which he lives. In other words, he has implicitly guaranteed a comprehensive level of moral and administrative competence in the functioning of his public role as politician.

Although the public has not the right to have a television camera present for his every action, the politician has committed himself to having his private and public character continually under scrutiny. If the politician wants to carry on an extra-marital affair then it is well within the province of the media to report that activity to the public. The public has a right to know of the character of the people they are electing to look after the common good of society.

Now I could labour the point with a variety of examples but I think I have said enough to make clear the difference in the moral commitment between the politician and the entertainer, between the entertainer and other professions. It is not reasonable to expect to scrutinize all professions equally in the public sphere. There are different commitments and corresponding responsibilities. The editorial writer falls short of making his case to justify the intrusive behaviour of the media in the lives of people by appealing to the example of the politician.

Besides failing to sustain the argument, the editorial inadvertently unmasks the fundamental motives of the media. It is one of those occasions where all the care taken to present the right image, all the effort to manipulate the mind and sentiments of the reader fall down badly. In saying that the media is only responding to a market, that the media activity is determined by the response of the public, the editorial writer is implying that media activity is purely and simply a business, that the lives of people are simply products that can be considered like any sort of detergent to be promoted and sold — no mention of moral restraint — only mention of the functioning of the impersonal forces of the market. Human action is reduced to economic activity. The moral vacuum of the argument is evident in the claim that the market interest supposedly generating the repugnant intrusion of the media is 'prurient' in objecting to the manner of satisfying that interest. What sort of mind would claim that market interest condones any manner whatever in satisfying that interest? The editorial writer continues.

> *The Princess of Wales* **claimed** *to hate media intrusions. She could not leave her front door without encountering the glare of the spotlight. Outside the confines of private premises she had virtually no opportunity for spontaneity and relaxation which must often have been hard for an obviously vibrant and fun-loving personality to bear. It was tougher still that images showing a slip up, a yawn, tears or an indiscretion commanded a premium. The princess's death will obviously add to pressure for greater regulation to prevent some of the more egregious media intrusions.* **Yet it is hard to see how this would function without seriously compromising the principles of freedom of the press.** [My emphasis.]

Diana *claimed* to hate media intrusion? Was there any question about this? We all know that Diana was severely tormented by the unrelenting, ungovernable actions of the media who hounded her. She was visibly affected by the constant pressure, as most of us would be. The purpose in subtly throwing doubt on Diana's attitude to the media is to remind us that in the end Diana 'asked for it', she got what she herself courted. The editorial writer then goes on inconsistently to offer a reasonable picture of the unrelenting emotional torment Diana was subjected to. The purpose here is also clear: the acknowledgement of the torment is balanced against the main issue of the editorial: the possible legal curtailment of media activity. When there are dollars and power at stake the *Disgusting Empire* will try every tactic regardless of the inner coherence of moral argument. Of course, there is no mention of money and power. That is hidden behind the grand 'principles of press freedom'.

What reflective person could possibly think that the principles of free speech are the central concern? It is only preserving their power base and securing the ability to disseminate the principles of their particular faction that is of concern. Those of us who hold political and moral views not permitted by the ruling elite know how cynically the principle of press freedom is utilised to suppress those whose views are unacceptable. The stark reality is that there is no unrestricted freedom of speech. There will always be a ruling elite whose views will be imposed on society and who will use their power to suppress views considered inimical to the state. The issue is not about free speech but about what may be said and who may say it.

Yet the editorial writer has gone too far even for the reader who may browse over the argument. Is he seriously asserting that the ungovernable state of the media is to be maintained, is to be preferred, even at the cost of wrecking lives? Undaunted, the editorial writer continues to develop the argument that Diana really 'asked for it'.

> *It must be said that the princess flirted with the media and courted media attention when it suited her. Princess Diana may have been the most photographed woman of all time but she was not a media creation.* **She was a person used to constant attention** *from the first days of her involvement with the heir to the British throne. One can well believe that she was at first shocked and overwhelmed at the level of attention. Later — especially after her separation from Prince Charles — she became adept at exploiting the media for her own purposes. Often this was to publicise the many worthy causes to which she attached her name. But it was also to win public sympathy for her side of the sad story of a troubled marriage and to re-establish her independence from the royal family. There is no other explanation for the Panorama interview she did with the BBC in 1995. She could have chosen to lead a life away from the public glare, in much the same way as her former sister-in-law Princess Anne has done. Instead many of the private aspects of Princess Diana's life which became public did so through her own words.* [My emphasis.]

Imagine if a male who had been apprehended for rape claimed that the victim in flirting with him had really asked to have sexual intercourse. The victim had only got what she had asked for! Imagine the justified uproar of ordinary people in the community. It is a sad fact that many males in the amoral atmosphere of Western society in the 1990s believe that the mere friendliness of a female is an open invitation. Many men have to learn that a friendly gesture is no more than that. A friendly gesture is not to be rewarded with rape. In the same way the gentlemen of the editorial board of *The Australian* have to learn that the mere friendliness or co-operative spirit of a media victim does not, cannot, morally justify activity with no restraint whatever. It can never justify media rape.

Diana 'used to constant attention'? If you repeat a lie often enough some people are bound to believe it, despite the overwhelming evidence against it. Diana was never used to the tormenting activity of the media. To her very last minutes she made this obvious. The media had soured her existence. Her so-called manipulation of the media was anything but adept when it came to pleading her own cause. It was transparent, imprudent, clumsy, self-defeating, unprofessional. Most media commentators seemed to give her the thumbs down after the Panorama interview of 1995. My reaction was certainly one of sympathy for Diana, but not in the way she apparently intended. In a tragic display of bad judgement she had put both feet in shark infested waters. Diana evoked a great deal of sympathy precisely because she showed herself to be one of those fragile, self-defeating, tragic figures of this modern age.

Again, it needs to be repeated that Diana in presenting her case through the media was simply using the same channels of communication that others were using to scrutinise and attack her. Should she have relinquished the current means of communication to avoid the accusation that she was manipulating the media and thus giving the green signal for the desperate, unrestrained behaviour of the media? That's an absurdity and an outrage that the media evidently have no trouble in proposing, as they also do in using the publicity for her charities to justify their intrusive behaviour. To cap off the complete lack of moral consciousness, the editorial writer finishes with this gem.

> *Today, the world grieves for Princess Diana, for a life cut short, for her sons without their mother, for the rest of her family and her friends. But it is simplistic to lay the blame for her death with the pursuing paparazzi who, in reality, appeared to be seeking to do no more than take new photographs of a woman who was already the most photographed in the world.*

The poor innocents of the media merely going about their selfless task of providing information and photos of the most photographed woman in the world! What spoil-sport wretch would complain that in this case they just wanted to take some more harmless photos of the same object? One struggles to hold one's stomach in place. The media mind knows no shame.

The *true* 'reality' is that the vultures of the media (the editorial/paparazzi team) were acting as they usually do, without any moral restraint whatever, without any consideration for their prey as real persons with feelings, families, friends and life of their own, but only with their self-interest in view where all was permitted. The apportioning of blame by the ordinary person may be the simplistic judgement of irreformably ignorant folk but let us rejoice that we have not yet been educated as the theoretic-republican media have, that our hearts have not been ripped out by self-interest, that our minds have not been so corrupted that we no longer recognise what is good, what is decent and what is right.

The editorial committee of *The Australian* is not prepared to rest with this defence. The threat to the grand 'principles of freedom of the press' is so serious that too much argument is not enough to defend their position.

13. The Media Heavyweights Brought in to Back Editorial Writer

On the facing page under the title of OPINION *The Australian* editorial committee calls in the professional big guns. Here's how they headline the section:

The deaths of the Princess of Wales and her companion have reminded other celebrities of their vulnerability and revived calls for a crackdown, but not all believe the fourth estate should be held accountable

Blame the Media or Blame the Public?

The unsuspecting reader would think from the headline and introduction that the reader would be presented with a balanced debate about the issue. Not a bit of it. *The Australian* is always at pains to give the impression that their reporting is balanced, that opinion and information cover all sides of the issue or event. What appears here is a good example of how they really see 'balance' in an issue. First of all, the 'media-theologian' (the academic) must be called on to boost and give credibility to their position. The academic that has been roped in for this purpose is Queensland 'journalism academic', Kerry Green. Green certainly rises to the task. She repeats fundamentally the same arguments so tortuously outlined in the editorial. The difference is that she expresses the arguments far more clearly and adds some features of her own. In the long run, the same answers I have given to the editorial can be repeated. But it is worth looking at the particular spin she puts on her arguments. Remember that Green is responsible with her colleagues for forming young minds for the work they will have to do in businesses owned by such as the *Disgusting Empire*.

As with the editorial, she starts off by suggesting that we are apt to get carried away by our emotions in such an event as the death of Diana. The impulse is to seek 'to punish the destroyer'. She asks who the 'destroyer' is. The first (blind) impulse, she indicates, is to blame the paparazzi and, 'by extension, the mass media'. But if we (i.e. the ordinary folk way down there below the academic) could rise above our blind emotional reaction we would see that 'the audiences' of the mass media are at least equally culpable. She goes on, in the face of the evidence, to claim that Diana 'was a consummate media performer and manipulator'. Both Charles and Diana used 'compliant British columnists' [*sic*] to present their case to the public, to 'shape public opinion first one way, then the other'. We can only gasp when we read the conclusion drawn from all this:

> *In the face of such sophisticated use of the media, it is naive to suggest that celebrities such as Diana have been victimised unmercifully; the media has also been abused.*

Alas, the poor, pitiful media! And we the stupid public who are complicit in abusing those innocent, zealous, righteous souls of the media empires. How stupid can we be to think that the release of private information through current public communication channels is totally different from the swarms of journalists day and night unrelentingly pursuing media prey, ever ready to write and broadcast whatever suits the objectives of the particular media empire! How stupid are we to think that an interview with a TV journalist broadcast internationally is different from the lies, the mockery, the ridicule, and smear that is levelled at a media prey day and night! How stupid are we to think that an interview in a coffee shop with an editor of one of the great London newspapers is different from a media prey being pursued up and down a dark street after she has left her therapist to be at last cornered, and in tears and desperation to feel the blinding flashlights from inches away! We need a media academic to come down from on high to disabuse us poor simple folk of our ignorant feelings about the justice and morality of such behaviour and events. So that we are under no illusion about Green's moral reasoning, we are presented with the only form of restraint on the actions of the media who are responding to the interest of the public in a particular person.

Once the interest of an audience has been aroused, the audience will decide when enough is enough.

The rhetoric of natural rights has filled volumes with the indignant discourse of the supporters of the 'Rights of Men'. The theoretic dogma of such natural rights has been bequeathed to our 'liberal-democratic' society by the great thinkers who built the scaffolds of 1789. It is regurgitated parrot-like whenever an agitating individual makes a claim against any properly constituted authority. Green, who is evidently a child of the oratory of such people as Voltaire, Robespierre and Rousseau, has no hesitation in suspending the person who is in the unfortunate position of exciting the interest of the public, of every natural right so jealously protected by the philosophers of individualism. Where other moral theories have been judged to fail in pointing out the incoherence of abstract individual subjective rights, Green thinks she has succeeded. The 'Rights of Men' have been at last defeated by the passing 'interest of the public'. The moment the famous person 'uses' the current channels of communication to publicise their views or person, that is the moment they have implicitly given up their rights as an individual. That is the moment they pass from person to non-person. During their hounding and torment they may only pray that some whim will deflect the attention of their pursuers and suspend their persecution. Those satisfying the public interest have been released from every moral injunction and restraint. But this is to use the rhetoric of abstract rights against their supporters. I will come back to this issue from a different angle shortly.[9]

Ms Green's obsequious support of the arguments in the editorial is evidently deemed insufficient, for a little below and in the centre of the page we find an article from *The Times* correspondent, Simon Jenkins (**The smell of the celebrity, the roar of the crowd**). The headline writer has again displayed his talent but, as we shall see, the emotive propagandist colour of the heading demeans a serious, intelligent examination of a real dilemma for the theoretic-republican mind. Jenkins brightens the unabashed propagandising of the Australian contributions by beginning with some amusing send-ups of the worldwide anger directed towards the media.

> *Bastards, reptiles, vultures, vermin, sewage in the gutters of the press. If I were a paparazzo, I would be keeping my head low today …*

The reader does not have to go far into this well-written piece before realising the amusing, ironic manner of dealing with the subject is covering the same arguments run hard in the previous piece. Jenkins writes that the very people responsible for 'eulogising' Diana are being seen as having driven her to her death. Grief follows, but then the people (in their emotion) look for blame.

> *… Blame is sovereign lord to every misfortune and demands swift recompense.*
>
> *That appears easily satisfied. The photographers who dogged Diana and Dodi Fayed for the past two months appear to have transgressed all professional restraint. They were insistent, cruel and murderous.*
>
> *With them around, she had no privacy and no dignity. She was imprisoned behind a grille of flashing cameras …*
>
> *Yet blame has not done with hunting. Behind the ghouls [paparazzi] lie other denizens of this underworld. The editors, picture editors, circulation managers, and bosses of the press have driven the market for the intrusive pictures ever higher.*

The cover of irony may be an ointment for those of the media who are honest enough with their natural feelings to think they may be culpable, but it will not do for most of us. When Jenkins applies the epithets *vultures, reptiles,* etc., to the paparazzi and the whole bunch of editors and media bosses hiding behind them, most people will applaud. It is a true description of the circumstances. Jenkins knows this and his thrust at the anger towards the media is subtle but clear. The colourful ironic description of the group held responsible for Diana's death is there as the implicit counter description of the partner in blame. That partner is 'the obsessive world-wide appetite for any news about the lady'.

> *If paparazzi are at one end of this sewer, at the other sits a salivating, prurient public. He among us who has no eye for such pictures, let him cast the first stone.*

There we are as the public: the equivalent of the vultures and reptiles at the other end of the sewer pipe. Well, it won't do and quite happily will I continue to pick and throw as many stones as are necessary to answer the self-serving defence of the media — as I have been doing. Jenkins does not bother to pursue any further the argument that the public is equally responsible for the death of Diana. He takes this as a given. It seems that Jenkins is not alone in his inability to get his mind around the simple proposition that the act of media persecution is wrong in itself. What he proceeds to discuss is the action that can be 'reasonably' taken to deal with the problem. He will discuss what *measures* can be *imposed* on the *unordered* situation. This is an interesting short piece of theoretic-republican reasoning. Firstly, he does acknowledge the obvious:

> *… a public thirst for intrusion is not reason enough for supplying it. Free markets need regulation. Damage needs redress. There are many products that sections of society may enjoy but that public safety or the right of the individual cannot allow.*

This is an obvious answer to the claim that the media is only satisfying the demand of the public and that the public is at least partly culpable for whatever happens in the act of satisfying public demand. The demand for heroin does not justify to any extent the drug barons who import the drug, use flunkeys to excite demand, and trap weak people in an addiction. The drug baron's acts are wrong in themselves. Society rightly reserves severe punishment for those that exploit the human occasion for illegal drug supply. But Jenkins's point is not the one that I have been developing, that is, one of moral responsibility. Media harassment or persecution is wrong in itself. What he proceeds to discuss is the justification for legislative action to curtail the circumstances that led to Diana's death, and the nature and limits of such legislative action.

In other words, he is not concerned with individual moral behaviour but how far the state can go in imposing rules to restrict public action in these particular circumstances. As I outlined in the beginning, this is the only way that the theoretic-republican mind can approach such problems. There can be no talk of a morality that does not exist. But some of us are stupid enough to insist that the individual is morally responsible for his behaviour, that if the individual must rely on state rules to keep him from persecuting a fellow-human being merely for the sake of material gain, then that individual is systematically corrupt and a member of a systematically corrupt society.

In the theoretic-republican context Jenkins has set himself to argue in, he cannot get far with the nature and extent of the legislation to deal with media intrusion. He exclaims ultimately that it is difficult to legislate for public taste.

> *How far a newspaper should go is ultimately a matter not of fact, like libel, but of taste. Legislating for taste is notoriously hard.*

Of course it is difficult to legislate for taste. But this is not a question of taste, as I have been arguing. Denial of a person's right, not just to privacy, but to happiness and well-being is a moral question. The question of media intrusion, as is apparent in all TV footage of Diana's harassment, is a question fundamentally of respect for one's fellow man. Nevertheless, it is even more difficult to legislate for individual moral behaviour. Human (positive) law is essentially to protect the citizen and apply sanctions to the wrong-doer. The natural law philosophers of the medieval times thought that legislation, whatever its limits, should reflect the natural law imposed by God through His order in the world. Individual morality must also reflect the objective laws of God but is *prior* to any particular human legislation. The moral conduct of the individual, based on the laws of God, is prior to the act of formulating society's laws and is the point to which the particular human law must continually refer. If the individual is taught through the educative instruments of society to deny the natural moral limits imposed on his behaviour, the human law of society will fall way short of curbing his desire to fulfil unlimited wants which essentially belong to an amoral realm. This is the dilemma Jenkins recognises implicitly — and whose remedy he ignores.

The consolation for the ruling class is that the human legislators will have a great deal of fun and earn a lot of money refining a set of rules for parliament to ratify for members of a society many of whom will only pay attention to them through the haphazard application of sanctions. Whatever can be got away with, will be got away with. If there is any retribution or punishment exacted for the death of Diana, those responsible will certainly not be those that have to bear it. Their power and position will protect them. The legislative process, not grounded in the eternal laws of God, is always capable of working cruelly and unjustly.

Jenkins, on the whole, argues his theoretic-republican case intelligently. It is unfortunate that it should ultimately degenerate into the suggestion that the royal family, in not choosing to protect their privacy, are really responsible for the intrusion of the media. Again, it's the 'you-asked-for-it' argument. If the royal family had not chosen to 'go public' from the 1960s onwards, Diana would be alive today! If Diana had chosen to retire from the public arena when she said she would, she would be alive today! Jenkins's final comment is that the whole dilemma of privacy vs. free speech may be resolved if the royal family chose to withdraw into a less publicity-generating mode.

Perhaps royalty might settle back into a mode in which privacy is easier to attain. Perhaps, perhaps.

The mind boggles yet again. Quite apart from the fallacy of generalising about media intrusion from the case of the British royal family, there arises a whopper of an inconsistency to slap the reader in the face. I thought that one of the main accusations levelled at royalty was that they were stiff, closed, aloof, cold, etc. The theoretic-republican call was for them to open up, lighten up, modernise and come down to the level of the people! You see, the royal family will never satisfy the theoretic-republican mentality. The republican obsession with royalty will only end when all royalty is deemed to have disappeared — when the theoretic-republican hierarchy prevails. Then they will turn their bored minds to some other 'issue' — if the 'world' they are trying to create has not yet brought about the total collapse of our liberal-democratic society.

As a reply to academic Kerry Green and *The Times* correspondent Simon Jenkins (plus all the other self-interested pleading) *The Australian* has allowed Antony Kidman, clinical psychologist, father of Nicole Kidman and father-in-law of Tom Cruise, to have a small say. One cannot help wondering whether Dr Kidman contacted or was contacted by the editorial committee of *The Australian*. Dr Kidman says that he is normally reluctant to comment publicly about his children's affairs. But in this case, Nicole had asked him 'to do what [he] could to publicise the harassment [by the media] her family has experienced ...' As a father who is proud of his daughters, he says, he does not hesitate to speak on her behalf.

A father speaking from the heart about the welfare of his children may have caused some apprehension in people who evidently put business, power and ideology ahead of the welfare of any particular individual. A display of heartfelt worry over the predicament of someone quite real (Nicole and Tom) in the minds of the public might end up arousing feelings that are unsupervisable and ultimately harmful to the interests of the media empire. Such apprehension would have been momentary for Dr Kidman's plea on behalf of his daughter and her family is mildly and softly put. It is an appeal to the decency and good feeling of one's fellow man. He outlines simply the main moral argument against media persecution: the use of the media by entertainers to promote their careers does not eliminate the normal moral standards of human behaviour. But it is utterly useless for Dr Kidman to approach the media in this manner.

As I said in the beginning, the media are like hyenas who dog their victims unrelentingly and have to be beaten back and left cowering. To be held in check they must be struck where it hurts most. They will cower only under a real threat to the boundaries of their power position. Dr Kidman's appeal to the media would have the same effect as an appeal to hyenas circling a cow protecting her wounded calf. Unfortunately, few possess the ability to mount a real threat to media power. In fact, only those authoriphobic types developing their own power position through media expansion could mount a real threat to the *Disgusting Empire*. For most of us the media are the modern 'untouchables'. Dr Kidman's polite article is in reality a sop to those who have a concern for the appearance of balance in reporting.

14. Diana — Some Pertinent Biographical Details

The 2 September edition of *The Australian* devotes the full **Obituary** page to Diana. In contrast to most other commentary on the life of Diana in *The Australian*, this account from *The Times* is mostly fair and balanced. At some point, for appearances sake, a true account of the established details of Diana's life had to appear. Much of the detail in the obituary is known to the reader who has had a passing interest in her life over the years. Even though one may sometimes dispute the interpretation of the events, the article has clearly been the product of some research. It is not necessary for me to examine the account in detail. I have already dealt with any disputable information or assertion appearing in it. I will be content with highlighting information about Diana's life that clearly contradicts the nonsense so mindlessly served up by other contributors to *The Australian's* 'commemoration' of the life of Diana.

One of the most frequent assertions about Diana is that she was essentially republican in her views. Her criticism of the royal family, of Prince Charles and of the stiff formality governing royal activities is meant to point to a mind that is fundamentally republican. I have shown that for the nonsense it is. This short biography of Diana on the obituary page recounts a family background that would make it highly unlikely that Diana, in a philosophical or political sense, espoused a jot of real theoretic-republican principle, especially if one holds that social environment is determining in the formation of a person's social and political orientation. Here's the short account of Diana's dazzling pedigree from the obituary:

The Hon Diana Frances Spencer was born at Park House, Sandringham, in Norfolk. She was the third and youngest daughter of Viscount Althorp, later the 8th Earl Spencer, who died in 1992, and his first wife, the Hon Frances Roche (later married to the wallpaper heir Peter Shand Kidd). She became Lady Diana Spencer on the death of her grandfather in 1975. Her Spencer forebears had been sheep farmers in Warwickshire who settled at Althorp, Northhamptonshire, in 1506. Cousins of the Spencer-Churchills, they included many connoisseurs and patrons of the arts. Having inherited a considerable fortune from Sarah, duchess of Marlborough, the family was able to spend large sums on antiquities, paintings and sculpture.

For many generations the Spencers served their sovereigns and the tradition continued. The princess's father was equerry to George VI and to the present Queen. Both her grandmothers, the late Countess Spencer and Ruth, Lady Fermoy, were close members of the court of the Queen Mother, as were no fewer than four Spencer great-aunts.

While the princess's paternal ancestors were representative of the Whig oligarchy of the 18th century, she also descended through several lines from the Stuart kings, Charles II and James II, who were not ancestors of the Prince of Wales. Other paternal forbears included the great duke of Marlborough, Sir Robert Walpole, the marquess of Anglesey (who lost a leg at Waterloo), and the earl of Lucan. On her mother's side there was Irish and Scottish blood with a sprinkling of New England stock.

All the evidence suggests that Diana was not in denial of her background, that the glorious ancestral lines repeated here were an essential part of Diana, the person. Earl Spencer referred to his sister as 'a very British girl'. More accurately, she was a very British *aristocratic* girl. The issue about warmth and openness was one of character and temperament. Apparently, some people cannot think of dignified, elegant behaviour being coupled with warmth and openness. Readers of Jane Austen's novels would know that the healthy character in her stories is the one who is able to combine elegance and dignity of person with a natural ease and warmth in their dealings with their fellow man. The theoretic-republican who keeps repeating the fanciful notion of Diana, the republican, is either engaged in mindful propaganda or mindless propaganda.

Diana, up to that fateful meeting with Charles in the field, had an undistinguished upbringing and education. The vital event in this period was the breakdown in her parents' marriage — the pain of which she never rose above. All reports about her character indicate that she was kind and enthusiastic about the 'small' things in a person's existence such as friendships, children, household activities. All this was tinged with a charming naivety and ingenuousness. It was especially this part of her character that the cynical, heartless members of the media mistook for 'manipulation' and manoeuvring. Where Diana was trying to reach out with friendship and conciliation the media was responding with guile and stratagems. This private world of Diana's virtually came to an end when (as the story goes) Charles ran into Diana in a ploughed field at Althorp. Charles at the time was reported to have been in a close relationship with Diana's sister, Lady Sarah Spencer. *The Times* biographer comments:

> *The younger sister [Diana] fell in love with the prince, was keen to be Princess of Wales and saw him as a challenge. She knew from an early age that she would have to tread carefully and she never put a foot wrong.*

If this account is true of Diana's feelings towards Prince Charles, and all the evidence suggests it is, then the claim about the royal family and Charles railroading the poor innocent princess into a loveless marriage because they, first and foremost, had their eyes on an heir to the throne is just malicious nonsense.

The meeting in the ploughed field at Althorp was to unleash the hounds of hell. In 1980 Diana's name was known to the world and the torment had begun. There would be few people with a television set who have not seen the manner in which the media pursued Diana from the start. Even in those early stages the pursuit was so unrelenting and unmerciful that Diana's mother and later the Queen had to appeal to the media. We all know that the appeals were in vain. One would have elicited a more favourable response from an appeal to Pol Pot about the suffering of his people. The courtship was conducted and the wedding took place. Then there was the normal period of marital adjustment. The adjustment most tragically did not take place. What were the reasons? One can speculate but, as I have already said, nobody will ever know which deficiencies in Diana and Charles would have contributed most to the marriage breakdown. The campaign by the media destroyed any chance of a successful marriage — as it would in the case of any other couple.

Diana went to her death with the cowboys of the media hot on her heels. It has been reported recently that Trevor Rees-Jones remembers Diana calling Dodi's name as she lay crumpled and dying in the back seat of the smashed Mercedes. What were her thoughts? Of her children? Surely. But just as surely those calls for Dodi were for some comfort in the realisation that what had happened was always going to happen. Diana's sometimes cool response in the face of the media frenzy bore signs of a fatal resignation.

5

Wednesday, 3 September 1997:
A Drunken Driver is to Blame

1. Grief and Consternation Around the World

While *The Australian* and other print media were busy shifting the blame for Diana's death, the more immediate instruments of the media — TV and radio — could not avoid reporting the feelings and views of the 'man in the street'. During this week I was scarcely out of range of a radio or television set. Reports on the reaction to Diana's death came from all manner of people and places. Looking back I cannot remember one voice that said Diana had been 'asking for it'. Talk-back radio was full of voices praising Diana's warmth, her open character, her charm, her beauty and the tragedy of her life. Not surprisingly, in this age of marriage breakdown, many women rang radio stations to say they identified with her tragic life. It seemed to be a consolation for them that a person of Diana's status had experienced the same misery in her life. As I remember, most of these women did not use the occasion to denounce men in general (as the professional feminists were doing). They were simply identifying with the struggle to cope with the demands of life.

Such an outpouring of grief and admiration for Princess Diana could not be ignored. *The Australian* devoted space on page 2 of its 3 September edition to the displays of ordinary people's grief both in Australia and around the world. There were also details of the planned TV coverage of the funeral and the enormous television audience expected. These rather perfunctory reports about the ordinary person's reaction took second place to the main concerns of *The Australian* on this third day following the accident.

2. At Last the Culprit: A Drunken Driver from the Ritz Hotel's Security Staff

One could almost feel the relief in the headline of this day's edition of *The Australian*. It advertised triumphantly in big black letters:

Britons vent fury on drunk driver

Its subheading was taken from the words of British Conservative MP, Peter Luff.

> *'It's all very well to protect people from the IRA, but we should be able to protect them from drunkards.'*

The wild headline is certainly attention grabbing. But is it true? Sure, people were dismayed at the possibility that alcohol may have been involved in the accident. That was my immediate reaction. But more information was needed. Confirmation was required that it was indeed true that the driver, Henri Paul, was 'drunk' and that his drunkenness was the determining factor in the accident. There was no indication from the TV or radio reports that the whole of Britain was 'venting its fury'. Some people were expressing a natural dismay, but that hardly adds up to 'fury'. Do the 'journalists' in the *Disgusting Empire* really believe that most people would immediately forget the thousands of images of media people hounding Diana? No, this headline is tabloid 'journalism' at its usual level. I'm sure, too, that Peter Luff did not realise in the heat of the moment to what use his words would be put, and that he did not realise he was helping the media to evade responsibility for the accident. It was a nice touch to bring the fearsome IRA into the image. That certainly made Henri Paul and the Ritz hotel (and thus Mohammed Al Fayed) look doubly bad.

Ean Higgins must have been pulled up for his hitherto dispassionate reporting on the accident for he now swings dutifully into the right mood with the sort of report that pretends to be offering a balanced view of the event but in reality is hammering a particular interpretation. He opens his front-page report with this highly charged paragraph.

> *A French court was examining laying manslaughter charges against three photographers last night as Britain vented fury over why a*

hopelessly drunk casual driver had been allowed to speed the mother of the future king to her death.

Higgins has started to draw on his bag of journalistic tricks. Suddenly, 'republican' Diana has resumed her high aristocratic status and become 'the mother of the future king', as if the members of News Ltd are at all concerned about the welfare of a future king and his mother. This is to tug at the heartstrings of the reader. Notice also how Henri Paul is 'hopelessly drunk' and his status as driver 'casual'. If the reader has not got the image of a staggering, slobbering drunk struggling into the Mercedes without any objection from an irresponsible, unprofessional Ritz staff or from Dodi's personal bodyguards, or resistance from Diana and Dodi, only to drive them off to their deaths, then the reader must be very dull indeed. I will come back to the credibility of this picture shortly.

Higgins has taken his manner of reporting down market. Instead of a cautious re-stating of the detail surrounding the crash in the light of the new information about Henri Paul's blood-alcohol level, instead of coolly examining the new information in the overall context of the accident, he has gone straight to a sensational and propagandist mode of reporting. It's not hard to imagine the reasons for the switch. The drunk driver has got the media off the hook and this has to be rammed home with all the energy News Ltd can summon.

Higgins follows on from the first highly charged paragraph with some more journalistic tricks. He presents preliminary opinion or wild speculation as compelling evidence. He draws support for the view being hammered from unnamed 'sources'. And suggestions introduced with a 'maybe...' are presented as fact. And so the estimation of the speed of the car is put at 'up to 200 km/h'. More considered judgements not long after put the speed at between 110 and 145 km/h.[1] Employees (unnamed) at the Ritz hotel 'alleged' that security staff had 'allowed' Henri Paul to get behind the wheel of the Mercedes 'even when they may have known he had been drinking heavily'. 'May have known ...'? Either they knew or they did not know. Surely it's important in this serious case to get it right, and not report the matter unless it is known for sure that security staff were aware of Henri Paul's alleged condition. But it's good enough for speculation to be given the colour of fact. Higgins reports other unnamed sources as claiming that Paul was 'over-excited' and 'as drunk as a skunk'. He goes on to say that he 'may even have taunted the photographers to a race ...' Again, did he or didn't he taunt the photographers? Speculation or innuendo is being presented in a way that the reader is meant to find persuasive.

Conservative MP Peter Luff's exclamation about the lack of protection for Diana is repeated and Higgins adds that the blame for the failure of security cannot be laid at the feet of the British Government because Diana had firmly rejected official security. That naturally turned the attention to the Al Fayed group which owns the Ritz hotel, and to Mohammed Al Fayed. At the mention of Mohammed Al Fayed Higgins must also tack on '... who has been angered by the refusal of the Government to grant him British citizenship'. At every mention of the owner of the Fayed group the reader must be reminded of the 'unsavoury' nature of the person being dealt with and of the motives implicit in his 'unsavoury' dealings with the British Government.

News of the blood-alcohol level in Paul had put Al Fayed on the defensive and his case against the paparazzi as those responsible for the accident was seriously weakened, according to Higgins. Higgins downplays the response of Michael Cole, spokesman for Al Fayed. Cole 'insisted' that Henri Paul was a 'reliable security employee who had specialist driver training'. When someone is reported as 'insisting' on their innocence we know that to be the media's way of indicating that they are dealing with a guilty person who is trying to get away with his crime.

Why didn't Higgins devote more time to the testimony of Michael Cole who certainly said far more than Higgins reports? TV footage showed several interviews with Cole during which Cole repeated the Ritz's opinion of Paul as professional, conscientious and hardworking. This picture of Paul was later confirmed in careful research into his life. It was also established that Paul had specialist driver training. Why didn't Higgins find out these readily available details before he wrote up his report? Why didn't he raise the very obvious point that nobody came forward to say definitely that Paul was behaving like a person who was 'hopelessly drunk'? And why would an organisation that wanted to project an image of professionalism allow a 'hopelessly' drunk driver to be put in charge of the life of the beloved son of Mohammed Al Fayed, and the life of the most high-profile person in the world? All the evidence available is that the Ritz hotel in Paris is tightly organised and very professional in its workings. On the face of it, even at this early stage, it is simply not credible that a 'hopelessly' drunk person would not have aroused the attention (and apprehension) of responsible people on the Ritz staff.

Later developments, most particularly the security camera footage and the growing testimony of Trevor Rees-Jones, demonstrate clearly Henri Paul's behaviour was not that of a person who was hopelessly drunk. The security cameras at the Ritz hotel showed a steady Henri Paul engaged in businesslike conversation with his colleagues. Most people reading this account of Henri Paul's alleged drunkenness would have observed somebody who was 'hopelessly' drunk. Many would have been in that state themselves. They would know that the security camera footage of Henri Paul that night showed somebody who did not fit the picture of a hopelessly drunk man. Kes Wingfield, one of Dodi's bodyguards and driver of the decoy vehicle, rejected all claims that Henri Paul looked drunk or was behaving in a drunken manner. Trevor Rees-Jones states that Paul was 'just fine' and talked normally about the tactics aimed at evading the media crowd outside the Ritz.

In a report on page 3 (**Driving three times over the limit raises odds of dying 40-fold**) Ben Hutchings writes that a blood-alcohol reading of 0.175 per cent (Paul's alleged reading at the time) would increase the risk of dying in an accident 40-fold. Hutchings is quoting from expert opinion. A blood-alcohol reading of 0.175 per cent would have greatly reduced reaction time, slowed the reflexes, dulled the understanding, and reduced judgement and anticipation of danger. A person in this condition is 'an accident waiting to happen'. If this is true, infallibly, then how did Paul manage to walk around the Ritz hotel in a steady manner, engage in conversation, climb into a car without arousing *named* suspicion, and then drive allegedly in a frantic manner through the winding streets of central Paris and get as far as he did? Surely, his car would have found the first lamp post at the first bend in the road. One must think at this point that there is something strange and inconsistent in all this. I will be dealing in detail with the issue of Paul's drunkenness and what it means in the final chapter of this book (Chapter 11).

Higgins's front-page report was evidently not sufficient. We find him rehashing the same 'details' in a report on page 3. In order to hammer the message home the headline reads:

Staff at Ritz 'knew he was drunk'

We know that the quotation marks in this headline are meant to be ignored. Higgins repeats Michael Cole's and the Ritz hotel's insistence that Henri Paul was an exemplary employee and well trained in defensive driving. Others are reported as saying that Paul was an affable man always conscious of the duties his job entailed. But this is mentioned only to be shot down by unnamed sources at the Ritz hotel who are referred to expansively and confidently. For what testimony, however obscure and unreliable, could not fail to make an impression against the 'unsavoury' group of people connected with Mohammed Al Fayed? The following paragraph is meant to provide the compelling evidence for Higgins's case.

> According to several reports, however, the driver's drunken condition on Saturday night was apparently well-known to Ritz staff, who were believed to have alerted the photographers' lawyers several hours before police confirmed the blood test results.
> One of the paparazzi's solicitors said last night: 'An anonymous person called our office a 1pm today and said everybody at the Ritz knew he was drunk when he left the hotel. It seems it was common knowledge. We planned to bring this to the attention of the investigating magistrate as soon as we were able to meet him.'

Why is all this assertion and speculation without a source? Surely, if it was common knowledge, people would be falling over themselves to testify. At least, if it was common knowledge pressure would have built up to say something openly. Why couldn't Higgins at that time offer just one reliable supporting detail? Who exactly is the source in the Ritz? Why doesn't Higgins raise the possibility of a connection between a Ritz hotel employee and an interested media organisation who could profit from such claims? In fact, why doesn't he raise the possible connection between the claims of Paul's drunkenness and others that may have an interest in projecting such a story. After all, wild speculation is the staple of media reports. This suggestion would probably be dismissed by the media bosses as populist prejudice against the media. They are certainly in a position to recognise a display of hypocrisy and prejudice. It is indisputable that the chequebooks come out when that is the easiest way of gaining the 'journalistic' advantage — or any other sort of advantage. You do not have to be very smart to realise what advantage you could gain by having a paid informant on the staff of the Ritz hotel — indeed, in any of the places Diana and Dodi frequented. Fat sums were being paid for crucial information about the pair.

It is plain that Higgins in his two reports is not concerned with presenting the facts about the case. He is not concerned about raising the obvious questions about the inconsistencies or odd concurrent details. He is only concerned with delivering a message of his and his masters' making.

3. Lawyers Come to the Rescue of the Paparazzi

Over the last thirty years the public has witnessed the once respected profession of journalism descend into the pits of bad taste and nastiness. But journalism is not the only profession that seems to have taken this course downwards. Lawyers as a group seem bent on narrowing the gap between themselves and journalists in their apparent desire to arouse public disgust. The lawyers defending the paparazzi arrested at the accident scene have given the public a fair glimpse of the way they go about their business. In a report by Stephen Farrell on page 5 (**Paparazzi's lawyers go on offensive**) we are privileged to witness the level of integrity and selflessness with which they defend their paparazzi clients. In the end, one could say that the lawyers are in good company. As the heading of the report suggests, the defence has become offence, in more ways than one.

The news of the blood-alcohol level of Henri Paul was not only good news for the media. It also provoked a jubilant response in the teams of lawyers representing the photographers arrested at the scene of the accident. William Bourdon representing the Sipa agency came forward with this suitably sanctimonious announcement.

All the people who wanted to accuse the photographers and blame them for this should have been more cautious and prudent. The fact that the driver consumed alcohol ties in with the crazy speed at which he was driving.

It just shows that no photographer was directly or indirectly involved with causing this accident. People should have been more careful before accusing them.

It may be assumed that these words were uttered on behalf of all the lawyers representing the photographers arrested at the scene of the accident. William Bourdon may get away with this in a court of law but the ordinary person is not fooled for one moment. Bourdon's sanctimony and special re-assembling of the events are transparent. Whatever Paul's state of sobriety, the behaviour of the media in hounding Diana to the point of desperation will not be forgotten by the person who still has normal feelings of decency and fair play. Furthermore, if speed and wild driving is an indication of a drunken state then most of the media representatives pursuing Diana were permanently in a drunken state. Other famous people, including Tom Cruise and Nicole Kidman, have spoken of the dangerous manner in which the paparazzi pursued them, even in the same way and in the same place as Diana and Dodi.

Bourdon may be able to manipulate a court of law but he cannot in this case have an effect on the court of normal decency. This may not bother Bourdon but subsequent events have made things materially difficult for him. Continuing investigation by the Paris Police Department has kept the spotlight on the direct involvement of media vehicles in the crash. It would be useless to say to Bourdon that he had spoken too soon. Honesty is not the objective in his defence of the media agency he is representing. His objective is to manipulate the detail of the circumstances in whatever way that will exonerate his clients *in a court of law*. The rest is of no concern.

Other lawyers took a different approach. The legal team representing award-winning photographer, Jacques Langevin (Sygma agency), ran the line that Langevin just happened on the accident. He was not even on a motorbike. He was in his car and was driving in the same direction as the Mercedes carrying Diana and Dodi. It was pure coincidence that he ended up at the scene of the accident! Really? His legal team also accused the police of acting under pressure from an hysterical public, which only goes to show that lawyers and media people share the same lack of moral feeling. If readers had been watching television at this time they would have been able to see the Parisian hotshot lawyers standing before the international cameras arguing on behalf of their media clients. Their slick arguments did not in the end differ from each other, the one being as unconvincing as the next.

4. Return of the Fairytale: The Beautiful Princess, the Cruel Prince and the Wicked Royal Family

If *The Australian* editorial board thought that an account of the lawyers' defence of their media clients would add strength to efforts to shift the blame for the accident away from the media groups, then on balance they have miscalculated. The lawyer's obviously partisan action in defending their clients leaves too much out of the picture. There is only so much a newspaper can say about the blood-alcohol level of a driver in an accident. The fact that Paul had a high blood-alcohol level raises in the end the crucial question of whether he could have controlled the car. Despite the colourful speculative manner in which Higgins dealt with the findings, there still lay a great deal of investigation ahead. In waiting for further information to come to hand *The Australian* could return to their main objective: smearing and ridiculing the royal family and the institution of the monarchy. *The Australian* chose to do this in a double-page spread (pp. 4 and 5) under the heading:

Legacy of a Princess

On these two pages there is queue of characters to have a go at Prince Charles and the royal family, all under the guise of praising Diana. If readers think I have made a good case from the articles and reports looked at so far for a less than impartial media, and if readers are surprised at how barefaced and simple-minded the partiality is, then they are yet to be surprised at how low *The Australian* can go in its reports. With the report by Deborah Hope that leads the section, **Legacy of a Princess**, we have reached the lowest levels of journalistic competence. The importance of this simple-minded piece is indicated by its being splashed across both pages, in bold type, and with a typeface several points larger than that in the surrounding articles.

Ms Hope's commentary is underpinned by the sort of contrasts made in Juliet Herd's fairytale articles about Diana, Prince Charles and the wicked royal family. To brighten the contrasts she adds her own special entertaining style. The subject is tackled with the warmth and enthusiasm displayed by schoolgirls gossiping behind their hands about their friends. Like most Australians, she said, she was deeply affected by the news of Diana's death. *Although republican*, she said, she found Diana's passing shocking 'almost beyond belief'. We see what trivial animosities the simple theoretic-republican mind entertains. The death of a republican is to be mourned; all those of royalty are not to be mourned. Ms Hope is deeply ashamed that she could have feelings for a person whose circumstances provide her with the title of princess. To her feelings of shame she adds some naughtiness as she marches before the reader the caricatures that proceed from her fantasy:

> *Like most Australians I found myself glued to the screen to watch lacklustre lords, boring baronesses and fast-talking Fleet Street hacks pour out their memories and judgements of the life of Diana. I drank up every word.*

She wonders guiltily why she was so 'absorbed' by it all. Her first thoughts, though, were not about the 'political consequences for the monarchy', but about Princes William and Harry. She does not seem to feel ashamed about her feelings for the future king of England. Prince William is evidently not yet part of her fantasy about 'monarchy'. She was concerned that the princes were now robbed of the warmth of their mother and thrown to the mercy of the cold, cruel upbringing that the wicked Windsor family would subject them to. Diana's life was like a fairytale, she says, and she expected a 'happy ending'. But that did not happen and the world was going to be 'a darker place because of it'. To contrast the warmth of the upbringing Diana would have provided for her children (of which they were now robbed) with the cold, feelingless treatment they would receive at the hands of the wicked Windsors, Ms Hope relates a terrible experience from her childhood.

> *Like other baby boomers I spent many soggy childhood hours waiting in the crowd at Circular Quay to wave a Union Jack at the Queen as she passed by, the only reward a fleeting view of a gloved hand at the window of a glossy black car. The disappointment never faded.*

She goes on to say that 'in contrast' Diana was 'every-woman', and she lists all the different aspects that a thoroughly modern woman like Ms Hope can appreciate, in contrast to the cold, feelingless Windsors. The contrast offered here is, to say the least, a strange one indeed. The poor Queen riding by in a limousine which is meant to show her to thousands of people in a limited space of time is contrasted with the life-actions of Diana! But the baby-boomer experience is worth examination.

Like Ms Hope I am a baby boomer and, also like Ms Hope, I was amongst the thousands of school children taken to wave at the Queen and Prince Philip as they rode by in the black limousine during the royal visit of 1954.[2] I have very clear memories of the occasion. Unfortunately, the detail of my recollection does not coincide with that of Ms Hope on all points. I was attending the Mercy Convent, Lane Cove, in Sydney. On the day the young Queen was scheduled to drive by in the vicinity of our school, our teacher interrupted the class program and took us to a position on Longueville Road, Lane Cove. There we waited, flag in hand, for some time. For a young active boy it seemed like a long wait but on reflection it would not have been more than an hour. It was long enough for the nuns to tell us boys several times to behave ourselves. It was definitely not raining. In fact, it was a fine day and the atmosphere was rather festive. I thought that the flag I held was an Australian flag, but I can no longer be sure of that. At a certain point it became clear from the movement up Longueville Road that something was about to happen. Then amidst much furious flag waving and cheering the open limousine burst into view. It was going at a fair pace but it was in view long enough for me to gather images of the Queen that have never faded. The fine day, our position at the kerbside, and the open limousine gave us all a good clear view of the young monarch of a constitutional monarchy.

Even at my young age, I was struck by her girlish appearance. The images of royalty that had been fed to us as children were those of regal bearing, austere looks and solemn expressions. Queen Elizabeth did not at all fit that picture. Her expression was that of a sweet young woman, a little on the reserved side. There seemed none of the stiff elegance commonly attributed to royalty. As she passed we were greeted by a pleasant smile from the fresh young face of a person who was waving in a friendly manner in response to the warm reception she was receiving from all around. I remember being especially taken by the colour of her hair. It was a distinctive brown. I do not remember a gloved hand. In a few seconds she was gone, and we were left to be taken back to class by the nuns who had a handful in keeping us boys in check.

Now it is clear that Ms Hope saw the occasion quite differently from me. One is inclined to wonder whether she is talking about a different time and place, or even a different Queen. But no, we are dealing with Ms Hope's fertile imagination. Even so, it is strange that Ms Hope's experience (nobody could dispute that she actually had an 'experience') should have left such an enduring scar. Was the occasion, as she describes it, serious enough for that wound and for the conclusions obviously drawn about the Windsors and the monarchy? The Queen could not help the rain, just as no famous person can help it when they are expected to appear before a big crowd in the open air on a particular day. The Queen could not do anything about the physical limitations imposed on someone who must see a lot of people in a short space of time. She certainly did not behave like a lot of rock and movie stars who think nothing of ignoring their fans when it suits them. I imagine the rudeness of a rock star would not scar too many people psychologically, at least not those with a healthy psychological profile.

The great question here is how the one apparently minor event of seeing the Queen's gloved hand on a rainy day during an official tour could cause so much consternation in the mind of Ms Hope and serve as a basis for condemning the character of the Queen and the institution of the monarchy. The answer is that it is all part of Ms Hope's theoretic-republican fantasy and not a part of the normal operations of reason.

Ms Hope goes on from her illustrative contrast between Diana and the Windsors to draw salutary (republican) lessons from the treatment of Diana by the royal establishment. The royal establishment's manner of dealing with Diana showed it to be 'a shark pool for the uninitiated', but more importantly it revealed to the Australian people 'the nature of the British monarchy and its relevance to Australia'. If the Australian people are susceptible to republican fairytales, as told by Ms Hope, they might indeed swallow the colourful product of her fantasy. Apart from anything else, these comments open up a world of misapprehension about systems of government and Australia's particular governmental arrangements that can hardly be handled in this limited space. I will come back to this shortly.

Towards the end of her piece Ms Hope does touch on the role of the media in Princess Diana's death. She says there are 'uncomfortable questions to be asked about the role we [the media] play in invading people's privacy'.(!) She does not ask them, of course. Instead, she continues her fantasy about Diana, the monarchy, and the wicked royal family. She starts her penultimate paragraph with the comment that Diana's work against landmines showed that it is still possible to change the world, but then without any obvious connection goes on to add the following:

> ... *I had to ask myself on Sunday evening whether I did not feel hypocritical, having schooled my children in the perils of constitutional monarchy, in demanding they tape Sunday's episode of The Simpsons so I would not miss any of the television coverage of Diana's death.*

'Perils of constitutional monarchy'? Whatever could Ms Hope be talking about? I must feel sorry for her children who have obviously been subjected to the lessons of simple-minded political bigotry. One can only hope that their home schooling will be balanced by some factual lessons in British and Australian history, systems of government, and what is meant when sensible informed people talk about a country's 'constitution'. It is clear that the appearance of the word 'monarchy' conjures up all sorts of political horrors in Ms Hope's imagination and I doubt whether some straightforward information about the different forms of rule and how they relate to a 'constitutional monarchy' could penetrate the clouds of her imagination. Nevertheless, some few observations may not go astray for the reader entertained by Ms Hope's article.

If Ms Hope equates the system of monarchy with tyranny and terror, and lumps 'constitutional monarchy' of any sort with such tyranny and terror, we must think in the first place that Great Britain and Australia have endured under a peculiar sort of tyranny and terror for some hundreds of years. This regime of tyranny and terror has brought with it a stability of government and a standard of welfare that all modern experiments in theoretic-republicanism can only look at with envy. This is just the point. The empirical evidence is overwhelming. Since the first great experiment in theoretic-republicanism ushered in the modern era of republics with murder, blood and mayhem, most succeeding efforts seem to have been vying with that revolution (1789) in the levels of barbarism the human person can attain. It is a cherished dogma of the theoretic-republican mind that religion is the cause of most human conflict, that religion is responsible for most wars. So successfully has this dogma been propagated that most people accept it without giving it a second thought.

I doubt whether anyone can really point to one war that has had religion purely and simply as its cause. To the reader who has leapt from his chair in amazement at this claim I would say that each of the 'wars of religion' he will name were actually conflicts of state where religion was either a pretext for power play or was already absorbed by the affairs of state. In individual conflict about religion it is not religion that is the problem but intolerance. It is an empirical truth that tolerant people of good will can live peacefully with people of a different religion. Conflict arises from individual acts of intolerance; wars arise when the intolerance changes in the community and state context to a question of state power.

No, since the French Revolution most wars have been caused by the effort to implement a regime based on a particular interpretation of the basic tenets of theoretic-republicanism. Because it is the fundamental belief of theoretic-republicanism that all other forms of government, all other structures of society and state are illegitimate, the implementers of the theoretic-republican regime declare total war against their opposition. Total war is declared against all society that is based on traditional morality, traditionally formed governments and the philosophies that assert there is a structure to reality that is prior to all those of human invention. The measures that can be taken by theoretic-republicans against such opposition know no limits to the destruction that can or must be wrought. Indeed, many implementers of theoretic-republican dogma declare proudly that it is better to completely destroy an unacceptable society and start from the bottom up rather than try to fix an essentially corrupt regime. It is with an impressive equanimity that such theoretic-republican heroes can look on the destruction of the people they hold so dear to their hearts.

There are a great many wars and conflicts one could point to in the history of the 20th century to exemplify what I am claiming. Let me mention just one illustrative case that has been of recent newsworthiness. Most theoretic-republican propagandists are never finished telling us that the conflict in Northern Ireland was a good example of the violent conflict caused by religion. The theoretic-republican media refer always with relish to the 'sectarian violence' of Northern Ireland. The underlying message is: 'See, look what religion brings about!' Now let me point out an obvious detail. 'IRA' does not stand for *The Irish Traditional Catholic Belief Army*. It does not stand for *The Irish Vatican Army*. And it does not stand for *The Irish Monarchical Army*. It stands for The IRISH REPUBLICAN ARMY.

The Irish *Republican* Army has not fought under a banner of the Papal crown. It has not raged against Protestant belief. It has not set up propaganda cells aimed at subverting protestant belief in the heart of protestant parishes so that protestants may be brought on Sundays to the Catholic Mass. It has not used the international media to disseminate the doctrine of papal infallibility or to disseminate the latest edition of the Catholic Catechism. Nobody can imagine members of the IRA subjecting their prisoners to questions from the Catholic Catechism until they got it right. No, the last thing the IRA want to know about is the central message of the Catholic faith. That message is the message of peace as preached by the Saviour — the Saviour who is 'meek and humble of heart' and wants individuals to love one another, to turn the other cheek, and to forgive the transgressions of others 77 *times* if necessary.

The message of the IRA is indisputably political; its goals are to be achieved by any effective means at its disposal. That has usually meant by violence. In typical theoretic-republican style they declared total war against their opponents. Think of the murder of British citizens who merely spoke out against them. The only religious feature about the members of the IRA is that they hold to the doctrine of their political belief with religious fervour. They preach the doctrines of theoretic-republicanism and dress it up in a campaign to re-unify Ireland. They are the Irish descendents of the Irish agitators that were aligned in the 18th century with the Jacobins of the French Guillotine. Of all the republican groups of the 20th century few have implemented their campaign with more ferocity and cruelty. In the classical theoretic-republican manner they formed themselves into an elitist group whose acquired power enabled them to dictate the political agenda despite the majority of Irish, both nationalist and loyalist,[3] wanting to resolve the conflict with peaceful methods.

It is the greatest of tragedies that on 15 August 1998 IRA terrorist action in the town of Omagh, Northern Ireland, confirmed exactly what I have written here. The town of Omagh is celebrated for the tolerant and harmonious relations between the Catholic and Protestant communities. While on that Saturday the peaceful people of Omagh went about their family business, a small group of fellow

Irishmen who call themselves the Real IRA were loading a 225 kg bomb into a car. While people (among whom were pregnant Avril Monaghan and her 18-month-old daughter) crowded Market Street on Saturday afternoon, the men of the Real IRA with their heads full of theoretic-republican principle were driving the car loaded with the 225 kg bomb to the junction of Market and Dublin Streets. While husbands and wives, sons and daughters, girlfriends and boyfriends, tourists and visitors enjoyed their shopping, the men of the Real IRA parked the bomb. When they left that car with the bomb they did not see people like themselves milling around it. All they could see was their theoretic-republican vision.

They were the purists; Gerry Adams, President of Sinn Fein, had been corrupted. They would implement the full logic of their vision. At 3.10 p.m. the bomb exploded, tearing people and the surroundings apart. Among the 28 people who died were Avril Monaghan, pregnant with twins, and her 18-month-old daughter. Later, Irishmen of different religious faiths came together with their ministers of religion to mourn the dead publicly.

When it comes to talking about the 'perils' of any particular system of rule, the evidence is such that people in the 20th century should start to quake in fear at the talk of an advancing republic. They risk the descent into barbarity, or being imprisoned behind the barbwire of the gulag, or being fettered in their basest passions. The sad fact is they don't see the 'perils' — and the reason is that the propaganda instruments of the theoretic-republican elite are so powerful and successful that people like Ms Deborah Hope can talk in their infantile way about the 'perils of constitutional monarchy' and not be laughed out of normal intelligent public discourse.

We know that in Ms Hope's confused imagination 'constitutional monarchy' looms as a nasty system of rule, but what in reality is it all about? How does it fit into the general division of forms of government: monarchy (rule of the one), aristocracy (rule of the few), and democracy (rule of the many)? A quick review of the constitutional monarchies best known these days (UK, Australia, Holland, and Spain) would tell one that constitutional monarchy is none of these purely and simply. In fact, on the surface it appears to be a mixture of elements of all three forms. Those minds that cannot think past a series of abstract propositions about forms of government may claim that this is its worst feature. It is hybrid. It is essentially inferior being not one or the other. But when one examines the concrete circumstances of existing constitutional monarchies rather than wandering around a series of rationalistic propositions in one's head, then it becomes clear that a particular constitutional monarchy is not a theory but an *actual* arrangement by that particular society as to how it governs itself.

A constitutional monarchy is not the result of the implementation of a theory that aspires to perfect government and society (something that is a political pipe dream) but an arrangement born out of that society's people, its manners, its history, its religion and all those *unseen* and *unforeseen* elements that contribute to its organic growth through time. A particular constitutional monarchy is not to be judged on how well it measures up with the provisions of a rationalistic theory dreamt up by some theorist in the coddled comforts of a university office, but by how well it provides for the moral well-being and ambition of its people. The tragedy of the modern era is accepting the insanity of damning a healthy, stable, happy society because it does not correspond with the theoretical prescriptions of a powerful intellectual elite.

In the case of Australia, we have a governmental system connected with Australia's heritage both as it is drawn from the northern and southern hemispheres. We have a system that does not answer to the theories of its critics but one which has provided a level of well-being and social development that few countries can boast. Australia's social history is not one of ideal moral behaviour. No nation can lay claim to this status. In the judgement of performance of basic moral duty and provision for the common good of its people, Australia ranks highly in comparison with other countries of the modern era, especially when compared with those countries that have been established on the tenets of theoretic-republicanism and the blood of their people. These are the facts. The great political lie propagated and accepted in Australia today is that we are not an independent country, that we will become independent by changing a written provision of the constitution, and that casting off the constitutional connection with the British monarchy will change us from a monarchy to a republic.

Australia's form of government in reality bears little resemblance to that form of rule known as 'rule of the one'. Australia's constitutional connection with the British monarchy has no meaning at all in terms of the executive decisions that are made by the government of the day. Its meaning is now derived from Australia's social, moral and political structure which has been born whole and unique out of the crucial elements of its history and heritage. Changing the present Constitution in the manner prescribed by the elites will be a blow against the integrity of this unique existing structure. It will mean the handing over of more power to the elitist groups that already infect the organs of the Australian nation. What a tragedy if the simple-minded political bigotry of the Ms Hopes of this world succeeds in the agitation for 'change'.

Ms Hope's feelings of shame and hypocrisy at being so entranced by Diana's death are nevertheless quickly overcome. Why? Because the 'royal glitter' and the 'short-lived brilliance' provided by Diana may mean that 'the dreary Prince Charles [is] forever unacceptable as a future king'. Those that suffer from a form of political Attention Deficit Disorder (pADD) may find the effervescing glitter of Diana entrancing enough to draw their attention from things more solid, more enduring, and of more inner value. But there are many who recognise the social and moral efficacy of steady respectful manners, of respect for people, traditions and institutions. These are not things that sparkle and glitter before the restless naked eye. These are things that reveal themselves to the calm, mature reflections of steady minds. There are those of us who understand the pain that Princes William and Harry would be going through but hope also that the calm fortitude of their father will be a help and an example in working through this pain. I have seen enough of the princes during the last year to know that they understand it will profit them nothing to succumb to the feelings that overcome weaker spirits in times of difficulty. They have shown they stand four square behind their father in his striving to deal with the tragedies of recent years.

5. A Family Photo

One of the oddest features of the double-page spread on Diana's legacy is the photo of the royal family situated just under this headline article by Ms Hope. The reader comes to the end of a rubbishing of the royal family and the system of monarchy and is immediately confronted with the smiling happy faces of a group of people who could be just about any other family lining up for a family photograph. Everybody looks relaxed. The Queen herself is positively beaming, as would any mother and grandmother proud of her family. Princes William and Harry, one on either side of Diana, are looking confident, at ease and happy. Diana is separated from a smiling Prince Charles by Prince William. She smiles also but with a hint of reserve. Under this photo is the following caption:

> *That was then … Diana with royal family members, a reflection of the outside world during her time in the house of Windsor.*

I ask myself what this caption means exactly. What is meant by 'a reflection of the outside world'? It is very clear that the photo was taken no more than a year before Diana's death. I would put it in fact at a couple of months before. Indeed, a year later Princes William and Harry seem no more than a year older. It was a time when the trauma of the separation was behind them and Diana and Prince Charles had reached an accommodation with each other. Does it mean that the photo was presenting the 'phoney' appearance of the royal family for public consumption and that it was hiding the torture Diana, *still a royal family member*, was suffering at the hands of people smiling so amiably into the camera? Or does it mean that Diana was representing the (warm) real world outside the cruel, heartless world of the Windsors? Either way it looks like another case of media lies and manipulation.

6. Diana, Friend of the Suffering and Heroine of the Nineties

The editorial committee of *The Australian* evidently judged Ms Hope's contributions to the double-page spread of Diana's legacy so valuable that she was worth more space. Two short commentary pieces follow her *tour de force* splashed in bold above the other contributions. The first, **Simple handshake cured AIDS phobia**, is a more or less straightforward account of Diana's praiseworthy charitable activities. There would seem little scope for Ms Hope's political fantasy in dealing with this subject. Nevertheless, as the heading to the piece suggests, she is able to have a go at what in her view was the (unjustified) 'social phobia' that followed the AIDS epidemic. It was tragic to see people afflicted by this terrible disease and the social isolation it caused. But it is understandable that such a deadly disease, not yet fathomable by medical science and without any medical cure, should cause widespread apprehension in the community. Such apprehension is not reducible to community ignorance and prejudice as Ms Hope and others seem to think. In fact, Diana's selfless behaviour is all the more praiseworthy because of the human inability to cope with the disease on all levels, not because she confronted the 'prejudice' of ignorant people.

The second piece, **Heroic inspiration for generations of women**, gives more scope to Ms Hope's political vision. She starts by claiming that 'Diana was a heroine of the nineties' and then proceeds to turn Diana's weaknesses into virtues. Diana's emotional instability and her inability to deal successfully with just about every aspect of her social environment are turned into the 'courage in standing up to the Queen and Prince Charles'. Again we meet the caricature so often the basis of commentary about Diana and her relationship with Prince Charles and the royal family. There is again the contrast of the warm, affectionate Diana with the cold, feelingless environment of the wicked Windsors. Women, according to Ms Hope, would have been especially impressed with Diana's refusal to accept the 'royal tradition of putting up with her husband's mistress'. This is all related in a cavalier manner as if the mythology of Charles's affair with Camilla Parker Bowles is gospel. Well, it is gospel according to Ms Hope's fantasy. I invite the reader to pause a moment and consider what's been claimed yet again about Prince Charles so unreflectingly.

The claim is, firstly, that it is tradition for wives to tolerate the mistresses of kings and princes. Secondly, that Prince Charles did have a mistress from the beginning of his marriage to Diana and that that mistress was Camilla Parker Bowles. The toleration of extra-marital affairs by both husbands and wives is not restricted to royalty. Republican elites are very obviously susceptible to the same temptations as royalty. The extra-marital affairs of presidents of republics may even be tolerated by the majority of the electorate. I only have to mention the name *Clinton* for everybody to know what I am alluding to. I won't labour the point. Tolerating extra-marital affairs (by husband or wife) is a question of force of circumstances. It cannot be a tradition in the true sense of (moral) tradition. Furthermore, in the philosophical framework that defends a monarchical form of government as legitimate as long as it concurs with prescriptions of the natural law, all extra-marital affairs are immoral. In the theoretic-republican framework there is no talk of moral or immoral, just what is preferable or not preferable to the observer. I wonder what we would find if 'the people' were able to look into the private lives of Ms Hope and her colleagues? I think in many cases we would find that what was a social outrage in the behaviour of Prince Charles, was in the case of a high-profile media figure something boring and hardly worth a second glance. When a student enrols in a course to become a journalist he must expect to undergo some intensive lessons in hypocrisy.

The second and more important part of Ms Hope's claim is that Prince Charles was conducting an affair with Camilla Parker Bowles from the beginning of his marriage. In fact, it is commonly asserted that the affair existed before the marriage and simply continued into the marriage. This is an extremely damaging claim for somebody of Prince Charles's status. Imagine now that a comparable accusation was levelled publicly in such an unreflective manner at a high-profile member of the theoretic-republican class. Forget about whether the accusation is true or not. It is most likely that all litigious hell would break loose. The accuser would risk being taken to the courts for defaming a person's reputation, for holding up an innocent member of the community to shame and ridicule, for the debilitating anguish caused by community contempt, for the loss of income caused by such debilitation and a variety of other claims whose theoretic-republican legal description I have not yet been able to master. The 'moral' basis for such legal action would be the *harm* caused by such an accusation. The fact that there are absolutely no qualms of media conscience about levelling the same sorts of damaging accusations against a powerless Prince Charles is another demonstration of the double standards of the theoretic-republican class.

For those subscribing to traditional standards of morality, it is not just the harm caused by the public accusation of marital infidelity and the hypocrisy shown by those tolerating it in some circumstances and not in others that is of interest. There are also the concerns flowing from the prior question of whether the accusation is true or not and, if true, whether the matter should be aired in the public forum. In Prince Charles's case it is at least questionable whether or not his alleged affair with Camilla Parker Bowles should be aired in the public forum. In reality, Prince Charles's influence on matters concerned with government is minimal. Indeed, any comment at all on public matters by Prince Charles is deemed by the sensitive theoretic-republican mind as intolerable interference. Marital infidelity in the case of Prince Charles would be of public concern if it could be shown that such immoral behaviour in a cultural and traditional context were harmful to the common good. I believe this would be a difficult case to argue, especially considering the widespread view in the ruling class that marital infidelity is *in itself* morally neutral. One could claim that Prince Charles's alleged marital infidelity is particularly pernicious in a social and moral sense because he will be the head of the Anglican Church. But I do not know whether the members of the ruling theoretic-republican elite would be so brazen as to argue this point. The last thing they would want are steps to preserve such a moribund institution as the Anglican Church.

On the other hand, when one comes to consider the question of marital infidelity committed by a person in Prince Charles's position, one cannot help taking into account the extremely heavy and restricting role a crown prince has to fulfill in the late 20th century. The pressures and demands of his position would make him more vulnerable than normal to such unfortunate moral lapses. But add to that the public torture he has been subjected to over the last 15 years at least, then one can sympathise and empathise with him. In the end it takes a cruel and vindictive spirit to make propagandist mileage out of such a lapse by a person in Prince Charles's position.

Now this attempt to mitigate the seriousness of royal marital infidelity as it relates to the common good and the public forum is predicated on the charge being true. Well, what if it isn't? What then? In moral terms, it represents the most outrageous calumny and character assassination. It is of far more serious moral import than the particular marital infidelity alleged against Prince Charles. In the person or the media organisation that reels it off mindlessly it represents the lowest levels of public behaviour. Prince Charles has asserted a number of times that his close relationship with Camilla Parker Bowles was deliberately and formally ended prior to his wedding. He has declared with much feeling that he maintained that fidelity until the marriage had irretrievably broken down and he and Diana were separated. I have not seen any solid evidence to contradict these claims. Indeed, as I have already said, you can be sure that if the affair with Camilla Parker Bowles had continued into Charles's marriage with Diana, there would be abundant evidence available via the foul means by which the media harvests its information. In these litigious times,

Prince Charles should be able to take his many calumniators to court like everybody else. In that event, he would be able to mount cases against individuals and media organisations around the world and win for himself millions of dollars, if we take other legal outcomes for defamation as a measure. But we all know that that's not possible for Prince Charles. His position as a member of the British royal family has suspended the 'universal, inviolable, indefeasible human rights' guaranteed to each person by the architects of the 'Rights of Men'. Prince Charles and the British royal family have been turned into non-persons.

7. Diana's Influence on Women's Magazines and Fashion

Ms Hope's three pieces are accompanied by three support pieces in this account of Diana's legacy. Under a section entitled, **Media**, D. D. McNicoll returns with a small piece on how Diana featured in the dramatic change in the format of women's magazines from the 1980s onwards. Compare, he says, an edition of *Woman's Day* or the *Australian Women's Weekly* with editions of the same magazines in the months before Diana's death. You could scarcely 'believe they were the same magazines'. I would say many of us do not have to complete this exercise. We were well aware years ago that the relevant media bosses had given orders for these magazines to take a perpendicular dive into the depths of the readership's baser inclinations.

McNicoll claims that Diana was responsible for 'revolutionis[ing] those and similar magazines'. But surely it was the other way around. Surely it was the case that the media bosses latched onto the person of Diana as the main tool to exploit the weaker side of human nature. Diana had no choice in the matter. It was obvious that she had to like it or lump it. Such magazines were saying: 'Diana, we'll do it the easy way or the hard way. Whatever way, we will have you in the end.'

McNicoll also gives space to the comments from well-known media figure in Australia, Ita Buttrose. He allows her to say that the changes in the women's magazine industry could be traced back to the deplorable greed of the 1980s. Ms Buttrose says 'it was distressing to see public figures hounded' by the media. But all this is to set up McNicoll's view on the Diana affair. Whatever way the images of the famous person are gained, he implies, that is of no concern to the readers. The readers make that image 'the week's highlight'. In other words, the readers are to take the blame for all the nastiness the media is capable of.

On the facing page beside a dazzling picture of Diana showing all her beauty, is a non-controversial article about Diana's influence on the world of fashion. This article is an exception in that its authors, Kristine Gough and Katie Meikle, do not sneer at Prince Charles or take a sideswipe at the royal family. Under the section heading, **Fashion**, the article, **An elegance that will live forever**, gives a good short account of the influence Diana had on the world of fashion style and design. The influence of Diana's beauty and character was such that the mere wearing of a certain style or design would ensure its success the world over. If Diana changed her hairstyle hairdressers around the world would be immediately confronted with customers, photo in hand, asking for Diana's latest look. The article represents a fitting tribute to this side of Diana and certainly has its place in an account of her legacy.

8. The 'Twisted' Gilded 'Cage' of the Royal Family

The final piece in the double-page spread devoted to Diana's legacy comes from an experienced journalist who knows how to express himself. His writing style is so refined and so much his own that he makes Ms Deborah Hope look like a kindergarten pupil scratching her name with a piece of white chalk on a badly smudged blackboard. Unfortunately, however, the Diana affair has found out his ideological and professional weaknesses. His short piece, **16 years that shook the twisted cage**, shows all the colour and fineness of his thinking and writing but it is put to work to regurgitate the media mythology of Prince Charles, Diana and the royal family. He writes that with Diana's

> passing all the royal family's precious allure and ageless appeal has been rolled up into one ball and sent, like a cannon shot, into a cartoon sunset.

It's a vivid image and has just the right amount of gentle disparagement. But it represents classic theoretic-republican thinking. Because the theoretic-republican mind sees only the material and calls the empty sentiment that surrounds the materially real 'spiritual', a person like Luke Slattery cannot see the strength and endurance of traditional arrangements that have been formed over the centuries. Such arrangements have been bred into the hearts and minds of the citizen not yet corrupted by the memory-erasing method of theoretic-republicanism. The sad fact for the theoretic-republican and the many embittered authoriphobic minds in Britain and Australia is that after all the railing and manipulation of the events surrounding Diana's death, the majority of the population still seems to show great affection for the people and institution of the British monarchy, whatever republican notions they have been duped into accepting by the propagandising media. Luke Slattery is deluded if he thinks that Diana has 'rattled the twisted cage of the British monarchy'. The failure in his reasoning comes with a series of misconceptions drawn from the usual prejudice about the British monarchy.

Firstly, the British monarchy is called 'a twisted cage' undoubtedly because it has reached its use-by date in a cultural and political sense. Presupposed is that the encroachment of 'democracy' has brought this about. (For 'democracy' read that particular system of government conceived by the theoretic-republican mind as if there is no other possible concept of democracy.) Secondly, Diana appeared on the stage to link 'the royals with a new generation' and to rejuvenate the 'fusty institution' of the British monarchy. Thus when Charles and Diana's marriage fell apart, the House of Windsor was given a 'fair shake'. The 'fair shake' was delivered by Diana. Slattery is not explicit about how exactly Diana gave the 'fair shake' but it is evident that her rebelling against the ways, attitudes and structure of the House of Windsor was the general means. Diana's campaign against the royal family was essentially contained in the break-up of the marriage which happened, according to Slattery, 'when Charles discovered an earlier love'. These are then the assumptions on which Slattery works.

The lie so breezily mentioned about Charles taking his (alleged) affair with Camilla Parker Bowles into his marriage with Diana not only has theoretic-republican propaganda value but it completely ignores Diana's demonstrable emotional problems which contributed greatly to the breakdown of her marriage with Charles, as they did in all her subsequent relationships.

It is interesting at this point to observe that Slattery thinks that Charles's preference for the 'rather equine older lover' over 'his young [beautiful] bride' would have turned most people off. Really, this is not at all worthy of somebody of Luke Slattery's ability. It just shows you to what extent even intelligent journalists feel safe in passing on their deep prejudices in the public forum. But it is the age of theoretic-republicanism and any doctrinal point-scoring occasion should not be passed off. I do wonder, though, what all those fiftyish women feel in getting the thumbs-down in the true-love stakes. In another context, the choice by an eligible man of great public importance of the true love of a woman showing her age over a young and beautiful thing would be applauded. If one of Slattery's theoretical-republican heroes made a similar choice, I have no doubts that the older woman would be described as mature, experienced, intelligent and the young beautiful thing as an air-headed bimbo. Slattery's manner of reserving the mythology of Prince Charles undermines his assumptions if one wants to pause and think about it for a moment. It is not Diana who was undermining the British monarchy but those who are permanently on the warpath against all social beliefs and social structures that are not consistent with their theoretic-republican vision.

In building his case against the 'moribund' institution of the British monarchy, Slattery hits on a philosophical notion that in my view is of capital importance in considering the health, legitimacy and endurance of any political establishment. After thinking that he has provided enough evidence that the British royal family is turning people off by their antics, Slattery asks how damaged they are at the point of Diana's death. He goes on:

> The point is that the modern constitutional monarchy, in both Britain and Australia, exists because people want it to. The ties that bind monarch and notional subject in the modern age are those of affection and regard. The institution itself is erected on tradition and fabulous fine-spun wealth, but it is sustained in this country, and perhaps in Britain too, by assent and popular will.

This is an excellent point. But it is not just the British monarchy that is bound to its people by affection and regard. It is not just the British monarchy that is sustained by assent and popular will. After the unalterable metaphysical background to government, indeed to all social structures, is acknowledged, then all government is bound to its people by affection and regard, and all government is further legitimised by the assent and good opinion of its citizens. After the laws of nature, which are the laws of God, are firmly fixed before the eyes of the citizenry all particular concrete forms of government arise as arrangements determined in various ways by the people acting as a people through time. By 'people' I mean a people acting as a moral incorporation, and not as an amorphous collection of individuals who have yet to decide their standards of morality and government.

Now the true meaning of democracy is to be found within the fixed metaphysical context and the particular agreement of a particular people. When the government and the people uphold their compact or their agreement, their virtual democracy is functioning for their benefits, for the benefit of their moral incorporation. When the people act against the laws of God, or against the foundation of their particular agreement, they bring about the corruption of themselves as a people. They work against their establishment as a democratic people. When the government denies the laws of God, as if they had no responsibility to the Author of our being, they delegitimise themselves as representatives of their people. When the government acts against the very tenets of their original compact with their people they remove the moral justification of their authority.

Attacks on the people as a people can come in many different ways. One fatal way is the corruption of the people's knowledge of their original contract, of the essential elements of their being a particular people at a particular time in history. And how can you corrupt this elemental knowledge? By ridiculing the foundations of society. By lying about a people's history. By debasing their achievements. By false propaganda about the prevailing system of government and by calumniating a people's legitimate rulers. But most of all, by organising and agitating to overthrow social structures that do not match up with the prescriptions of an abstract theory dreamt up by some 'intellectual' as to how government should be carried out at all times and in all places.

I suggest that Luke Slattery reflect not only on the concept of assent as binding the British people to their royal family, and as binding the people of Australia in a *fraternal historical bond* to the British royal family and the British nation, but on the lies and distortions he has propagated in his short piece about the 'twisted cage' of the British monarchy. Perhaps he should also reflect on how our traditionally-formed Australian democracy has just about had the life twisted out of it during the last forty years.

9. The 'Rape Plea Argument' Yet Again

The gentlemen on the editorial committees of the *Disgusting Empire* will never weary of presenting the rape plea argument, in whatever form. That's only to be expected. Just as rip-off merchants are the first to suspect a scam, so too are the manipulators ever ready to suspect and accuse others of manipulating them. The manipulative media are the first to raise their arms in protest when they imagine somebody is getting more from them than they think is justified, which is never at all. Secondly, the 'you-asked-for-it' argument levelled at Diana is perhaps the most persuasive of all arguments to deflect blame from the media. After all, if opposing parties are locked in a struggle using the same methods then it is just bad luck when one of them succumbs. In this case, it's a pity for Diana, but that's the way it goes. So taking the opportunity to invoke the rape plea argument whenever possible, the *Disgusting Empire* calls on one of its grandest, Mr Peter Stothard, editor of *The Times*, London, England. The headline writer goes to work. Now it's not just the Princess who manipulates the media, but the whole royal family.

Icons on the menu at lunch with princess

Even followers of the royal soap opera would not realise how adept its players can be with the media. The late Princess of Wales was superb.

The demonstration of these ridiculing headlines unfolds in a lunchtime meeting Stothard had with Diana. The editor of *The Times* gives the reader the benefit of his thoughts in a rather bemused manner all the time indicating that he was not at all at home (down) on the level of triviality where the royal family are to be found, and where the sensible and refined, like an editor of *The Times*, would never go unless it was necessary. After setting up the atmosphere of the meeting place, (a Park Lane restaurant), in a mock *Woman's Day* mode, Stothard gets to the purpose of the meeting. Diana was there to plan a response to a damaging news story, she claimed, originating from Prince Charles and his supporters. This bare-faced approach by Diana brings Stothard to exclaim:

> *Whatever else is said about Diana, Princess of Wales, in this dreadful week [of the accident] let it not be said she lacked sophistication about*

the media, her use of it and its use of her. She was as 'on message' as the most disciplined, determined New Labour apparatchik.

She was as charming that day as everyone always says that she is. But she did not move outside the lines that she had most clearly defined.

Comparing Diana with a New Labour apparatchik indicates how well manipulators and propagandists think they can recognise their own motives and actions in another. Now to emphasise how determined, disciplined, clever, and full of media guile Diana was, Stothard proceeds to give an account of Diana's haphazard conversation. On Stothard's saying, Diana jumps from one subject to another offering indiscreet, personal details about the members of the royal family which we are to believe, as Stothard seems to have believed. The 'lines that she had most clearly defined' seemed very broad, the limits being set rather by temporal and physical limitations than by any clever purpose on Diana's part. She gives a childish, resentful commentary of the manner in which the royal household has operated for generations, as if a unique, enduring institution like the British monarchy should operate on the same basis as the kindergarten she worked in. At no time does Stothard seek to analyse Diana's conversation against the background of her known emotional instability; at no time does he stop to make a judgement about her obvious intent. Her indiscreet ridicule of the persons she perceives as connected with the conspiracy against her is swallowed with barely a hiccup by the illustrious editor of *The Times*.

Diana's objective in this meeting is so clever and sophisticated that the children in her nursery would immediately hit on it. It is this. Diana claims she has been victim of her husband's clique. She wants to retaliate in like manner. She rings the editor of *The Times* and after childishly badmouthing her perceived opponents asks him to run a story which will highlight her charitable side. She relates the circumstances of a particular charitable deed. Stothard comments that '[s]ome bits of her story did not fit together as well as a true story should'. But he thinks it 'churlish to cross-examine her...' Really? When has churlishness ever stopped a member of the media in going where he wants? No, it would spoil the objective of Stothard's article if he let Diana's failure to give a coherent account of her charitable action reflect on the desired implications of the rest of the conversation.

Again, the attempt to paint Diana as a superb manipulator of the media fails. Diana's attempted use of the media in this case is obvious and trivial compared to the talents of the real experts, one of whom was sitting opposite Diana during that lunch-time meeting. Stothard's account of the meeting, accepting that it is essentially a true account, only shows Diana at her worst: naive, resentful and childish, and unfortunately willing to misuse the good side of her character. It shows that she was on a totally different wavelength from the people whose aid she fondly thought she could enlist. In her contact with the media she bit the dust every time. This conversation with Stothard, which was meant to be friendly, co-operative and confidential, is ultimately used against her in the worst circumstances in order to protect the media's territory.

Having now arrived at the end of my examination of the 3 September edition of *The Australian*, I imagine some readers may think I have exhausted all the rotten things the media could say about Prince Charles and the royal family, and how it must mean the end of the British monarchy and Australia's connection with it. But it is just the opposite. By Thursday, 4 September, the media had worked themselves up to attempting a *coup de grace*. What followed between Thursday and the funeral on the following Saturday revealed the media at its rock-bottom level of despicability. One media commentator became so carried away by the apparent success of the media propaganda operating against the Queen and the British monarchy that he exclaimed there was a 'whiff of 1789 in the air'. His transports of revolutionary joy had obviously been prompted by fond imaginings of crowds of republicans storming Buckingham Palace.

Before I start to look at the media activity in this period, I want to remind readers of what they actually saw in television reports. For nobody could have missed those pictures. When the Queen, Prince Charles, the Duke of Edinburgh, and Princes William and Harry appeared at the gates of Balmoral Castle and later at Kensington and Buckingham Palaces to look at the floral tributes to Diana, the crowd showed nothing but affection for them and understanding of their grief. One woman gave a bouquet to the Queen saying she thought the Queen could at that moment do with a bit of comfort. The onlooker could see that this open, sincere gesture of affection brought tears to the Queen's eyes.

During the three-hour telecast of Diana's funeral there was not one gesture of ill-will or blame directed at the royal family. To the contrary, when the four male members of the royal family took their place behind Diana's casket for the long walk to Westminster Abbey, there were only expressions of sympathy to be seen on the faces of people lining the route. In the days after, no, in the months after the funeral, affection and understanding were the overwhelming reaction of ordinary people to the Queen, Prince Charles and the two princes wherever they appeared. It was only the media who soldiered on with their despicable campaign.

6

Thursday, 4 September 1997:

High-living Henri Paul and 'Callous' Prince Charles

1. The Driver

The 4 September edition of *The Australian* devotes less space than the previous editions to Diana's death. There are various articles and reports dealing with the preparations for the funeral, the ongoing sympathy from people the world over, and the implications for the media at the passing of Diana. This collection of articles functions in a supporting and supplementary role to the main thrust of this edition's treatment of Diana's passing. The intent, as is evident from the front page, is to continue to hammer the drunken state of Henri Paul as the one responsible for the accident that killed Diana and Dodi, and to paint Prince Charles as unworthy of ascending the throne of Great Britain. The headlines of the front page read:

DIANA
THE WORLD MOURNS
Public backlash against 'callous' Charles

Under the headline is a 21 cm x 27 cm colour photo of Henri Paul holding a glass with a brown liquid in it. This colour photo dominates the whole front page and is meant to convey a wealth of meaning that several pages of printed words could never do. Directly above the photo is the following heading:

Liked a drink, loved speed: the man who drove Princess Diana to her death

To the side of the photo and headlining the report on Henri Paul is the follow-on from the above:

But paparazzi still court target

The report comments briefly on Henri Paul, his character and his way of life. It then goes on to deal with the implications of Henri Paul's drunken state for the photographers arrested at the scene of the accident, the condition of Trevor Rees-Jones, and preparations for Diana's funeral. However, the short comment on Henri Paul is enough because the headlines together with the huge photo of him in party mode with glass in hand have said it all. The message is that Henri Paul was an irresponsible, heavy drinking, reckless party animal who was never happier than when driving at high speed without consideration of the time or place, or the state he was in; that the senior staff at the Ritz were aware of his profligate character but nevertheless let him climb into the car carrying Diana and Dodi and drive them to their deaths. Nobody could miss this message. By day four of the reporting on the death of Diana, the editorial board at *The Australian* feel confident enough not to worry about being too direct. Now let us consider the photo and report more closely.

The report tells us that the photo appeared in London's *Daily Mirror* and was 'undated'. *The Australian* editors in mentioning the photo as undated evidently think they have cleared themselves of the charge of misleading the reader. But saying the photo is undated without any further qualification still leaves the reader with the impression that it is of recent origin at least. That is the distinct impression I had when I first saw the photo. Most readers later would have been shocked, as I was, when they saw the footage from the security camera in the Ritz of Henri Paul. He was scarcely recognisable as the same man whose photo had been splashed in all its colour across the front page. The figure in the footage was almost bald, and what little hair he had was grey. He was also heavier and without a moustache. He was clearly a good deal older than the man in the photo on the front page of *The Australian* — at least ten years older. I wonder how many people would like an impression of them given to the public on the basis of a photo that was at least ten years old, and had been cropped and enlarged to project an unflattering image. Most people would think that a pretty grubby trick to play.

If we look closely at the photo it's clear it has been cropped to exclude all else and to highlight Paul with drink in hand. Under the photo is the caption:

Glass in hand ... Henri Paul, the driver behind the wheel when Diana died

It looks like the whole photo was of at least two people (you can see an arm of a friend around Paul's shoulder) taken at the sort of social gathering we all attend. It is likely that the friend also had a glass in his hand, which is what most people do when they attend a social gathering. If this was the whole photo then I suggest a completely different impression would be given, not the impression *The Australian* wants.

What are the contents of the glass? I defy anyone to name the liquid with confidence. It looks like neither brandy nor whisky nor like beer. Let's face it, it could easily have been a soft drink. A non-alcoholic drink would seem to match the expression on Paul's face and his general demeanour. Paul's eyes are clear and his expression steady but reserved. His clothing is unflamboyant. Over his shoulder in the background one can see a young man whose clothes are more with it. All in all, he hardly looks on the point of entertaining the gathering with party animal tricks. When I first looked at the photo I had the immediate impression the reader was clearly supposed to have. It was only on closer examination and after the later security camera footage that the impression fell apart revealing the deceptive nature of the report. This was further confirmed when reports came to hand of the real Henri Paul.

Sancton and MacLeod devote a full chapter to Henri Paul and his background.[1] A lot of their information is drawn from the same avenues of investigation pursued by the Paris police. This seems also the source of an article (**The secret life of Diana's driver**) by Philip Jacobson in the *Herald-Sun*, 7 March 1998. The picture of the character of Henri Paul arising from these two sources reveals a person directly the opposite of the caricature presented by *The Australian* on 4 September. I will be looking more closely at Henri Paul and his state and behaviour just prior to the accident in Chapter 11. It will be enough for the moment to sketch the main outlines of his character.

From all accounts given by his close friends, colleagues, employers, and the staff of bars he frequented in the neighbourhood of the Ritz, Henri Paul was first and foremost a sober-mannered person. He was neat, particular, ordered, conscientious and hardworking. He not given to over-indulgence in public and maintained a manner that seemed controlled and reserved. Those that he drank with or mixed with socially said that he never looked the worse for wear. Even his close friends were shocked to learn that he was undergoing treatment for a drinking problem. The drinking problem had to have been a mild and temporary one for the autopsy on Paul after the accident did not reveal the damage to the liver normally suffered by chronic alcoholics. With regard to his driving, those that drove with him (an ex-girlfriend and childhood friends) said that he was very careful. In fact, he was reluctant to take the wheel when he and his childhood friend, Claude Garrec, occasionally drove from Paris to Lorient, their home village, 500 km west of Paris. The circumstances of the accident and the finding of the blood-alcohol levels (first 0.175 and then 0.187) in Paul raise a lot of questions about Henri Paul on that day. *The Australian* was not at all interested in raising those questions and subjecting them to a critical analysis.

Instead it throws at the reader a sensational caricature of Paul and matches this with sniping comments about the necessarily reduced culpability of the paparazzi who were chasing Diana and Dodi when Henri Paul lost control of the car. To ensure that the bent message is thoroughly rammed home a second report at the top of page 6 is headlined:

Second test worse for binge drinker who loved the fast lane

The report comes from *The Times, The Australian's* senior stable mate in the Murdoch empire, and repeats in more detail the picture painted of Paul in the front-page report. The blood-alcohol levels are matched by claims that Paul was fast-living and boastful of his job at the Ritz. Given 'his inebriated ego' he could not have resisted Dodi's orders to take the wheel of the Mercedes. Unnamed employees at the Ritz are again quoted as saying that Paul was clearly as 'drunk as a pig'. The claims of the unnamed Ritz staff are to dismiss the claims by Ritz senior staff that Paul's manner was not that of a person hopelessly drunk. Whatever the question about Paul's manner and blood-alcohol level, the character picture of Paul splashed across the pages of *The Australian* can readily be refuted with some honest, impartial, steady investigation of the person Henri Paul and his actions on the day of the accident. Most of the information was so ready to hand that a competent journalist could have had it filed well before 4 September. One could not come across a clearer demonstration of a newspaper wanting to hammer a particular message rather than do the responsible job of reporting the truth. I will come back to Henri Paul and his condition on that night. There are many questions to be asked and many inconsistencies to be resolved. Let me now turn to the second message of the edition of 4 September.

2. Charles the Callous

Murdoch's people never seem happier than when they can attack and torment Prince Charles and the royal family. They put their minds to creating wonderful movements from the major themes of the media's grand symphony of the cruel and crippled Prince Charles. Ean Higgins evidently feels that he should match the products of Ms Deborah Hope's fantasy. In this present edition he shows that he has completely put aside his serious lapse in the 1 September edition where he reported the Queen's and the royal family's reaction to Diana's death in a dispassionate manner. His front-page report is headed:

Royals build iron cocoon for William

The first paragraph sets up the overworked theme to be further overworked:

> *The royal family is building a protective but rigid cocoon around Prince William that could shift the dominant influence in the future king's life from the more open and populist style of his mother towards the harsher traditionalism of Prince Charles and the Queen.*

Various people are called on to support the warnings about the sinister plans of the royal family. Prominent among these is Dr David Starkey who is given the impressive title of 'prominent constitutional historian'. As we will see later, Dr Starkey is hardly an impartial academic observer of the events surrounding the royal family. He is more like a grand political bigot ever-ready to pass on his political wisdom. The contrast between the cold wicked Windsors and the open, warm Diana (as propagated by such as Starkey) is evident according to Higgins by the Queen allegedly taking charge and imposing the 'traditions' and 'values' of the palace on William and Harry; by Tiggy Legge-Bourke (the young princes' professional carer) being called in to comfort the princes at Balmoral; and by Charles 'forcing' the princes to maintain 'a stiff upper lip' and attend the Sunday church service 'dry-eyed'. This last allegation is particularly ridiculous. It says more about Higgins's simple-minded bigotry than about Prince Charles. Can you imagine it? Prince Charles lining up William and Harry and commanding with wagging finger: 'You will go to church and you will be dry-eyed, and you will maintain a stiff upper lip!' I am sure William and Harry would laugh themselves silly at this childish fantasy if it did not concern the father they quite clearly love and respect.

No, I have answered these sorts of allegations in previous chapters. It is natural for the royal family to gather around the princes in their grief; it is natural and reasonable for the family to call in the help of a carer the princes like and are at ease with; and it is entirely natural, reasonable and in order for a Christian family who have lost a loved one to attend church to pray to God for the repose of her soul. Most importantly of all, the young princes show that they willingly go along with their father and their grandparents in the course of action taken after their mother's death. When the royal family appeared to inspect the floral tributes to Diana nobody could have missed the way Prince Harry held his father's hand. During the funeral procession nobody could have missed the way Prince Harry walked determinedly ahead of his father, brother, grandfather and uncle. It was as if the young 12-year-old prince was again purposefully defying the powerful organisations that are intent on burying his father. The ordinary person must continually wonder what sort of people can mount such vicious public attacks on the father of two young men who have just lost their mother in such tragic circumstances — those sons for whom the media pretend they have sympathy.

The front-page report is certainly not enough for the purposes of those wanting Prince Charles out of the way. Higgins resumes his attack on page 6 where the nasty front-page portrayal of Charles and the royal family is developed into full-blown agitation to force Charles to give up the crown in favour of son Prince William. In this report we are to witness the theoretic-republican media in full lying mode. The pretences have largely come down and the enemies of the British monarchy (as an inherited social arrangement that is inconsistent with theoretic-republicanism) can sniff blood in the air. The report is headed in big black letters:

Backlash threatens Charles's crown

Higgins begins with:

> *Speculation emerged yesterday that the crown might pass directly from the Queen to Prince William, amid a public backlash against Prince Charles in the aftermath of Diana's death.*

What he means is that the media have banded together to agitate for the removal of Prince Charles from the succession to the throne and that they are busy fabricating stories that would whip up feeling amongst the public for such action. There was no such speculation among people who would be qualified both in character and expertise to make such a judgement. There was no evidence of a widespread backlash and later events would prove that. Regardless of the actual state of affairs Higgins summarises what 'media commentators' are saying about the causes for the backlash. For 'media commentators' read 'unprincipled lying voices who have control of the instruments of public information'.

> *Media commentators said Charles risked popular reprimand for what they said was a failure to express adequate remorse for his contribution to the break-up of his marriage with Diana; a failure to provide sufficient protection for her after their divorce; and for 'callously' allowing his two sons to go immediately on to the public stage after their mother's death.*

This is a good example of the ways in which unprincipled 'journalists' and their media instruments can fabricate, twist, distort and beat up stories to support their material and political objectives. One can start by asking what an adequate expression of remorse would be for Prince Charles. The answer is that there would be no adequate remorse for the media. They show that they would not stop until they could twist the most inoffensive words or actions of the Prince into something black and nasty. But this is not the only point to consider. The 'adequate expression of remorse' in this context is predicated on accepting the lies and distortions propagated by the media about Diana's and Charles's marriage. I have said enough about this subject. You see, in this way Prince Charles can never win. He is damned if he does and damned if he doesn't. Of course, there's the fundamental issue of why Prince Charles should make public his feelings about the breakdown of his marriage. Most ordinary people would think they have heard enough about the tragedy of his marriage failure and that reasonably he would be allowed some privacy of feeling about this matter.

As for providing protection for Diana, anybody who has followed the course of Diana's life following the divorce knows that she was wanting above all to escape from the scrutiny of those she perceived as connected with her husband. She steadfastly refused any offers of protection from the British government and from Buckingham Palace. If Prince Charles had taken action to override Diana's wishes in this matter he would have been crucified by the media as somebody worse than a Nazi henchman. The media in Britain would have been well aware of Diana's wishes and her reasons. That does not stop somebody like Mary Kenny, 'heralded by [*The Express*] as "the voice of traditional values"'. This is what Higgins reports this 'voice of traditional values' saying:

> *Prince Charles is said to be racked with guilt and remorse after the death of Diana: so well he might be. The royal family and the entire establishment failed to protect the princess after the divorce, to which she was, remember, the reluctant party. [Regardless of Diana's refusal of Buckingham Palace security] ... surely the Prince of Wales could have devised some sort of arrangement which ensured properly organised protection for Diana, including 24-carat safe and sober drivers ... Many people feel that she was let down, somehow, in life. She was certainly let down in the way her life ended: unprotected and unshielded from the known perils of maniacal driving.*

If this is an example of Kenny's moral thinking, then it is evident she would not know a traditional value if she tripped over it. For her benefit I would suggest that amongst traditional values are honesty, empathy and fair dealing, values which are entirely lacking in these words. Indeed, accepting traditional values and being a media commentator would seem mutually exclusive situations.

Kenny, as is evident from Higgins's report, was not the only one to abuse and misuse in an inconsistent manner the reports of Prince Charles's feelings about Diana's death. If Charles was so callous, so hard-hearted, so self-centred towards Diana, surely feelings of guilt and remorse would not play a part in his response. But then for the media to admit feelings that contradict one of the main assertions about Charles in this report, and follow it with a sneering dismissal of what is a normal human response, demonstrates only the nastiness and morally empty minds of those who continually rage against a group of people dismissed as non-persons. Kenny's pompous discounting of Prince Charles's understandable emotional turmoil is based on a dishonest appraisal of Diana's security arrangements. It is based on a complete disregard for the harassment and hounding by the media that accompanied Diana everywhere. And it is based on turning a blind eye to the emotional problems and insecurities that plagued Diana through her life.

There is no lack of support for Kenny's twisted moral thinking. Anthony Holden, the royal commentator from *The Express*, demonstrates that those bearing the title of royal commentator are the royal family's bitterest enemies forever seeking to turn whatever circumstances prevail into a smear against the Queen and her family. Higgins reports Holden wandering through the crowds in London who were paying their respects to Diana, and sniffing in the air 'a shift in anger towards Prince Charles'. Holden claimed that people were wondering why Charles had 'uttered no apology for the way he betrayed her during their marriage ...'[2] There was no evidence that this was a widespread feeling. The people among whom Holden was walking were there to express their sorrow over Diana's death. They were also preoccupied with thinking about the feelings of her sons — as was evident in TV footage. No, it all points to a fabrication by Holden to whip up feeling against Prince Charles. He would have searched high and low for somebody so mean-spirited as to accuse Charles of callousness when he was wanted by his sons at such a difficult time. But the editorial board of *The Independent* would not be outdone by the casual smear of a mere royal commentator. It mounted its own public smear:

> *[the mourning public] would not have sent their bereaved sons to*
> *ordinary Sunday church services. Their emotional expectations are a*
> *world away from the self-deprecating and contorted dignity of the*
> *Prince of Wales or the amazing, iron self-discipline of his mother, who*
> *seems almost like an ancient Roman matriarch, stern-faced and*
> *unfaltering as the family tragedies pile up around her.*

If readers stop to consider these words, then they will think that they are getting a good view into the pits of the moral-less media mind. *The Independent* editorial shows us what scorn its authors have for religious belief, belief in the saving graces of the Almighty; it says what they think of dignified private sorrow on a tragic family occasion (they will know what praise and admiration Jackie Kennedy received for the dignity and bravery she showed during the funeral of her assassinated husband more than thirty years ago); it says that they have no regard whatever for the feelings of a family grieving over a horrible tragedy; and it says above all that they place the advancement of their power and ideological program above such considerations. The following day will show that this was all a softening up for the attempted *coup de grace*.

Just to show how ready Murdoch's men are to mock the canons of decency, they placed the report bagging Charles for his callousness so that it wraps around a 23 cm x 20 cm colour photo of Prince Charles and his sons. Charles, William and Harry are posing for the media at the Balmoral estate not long before Diana's death. The picture is of two sons looking happy and relaxed with their father, as they always do.

3. The Media Rat Pack Loses its Quarry

The final article in the 4 September edition is ostensibly about how the reporters who followed Diana's every move were stricken by her death, how they will never get over the loss of somebody they liked and got on well with, and how they are now being unfairly lumped together with those other unconscionable reporters who hounded the princess. It may have been true that some journalists had reason to feel this way. It is indisputable that Diana had a friendly relationship with one or two who showed some rare respect for her feelings. But with good reason the public will find it hard to separate them from all their unconscionable colleagues. This report, though, is not just self-pleading by a journalist. In fact, it (**Royal rat pack out of favour and at a loss for a quarry**) distinguishes itself not only by its reasonable approach compared with the majority of the reports dealing with Charles and Diana, but it also unintentionally provides confirmation of key points that I have been making against the media. Carol Midgley is the author of this report drawn from *The Times* and she should be congratulated for resisting the inclination to indulge in the all-out royal-bashing most of her colleagues give themselves over to. She opens with a description of the national mood:

> *'You murdering bastards,' spat the weeping middle-aged woman to a weary photographer on duty outside the gates of Buckingham Palace. 'You killed her, you pigs. You murdered her.'*
>
> *Ugly scenes such as this were being repeated at many venues across London this week as members of the public vented their spleen on the current object of national hatred: the press.*

It seems that part of Midgley's purpose in relating such incidents is to highlight the view of the 'informed' (i.e. media commentators, media academics, elite theoretic-republicans) that the mass of people are reacting in a highly emotive manner about Diana's death and are levelling their understandable (if not reasonable) anger against the media in bulk. I have already dealt with this media defence in previous chapters, so I need not repeat the arguments. The important point, however, is that Midgley recognises what most of us recognise. The national mood, indeed, the mood around the world, is directed at the media who are the people responsible for Diana's death. So while most of the media were breaking their necks to convince us that the people were directing their anger at Prince Charles and the royal family, the people themselves were grieving about Diana's passing and holding the media responsible. There were many who did not hesitate to show their anger for what they held the media responsible for.

Secondly, Midgley confirms how the media viewed Diana in terms of her usefulness to their business enterprises and in what manner they had organised themselves so that they could track her every move. The connection between the editor and the journalist in the 'Diana enterprise' is confirmed.

> *... no other public figure has had such an effect on newspaper editors. On a slack news day, a fetching picture of the princess beneath a snappy*

headline could solve the problem of a tabloid front page splash in a stroke.

Stories of photographers and reporters waking each other with 2 am phone calls, after being tipped off that she was 'on the move again', are legion.

What Midgley is telling us here we all know. We all know that the media viewed Diana as a money-making object, and not as a real person. We all know that they organised themselves using the most modern electronic technology to track her down and corner her. Finally, Midgley confirms what we also know about the manner in which the foul instruments of the media empires cornered their prey.

... British interest in the princess intensified in the 1990s to an extent which some found intolerable. Jane Fincher, a photographer who resigned from the royal roster because of the 'bad manners' of some photographers, says she felt ashamed when the cameramen would block the princess's way, 'trapping her in corners and hunting her down like hounds with a fox'. A sea change came, she says, when the princess separated and divorced her husband. 'After that it seemed the barriers went down,' she says.

Jane Fincher should be heralded as a heroine for her action. It would take a person of real decency and courage to walk away from the contemptible media scrum surrounding Diana, and risk her career by doing so.

Jane Fincher's display of fundamental decency and Carol Midgley's frank report are but momentary lapses in the media's main campaign. While we in Australia were busy reading the morning reports and commentaries of the 4 September editions, the media minds on the other side of the world were preparing the greatest display of gutless bastardry I have ever witnessed in the community in my life.

7

Friday, 5 September 1997:
The Gutless Bastardry of the Media

1. Feelings of Grief and Loss

I appeal to the reader. If your son's ex-wife who led a very public life was killed in a tragic car accident leaving behind her two young sons, what would you do? How would you react? As a normal person with normal feelings you would be struck down first by the trauma of the tragedy. After the initial shock your feelings would be overtaken by the grief and concern for your son and his children. Some people are for a long period incapacitated by such an event. The concerns are many and heavy. What will your son do? How will he cope with his children? And how will your grandchildren get over the trauma of losing their mother so tragically? Those that lead a public life and suffer from normal feelings would react in just this way. The demands on them publicly are great but the ordinary person would allow them time for adjustment and for taking steps to deal with the tragedy.

After Diana's death it was normal for the Queen to concern herself first and foremost with her son and her grandchildren. It was normal for Prince Charles to want to be with his sons to comfort them and to help them deal with their shock and grief. Most people would not only allow this but expect this action from the Queen and Prince Charles. They would be disappointed if the Queen and royal family placed public 'duty' above the welfare of the persons immediately affected by Diana's tragic death. As I have said many times, it was evident that most people in Britain and around the world were grieving for Diana and concerned about the feelings of the two young princes. But the media, who are always calling for the royal family to be less stiff and stuffy, would not allow this. With typical hypocrisy and inconsistency, they attacked the Queen for giving priority to private family concerns in exceptionally difficult circumstances over public appearance. I make a point of saying 'public appearance' because appearing in public as an alleged salve for public feeling could hardly be called a duty in the circumstances. In fact, it's more likely to be considered a public burden by most people.

After attacking and smearing Prince Charles for four days on end without the slightest consideration about how William and Harry in their grief would react to the nastiness directed at their father, they saw the chance to get at the Queen and the whole system of constitutional monarchy. In a frenzied and combined attack, they fabricated a picture of a callous and uncaring royal family who were selfishly ignoring their grieving people, and hiding themselves away in the comfort and luxury of Balmoral Castle. The media drew on the 'expertise' of those academic and political figures most bitterly opposed to the Queen as a person and to the structure of constitutional monarchy. It was an example of the naked manipulation of the instruments of information dissemination by a minority political group who had both material and political objectives in view. There was no end to the weaselling, hypocritical, mock-obsequiousness of the headlines.[1] This was truly the stuff to sicken normal people to the pits of their stomachs. *The Australian*, left to report the campaign from the frontline in Britain, opened its 5 September edition with the following headline:

Stung by criticism, 'hurt' Queen to address grieving nation

Ean Higgins is again given the task to report from the centre of the action. His front-page report begins by saying the Queen was said to be 'hurt' by the accusations that the royal family had been 'indifferent to the country's outpouring of grief at the death of Diana'. In both cases, where the word 'hurt' is mentioned we have it in quotation marks as if it cannot be true that the Queen could possibly experience such feelings. But Higgins does not need to regurgitate the frenzied outpourings of those claiming indifference on the part of the Queen. The message has been hammered enough. Besides, it would sound unbelievable to most Australians who could not possibly understand the media feigning concern that the Queen was not paying enough attention to their feelings of grief! He is left to report that the 'extraordinary attack on the royals from the media, Labour MPs and many among the tens of thousands of mourners flooding central London' had become so serious that British Prime Minister, Tony Blair, had to step in to defend the royal family and that spokespeople for the Queen had to respond on her behalf.

2. The Queen is Forced to Respond

In the end the Queen was forced to take action that made it appear that there was some substance to the frenzied accusations coming from the media bosses. If no other action during this week has demonstrated the nature of the media empires that operate today, then this episode should have shown not only what type of people inhabit the dark spaces of the media pit, but also what extraordinary power they can deploy in the right circumstances. This episode shoots gaping holes in the *free speech* arguments media chiefs employ to defend their disgusting activities. If ever there was an example of 'freedom' being used as a 'cloak for malice', this was it. The Queen's press secretary, Australian-born Geoffrey Crawford, was forced to state publicly:

> *The royal family have been hurt by suggestions that they are indifferent to the country's sorrow at the tragic death of the Princess of Wales ...*
>
> *The Princess was a much loved national figure, but she was also a mother whose sons miss her deeply ... Prince William and Prince Harry themselves want to be with their father and grandparents at this time in the quiet haven of Balmoral.*

Who with an ounce of sensitivity could doubt that this was actually the case? Higgins said that 'resentment had mounted steadily all the week over the royals' perceived detachment and coldness towards the memory of Diana'. This was an out-and-out lie. What had mounted during the week to reach a crescendo was the activity of the media for their material and political gains. If any of the public had felt such a selfish unsympathetic resentment, then they would have been a small number whom reporters had to search high and low for to get them on camera or to write down their words. Buckingham Palace released a statement outlining the obvious. This was forced from them to appease the campaign that had been whipped up against the royal family.

*All the royal family, especially the Prince of Wales, Prince William
and Prince Harry, are taking strength from the overwhelming support of
the public, who are sharing their tremendous sense of loss and grief.
They are deeply touched and enormously grateful.*

Imagine what the necessity of producing such a statement would
have done to the two young princes already crushed under the tragedy of their mother's death. To have added to this tragedy the lies of
the hard-bitten campaign against their father and grandparents was a
double blow for them to cope with. But it was not only the lies about
the coldness and detachment shown by the royal family that would
have caused such consternation. The media also beat up such trivial
things in the circumstances as 'not flying the flag at half-mast at
Buckingham Palace; for not initially providing sufficient access to sign
condolence books; and for refusing, until late on Wednesday, to extend the length of the funeral procession to accommodate the expected
crowds'. The mind boggles.

When a family is struck by the tragedy of a mother killed in a car
accident, is it reasonable to give such priority to access to condolence
books and a flag flying at half-mast? As for the extension of the funeral procession, this is pure beat up. The organisation of a funeral
on the scale of that proposed for Diana required a great deal of
thought. The planning would have necessitated a fair period of time
before fixing the details of the day. Did the Queen 'refuse' to extend
the procession 'until Wednesday'? Of course not. There is no reason
why, if the circumstances required it, the procession should not be extended — as the Queen did within three days following the death of
the Princess. The evidence is that if anybody was displaying hard-
heartedness it was the media collectively. It all added to the suffering
of the two young princes whose welfare the media were pretending to
have at heart.

The issue is pursued in a follow-up report on page 6 under the
heading, **Subjects demand their Queen speak**. Lord Blake, constitutional historian and evidently sympathetic to the situation the royal
family found itself in, attempts in his own way to mollify the media-
fabricated resentment by recommending the royal family demonstrate
with some 'simple gestures' that they care. The Queen should address
the nation on the eve of the funeral. Lord Blake makes his recom-
mendations in a spirit of goodwill. But officials attached to the

committee of 25 organising the funeral replied to the criticism against the Queen in a way that most would understand.

> *Officials involved in hourly consultations with the palace said criticism of its response was unfair and failed to take account of the unprecedented nature of the situation with which it was dealing.*
>
> *'The palace is responding to a developing situation, the reaction of the public and the massive outpouring of grief has taken everybody by surprise. The palace is aware of and is responding to the massive outpouring of emotions.'*

This is an entirely reasonable response and could have been made in the confines of a private conversation between those who had concerns and the proper officials. But the media is not interested in foregoing the opportunity to exercise their ingenuity for fabricating a useful scenario, and certainly no reasoned response could possibly penetrate the ramparts of their political bigotry.

8

Saturday, 6 September 1997:
The Canonisation of New Media Fabrications

1. The Cause of Canonisation is Formally Promoted

The day of the funeral of Diana, Princess of Wales, dawned. People around the world prepared their last farewells to a Princess they found they had an unexpected degree of sympathy and affection for. The news that the funeral would be televised and sent all around the world had people organising their time so that they could see it. We in Australia were fortunate in that the funeral would take place during prime-time evening television. While most normal people were making their arrangements mindful of the tragedy of Diana's death and the suffering it was causing the princes and the royal family, the morally empty minds of the media were still on a high from the week's campaign against the grieving family. *The Australian*, true to the course of action taken during the week, was setting itself up to ensure that the series of lies, distortions and manipulations of the week could be permanently fixed in the body of slander and calumny that constituted the media mythology about the British royal family. The additions would be formally canonised by proclamation. Ean Higgins, whose star rose rapidly during this week, again had the front-page report dealt to him. It was his task to begin the promotion of the cause.

The front-page headline is a bit of hard sell for the Saturday edition, easily the top revenue-earning edition of the week ...

PEOPLE'S PRINCESS
THE LORD SNOWDON PORTRAITS

The Murdoch organisation must have paid a packet for a series of photos of Diana taken by Lord Snowdon. They are collected into a 'unique 10-page commemorative keepsake' called: **DIANA, THE SNOWDON PORTRAITS**. It is this supplement that *The Australian* chooses to hawk at the top of the front page. To the left beside an exquisite Snowdon colour portrait of Diana, Higgins is thrown two 18 cm columns. His report is headed:

Billions to mourn as Diana laid to rest

Now you would think from this that the reader would be confronted with some sober reflective comments about the preparations for the funeral and the feelings of the people who would be present in London. But no, Higgins must twist and turn to mould the circumstances to the right propaganda line. He opens up with the comment that the television audience would be vast and that a multitude of people would be present in London not only to witness the funeral procession but (most importantly) 'to reclaim their princess and humble royal tradition'. Reclaim the princess? From whom? Well, of course, it's from the wicked Windsors that the princess will be reclaimed.

While the grieving family in Balmoral were trying to cope with the tragedy, the media were conjuring up a scenario that is now holy writ for them. But let's think about it. The idea in itself is preposterous and infantile. The actual circumstances of the death of Diana and the period following simply do not allow for any sort of *real* scenario that has the royal family 'stealing off' with Diana. And what about the people 'humbling royal tradition'? Higgins is finding it difficult to control his imagination. That very day the people would lap up royal tradition. Higgins and his masters could not escape the tragedy of Diana being most forcefully conveyed in an array of British royal tradition that would be the funeral as a whole.

Having repeated the fantasy of Diana being reclaimed from the feelingless Windsors, Higgins goes on to repeat the full fantasy. The Queen was forced back to London from her selfish hideaway in Balmoral where she had been plotting to place 'protocol ahead of raw emotion for Diana'. Her forced return to face up to the 'people' was aimed at preventing the funeral becoming 'a mass expression of anti-royal outrage'. What rot! When the Queen and the royal family arrived in London they were greeted with nothing but affection and sympathy wherever they went. Higgins calls on theoretic-republican theologian and propagandist, Dr David Starkey, to turn up the colour of the fantasy several degrees. Higgins throws to Starkey who says:

> *'The simple reason they took these actions is that they feel that if they don't break protocol, the people will start breaking the windows of Buckingham Palace ...' But, noting the emotionally charged nature of the event, Dr Starkey said he still detected 'a whiff of 1789 in the air'* — a reference to the French Revolution.

In reality, this was a risky moment for Starkey who was caught indulging unrestrainedly in his maddest theoretic-republican fantasies. If the appropriate medical official had happened on this delusive episode, he may have thought it so severe that he felt obliged to schedule the 'prominent constitutional historian' for a period in a discreet convalescent home on the west coast of England.

Was Starkey really conjuring up before his mind a crowd of thugs and brigands storming Buckingham Palace to release seven prisoners, two of whom were mad — as happened with the storming of the Bastille in 1789 when the odd indiscriminate murder accompanied this wonderful theoretic-republican event? Or did his delusive episode focus on the storming of the Palace of Versailles when, after murdering King Louis XVI's personal guard and fixing their severed heads atop spears, the same bunch of thugs and brigands forced the French king and queen to march back to Paris 'amidst the horrid yells, and shrilling screams, and frantic dances, and infamous contumelies, and all the unutterable abominations of the furies of hell, in the abused shape of the vilest of women'.[1] If Starkey had been observing the real events in London on Friday, 5 September, instead of playing out his delusions, he would have witnessed the royal family being received not by a bunch of murdering thugs but by crowds of people from all over the world exhibiting their affection and sympathy for the royal family. But we are not dealing with reality here. *The Australian* editorial committee clearly thought the front-page article had finished the final promotion for the cause of canonisation and moved directly to the solemn act itself.

2. The Editorial Completes the Solemn Act of Canonisation

At the beginning of this work I said I was setting out to demonstrate the philosophical assumptions of the theoretic-republican mind, how authoriphobic theoretic-republicans utilise their theoretical scenario as a weapon to destroy traditional structures in order to replace existing authority with their own systems of authority, and how essentially their motivation was for power and position. I was aware that the stock accusation of being deluded by conspiracy theories would be levelled at me. Well, I have traced the clear movement of the arguments of the week, and provided argument and evidence to contradict every point of the case being fabricated. Let's now see how Rupert Murdoch's propaganda instrument, *The Australian*, brings the confluent arguments to the expected conclusion. Let's see how expert *The Australian's* editorial writer is in summarising the key points of the week's fabrication for their assumption into the theoretic-republican heaven of myths. The editorial writer has done so well in this piece that it could have issued straight from the Murdoch mind itself. Herein are the main articles of the proclamation of canonisation:

Princes now best hope of The Firm

The House of Windsor is at a watershed. It is a poignant tribute to the Princess of Wales and her modernising influence that so many believe (or fear) that her sons — having lost their mother so tragically — will be subverted from the path of forging a people's monarchy — one which is concerned about the issues and troubles affecting everyday people, one which is not constrained from reaching out by ironclad protocol. So it is natural that the overwhelming sympathy for the princes flowing from their mother's death is coupled to worries about how they will cope in the immediate future — and beyond.

The reactions of the royal family, and of the people of Britain, show how outmoded is the rigid British class system, with its demands for an almost slavish devotion to duty. Consider the public personas of the princes' father and grandfather: stiff, publicly unbending and unable to utter simple expressions of compassion for the 'people's princess'. Prince Charles and Prince Philip must seem as relevant as the dodo to today's generation. The royal family retreated behind the gates of Balmoral and the walls of protocol, when the people wanted an expression of sorrow and an act of humanity. The retreat was natural but the signs that it was inappropriate were quickly and readily apparent. Protocol says, for instance, that the royal standard is not flown from Buckingham Palace when the Queen is away. But the royal family was incapable even of responding rapidly to public demands that the flag be flown half-mast to mark Diana's passing. The very idea seemed to be beyond the capacity of those around the royal family to understand. They could not appreciate that, at this tragic time, humanity might take precedence over protocol.

The Princess of Wales in death continues to pass judgement on the royal family, much as she did in life. That she was a celebrity in the media age rather than just another 'royal' is measure of how 'The Firm' failed to understand the changing expectations that the British had of the constitutional monarchy. Her celebrated remark that she found Prince Charles 'middle-aged' for much of their marriage points to the difficulties he will have in succeeding the Queen. Prince Charles, however much he has been trained for the job, is a person who will satisfy only a past era of public expectations.

The remaining five paragraphs of the editorial subject the reader to the sort of socio-political babble with which the theoretic-republican mind likes to stir up the emotions of what it calls 'the people'. It's the sort of babble that is appropriate to the solemnity of the occasion where new elements of the theoretic-republican scripture are canonised and formally placed within the media magisterium. I will make do with bringing out the main points. They follow on from the previous paragraphs.

Fame was once attached (says the editorial) to people of 'high achievement in some practical activity'. What is meant here, of course, is people who had distinguished themselves through their high degree of moral courage, self-discipline, unselfishness and skill. The editorial simply could not get that idea out and had to make do with the weaselling 'practical activity'. In contrast, fame now attaches to 'someone who is sympathetically exposed by cameras, accessible to the common people and, it seems, tragically flawed'. Diana was one such 'famous' person who functioned like 'the character in a novel'. Diana attracted attention through her role as a princess but her true fame came after her troubles became public.

But it was her bulimia, her unhappy marriage, her divorce and her battle with Buckingham Palace that ensured her public adoration, presenting her as a victim who yet sought to prevail against starchy tradition.

Diana's death ended the story of the tragic princess for the public but she may just achieve in death what her 'admirers' had hoped for. As the 'people's princess' she transcended the normal role of royal consort. She took charge of the future crown prince and his brother and proceeded to give them a 'normal life'. Bad luck if that meant 'bending' the royal rules. Breaking the line of thought the editorial then throws in this stock defence of the media's uncontrollable behaviour:

> *Her misfortune was to be famous at a time when the communications revolution was leading to the development of an insatiable media industry trying to meet the insatiable public demands for information about celebrities.*

Resuming the previous line of thought, the editorial goes on:

> *Diana latterly saw her celebrity status as a way of making sure her boys would know more about the pain and pleasures of the real world than adherence to protocol would allow. This, she had determined, would better prepare them for their future royal roles than the disciplined approach of their father and the palace.*

The reaction of people to Diana's death 'says more about the search for symbols that represent generational expectations than the direct relevance of the princess'.

> *Diana was more than a reject member of the royal family; she was a window for the vast numbers of people to a world of vivacity; of bright lights; of the search for love won and lost; of triumph over disaster; of compassion in the face of individual illness and social suffering. This is the essence of her status as the people's princess and those around the Queen have misread the people's mood. Their misunderstanding threatens the long-term future of the monarchy. If it is to survive, a wide section of the community must feel its relevance — Diana's achievement. And that is what her sons must achieve if the institution is to survive into the 21st century.*

Tony Blair's and the Labour Party's election in Britain heralds a new, open, modern age. The monarchy cannot 'cling to its insular traditions'.

In years past, the Queen was relevant to her generation and it was recognised that this was the great strength of her rule. Strength because a royal family out of touch is a royal family on the path to extinction.

Under the banner of 'relevance' the Princes William and Harry must carry on Diana's

task of reinventing the relevance of royalty to a media-savvy people; self-absorbed and cynical yet still looking for leaders.

The 'traditionalists' in the royal camp rejected this manner of reinventing royalty. They failed to see the 'wellspring of regard' generated by Diana for the royal family. Diana brought them a new level of popularity. The failure to exploit and understand this trend has affected the standing of the royal family to the extent that

the future role of the monarchy is a matter of serious debate. Such is the measure of the failure of the royal family to understand the void between their performance and public expectations. The princes are their hope for the future.

At every point, as I say, I have provided argument and evidence to contradict each article of this editorial proclamation. Instead of taking the arguments again point by point, I will present the editorial's assertions and their implications in propositional form and offer a brief rebuttal.

The Articles of Holy Writ as Newly Proclaimed by the Media

THE ROYAL FAMILY WILL SUBVERT THE PRINCES'
ATTEMPT TO FORGE A 'PEOPLE'S MONARCHY'
The 'people's monarchy' meant by the Murdoch editorial committee is no monarchy at all. Their 'people's monarchy' means the final act of subverting the existing constitutional monarchy. The subversion is undertaken by the theoretic-republican class not by the royal family. There will be no subverting a genuine monarchy commensurate with the traditions and wishes of the people as a 'people'. There is more about that below.

THE MONARCHY UNDER QUEEN ELIZABETH HAS NO CONCERN FOR THE PEOPLE

The Queen has shown at all times that she has the welfare and happiness of the people at heart. An effective healthy monarchy is as concerned with the welfare and happiness of the people as any other form of government. In the British constitutional monarchy, the queen has no formal executive power. But in maintaining and following the traditions of the nation she has shown how the concerns of the people are close to her heart. At the beginning of her reign she announced before God that she would be at the service of the nation. She has not faltered in this undertaking. There are few public figures alive today who can boast the strength of character and the devotion to the task allotted her in life. The rorts and abuses of office, the neglect and contempt for the people so evident today are not to be found in Buckingham Palace. The ordinary person knows where to look for such failings.

PROTOCOL IS IRONCLAD BY ITS NATURE AND IMPEDES THE ESTABLISHMENT OF A GENUINE PEOPLE'S MONARCHY

Protocol is a particular mode of centuries-old tradition. There is no opposition between protocol and a 'people's monarchy'. The nature of protocol and tradition is that it shores up and guards the continuity of a people's cultural identity. It is the vessels of the life-blood of the people as a moral incorporation. It guards against the assaults of its enemies, both internal and external. The internal enemies of the people know that in subverting tradition they strike at the heart of the nation. In the British nation there is no 'people's' monarchy to be established. It already exists. There is on the other hand a centuries-old healthy structure to be ripped down by those who want more power and position in the state.

PROTOCOL IS IN OPPOSITION TO HUMAN FEELING AND EMOTION

This is nonsense. No protocol operates uninterruptedly in the life of a person or an organisation. It enhances rather than inhibits or destroys the feelings of unity in a nation. It operates only during those times when the national feelings of the people expressed in their traditions require it. The Queen and the royal family have shown they follow protocol only as it has been prescribed in the continuity of the nation. Protocol not only operates in a royal setting but also in republics where plenty of boot-licking of the new czars is required for advancement.

THE QUEEN GIVES PROTOCOL PRECEDENCE OVER HUMANITY

This charge is made in relation to the flag flying at half-mast over Buckingham Palace. This is as mean-spirited and trivial as one can get. The public as a whole were not demanding a break in tradition. The keeping of tradition would rather honour Diana than the opposite. Those that place the material before humanity are the very ones capable of such nasty propaganda in such tragic circumstances. Murdoch's minions plumbed new depths of hypocrisy in the circumstances surrounding Diana's death.

THE MURDOCH EMPIRE EXPRESSES SYMPATHY FOR PRINCES WILLIAM AND HARRY

This is about as hypocritical as the human person can become. No chief, at whatever level in the Murdoch empire, really has genuine sympathy for the young princes. They have shown that by the all-out attack on the princes' father and grandfather at the most tragic time of their young lives. The expression of sympathy for William and Harry is merely a ploy to get at the monarchy and undermine it.

THE REACTIONS OF THE ROYAL FAMILY SHOW HOW OUTMODED THE BRITISH CLASS SYSTEM IS

This proposition is based on a lie about the reactions of the royal family and a misrepresentation about the way the aristocracy express their feelings. If there is unbreakable hardness of heart to be seen in modern society then one will find it within the towering walls of the media empires that oversee the social layers below them.

SLAVISH DEVOTION TO DUTY — THE ROYAL FAMILY

The royal family have shown during the years that they follow the wishes of the majority of the British people with regard to the centuries-old royal traditions. The way they have carried out their responsibilities has hardly been 'slavish' and 'unbending'. The film footage of the many royal walkabouts to meet the people is testimony.

The Queen and royal family have always done this in a willing and friendly manner. The Queen, even on formal occasions where she is expected to act as the personification of the nation, comes across as warm and considerate. Her popularity through the many years is proof. You see, during the week following Diana's death it was easy to paint the royal family as slavishly following protocol and duty. They were preoccupied with the tragedy and the grief of the young princes. It was easy to set up the royal family as slavishly following duty when the unusual circumstances and the vast numbers of people involved required time to form a complex plan of management. We all know how easy it is to blacken and denigrate the best intentions in the world.

THE PUBLIC PERSONAS OF PRINCE CHARLES AND HIS FATHER: STIFF AND UNBENDING

Notice how the editorial speaks of 'public personas' but goes on to criticise Charles and his father for personal failings. The appearance of both men in formal situations where a certain behaviour is expected by the majority of people in conformity with tradition or a proper sense of the occasion is extended to their personal characters. It is the contemptible tactic of applying one mode of behaviour to circumstances where another mode of behaviour is expected. It is like criticising a solemn Hindu ceremony for not including hard rock music. This is not all. Both Charles and Philip, because they *allegedly* did not 'utter simple expressions of compassion' at the time and place desired by Murdoch's men, are condemned 'as relevant as a dodo to today's generation'. Later much is made of Diana's comment that she found Prince Charles 'middle-aged' during their marriage.

Leaving aside the circumstances of this comment and the mouth from which it issued (see below), we have here as much discrimination against age and generational attitude as one could find. Such discrimination in an ideologically undesirable person would have teams of people running to the anti-discrimination board. The grand charge of 'irrelevance' is serious indeed. But to take a narrow section of the community (i.e. the young, the unstable, the bored, etc.) as the standard of relevance is a bit much. And to dismiss middle-aged people as having nothing 'relevant' to say and do in society is the grossest bigotry. Finally, we must grasp for words to describe the attempt to set up an opposition between steady, responsible, 'middle-aged' behaviour on the one hand, and humanity, compassion and social 'relevance' on the other. One would not get away with this if one did not belong to a ruling elite.

SLAVISH DEVOTION TO DUTY — THE UPPER CLASS

The term 'upper class' is a general catch-cry and weapon for those wanting to whip up envy and resentment against the people they want to remove from power. The people of the Murdoch empire, conspicuously among the most privileged and powerful on an international level, want to remove from power any person and any organisation that stands in the way of their expanding empire. The English upper class, with all their perceived traditions, manners and privileges, are a continuing source of bitterness for the authoriphobic, and must remain a prized target. But the upper class in Britain has long been in a state of decline in all respects. What the editorial writer is concentrating on here is the sense of duty and honour that was the ideal of 18th century British society, vestiges of which still remain in our crumbling social structure.

For people without any fixed standards of morality whose only guide is self-gratification, particularly in the form of power and position, the 18th century gentleman's code is an anathema. That code places decency, honour, respect and duty before the money-grubbing, power-seeking scramble of the modern elite. The modernisation of society or the making 'relevant' is the process of removing all standards from the mind so that the basest inclinations are susceptible to manipulation. The men of the *Disgusting Empire* are busy writing a 'George Costanza'[2] screenplay for the coming international society where a world of weak, spineless, aimless, despairing, self-indulgent people can rise in the morning to find their gratification in a cinema owned by the *Disgusting Empire*, in a TV show owned by the *Disgusting Empire*, in a sport stadium and sport teams owned by the *Disgusting Empire*, in a word, in all the forms of self-gratification all owned by the *Disgusting Empire* and its subsidiaries.

PRINCESS DIANA AS THE MODERNISER OF THE MONARCHY

There is no evidence that Diana had any genuine political agenda with regard to the monarchy. Diana's warmth and empathy with fellow-sufferers was the best side of her character. She acted out her role as the Queen of Hearts on the personal level, all the time calling for a conversion of heart in others. She continually showed herself politically naive and philosophically ignorant. And she admitted it. The raising of Diana to the role of political innovator or social reformer is merely another cynical tactic to undermine the monarchy.

To modernise the monarchy in the way envisaged by the theoretic-republican mind is to have no monarchy at all. Under their plan, the *appearance* of the royal family would be allowed to remain. What would go is all the privilege, wealth and property the royals have, and the theoretic-republicans don't have. Also gone would be the non-material world of national tradition and fellow-feeling, the soul of the people. In this scheme the Queen would be just another woman dressed up as the Queen to amuse the public who happen to display some interest in the history of Great Britain. At night the person who played the Queen would be sent home to an apartment in the suburbs. Buckingham Palace would become a gigantic theme park housing the departments of the *Disgusting Empire*. In one office would be the co-ordinator of royalty amusement, down the hall would be the office for children's TV, across from that the office for adult movies, down further the office for pornography, and so on. There would the educational theatres, one for creative scriptwriting for news, another for acting and image for TV reporting, and so on. All offices would be morally equal, that is, morally neutral. They would be valued on the basis of their revenue-generating power and their strength on the stock markets of the world. The Queen and the royal family could have a very comfortable existence under this scheme. For a start, the hounds of hell would be called off.

DIANA THE RELEVANT ROLE MODEL

Diana's open, warm manner was a general example for all. So was her concern for the suffering of others. These were personal qualities that everyone could admire whatever their preference for a particular form of government. It was right and admirable that Diana was concerned with passing these qualities on to her children. But, you see, so was Charles in his way concerned with passing on these qualities. Charles and Diana had no disputes over the children and shared in their upbringing, as the evidence makes clear. Their different characters actually were of great benefit to the princes. Charles had a 'warm, loving relationship with his sons' but provided a complementary example to his sons, and continues to do so. The passing of one year since

Diana's death contradicts all the malice directed at Charles by the media about how the princes would be educated. William and Harry earned the admiration of all through the courage and dignity they displayed during their mother's funeral. They have shown the extent of affection and respect they have for their father and grandparents. And they have retained the affection of the people. All this is the result of the family influence around them and not just of Diana. The crucial point is that they have not suffered from exposure to Diana's bad side. It is this bad side that Murdoch's people want sanctified and systematised in a program of education for the 'people'.

Diana, as her brother said in his funeral oration, was 'a very insecure person at heart with deep feelings of unworthiness'. She came emotionally damaged into her marriage with Charles, into her relationship with the royal family, and later put it on full display in the public domain. The episodes that were governed by her bouts of emotional imbalance mostly brought more misery to herself and those close to her. The editorial not only recognises the personal harm it brought her but eulogises the imbalance and the appeal it had to people similarly stricken.

It recognises that people are no longer attracted by the moral qualities of great people but have been brought down to the level where their wounded and scattered feelings find relief in gossip, in weak and shallow people, in glitter, and in fads. No doubt Diana connected with such people and their feelings. This earned her affection, too. But recognising a mutual misery is one thing; it is another to want to sanctify the causes and circumstances of that misery and impose it on the community. This is what Murdoch's people evidently want.

The recognition of the problem for them is not reason to correct it in order to make people happy; it is reason to claim the Queen and the royal family preside over the foundations of that misery and do not care about the unhappiness of the people. It is reason to say the Queen fails to recognise the mood of the people. It is reason to spread the malicious lie that the Queen is not in tune with the people, that the royal family is not 'relevant', that it must be feared that they will instil the same uncaring attitudes in the princes, and that there is now serious debate about the future of the monarchy! To eulogise the misery of the people, to promote its causes and then make the gigantic leap to the questionable future of the monarchy, is only something the all-powerful would dare.

It is not only a rational scrutiny of this particular editorial that will show up all the lies, distortions and manipulations it is guilty of, but time itself has shown that the princes love their father and grandparents, that they are happy and well-adjusted under their care, and that the people of Britain have high regard and affection for the Queen and Prince Charles also.

The media have regularly reported the ill-feeling Prince William has for the media because of the way they treated his mother. You can be sure that that ill-feeling has been raised several degrees by the malice shown towards his father and grandparents on the occasion of his mother's tragic death. But no one at this time has mentioned Prince Harry and the way he feels. What conclusions could be drawn from observing his behaviour in the TV images of that week? We saw a young red-headed lad with a look of determination when he appeared in formal circumstances. He walked out ahead of his male family members at the funeral. It looked deliberate. It looked like a challenge. In a less formal occasion he has studiously displayed affection for his father.[3] There are signs that this prince not only shares the contempt most decent people have for the media, but also that he will do something about it. I wonder what would lie in the future for a young prince with the spirit and moral strength of Shakespeare's Henry V.

While Murdoch's people were busy composing this malicious piece for the Saturday edition of *The Australian*, the young princes, their father and grandparents appeared before the gates of Balmoral Castle and later at Kensington Palace and Buckingham Palace. The warm reception given them and shown extensively on TV reports was hardly mentioned by *The Australian* in the following editions. The one brief report of the royal family's appearance to inspect the floral tributes to Diana was in the present edition (p. 11, 6 September). Nicholas Watt gives his account of the visit to inspect the floral tributes laid at the gates to Balmoral Castle. It was here that Prince Charles walked with Prince Harry clutching his hand. Harry pointed out the following handwritten message attached to a bouquet of flowers:

> *Diana, Princess of Wales, was a truly remarkable, vibrant, young woman, taken most tragically in the prime of her life. Grief will be both private and personal and as sons of this courageous, compassionate sister of mercy I hope they will stand strong and proud and as befitting young princes.*

SATURDAY, 6 SEPTEMBER 1997: **199**

This brief message says as much as need be said to dismiss the whole media campaign against the royal family. It was from Ann and Bob Blackery, of Benfleet, Essex. Ann and Bob's feelings were representative of everyone in Britain and around the world who had a heart and sympathy for those in distress. They recognised the tragedy and its meaning for the people connected with Diana. They knew that the loss of a dear one cuts hard and deep in a way that is uniquely personal. Grief is essentially personal and private. It would be a good thing if Murdoch's vassals could be sent to people such as Ann and Bob Blackery of Benfleet for some fundamental lessons in decency. But you need a heart for that. These people have a black space where the heart should be.

That the media take up canonised additions to the media scriptures in the face of contradictory evidence was well demonstrated in the days following the funeral. I will look briefly at two reports in the *International Express* (10-16 September, Australian Edition) dealing with the visits by the Queen, Prince Philip, Prince Charles and the two young princes to the floral tributes outside Buckingham Palace and Kensington Palace. The first report (pp. 32-33) by Sean Rayment is introduced with this headline:

SORRY YOU'VE HAD TO WAIT SO LONG

The report is generally sympathetic to the Queen. It acknowledges her calming effect on the crowd around the Buckingham Palace gates and the warm affection shown her, but it is all reported within the established media view that the Queen had done the wrong thing by 'hiding' away in Balmoral. She was now making up for her hard-heartedness.

> *In previous days, the people had pleaded with the royal family, and in particular the Queen, to give a public show of emotion.*
>
> *However, any feelings of disappointment over their lack of response evaporated at 2.40 pm with the arrival of the monarch.*
>
> *Whatever wound had been caused by the Royal Family's insistence on remaining at Balmoral and keeping its silence, was healed in a gesture that will not be forgotten.*

Remember Dr Starkey saying that he sniffed revolution in the air? — so angry were the people that the royal family had in their cold wicked way retreated into the luxury of Balmoral Castle and ignored the tender feelings of the public. That crowd who had been compared to the seething mobs that stormed the Bastille had now suddenly become pussycats purring in delight in the presence of the Queen.

When the Queen and Prince Philip descended from their car at the gates of Buckingham Palace there was quiet but instant applause. This was strange behaviour for an incipient revolution. Rayment struggled to get the message across that the Queen had erred badly in 'ignoring the feelings of the people'. He did his best to find people who would serve the purpose. But the best he could get was that it was 'important' for the Queen to share the grief of the people. He found someone who did not think the applause was appropriate because the day was Diana's. Otherwise he was obliged to report deep appreciation and affection for the Queen. Send in a thousand talented Murdoch editorial writers, it could not be ignored. Rayment quotes Alice Smith from Purley, south London:

> *I wanted to see the Queen and pay my respects. You only needed to look at her face to see that she is a woman consumed with grief.*
>
> *I have always believed that the problem with the Royal Family is that they have become public property.*
>
> *But in moments like this they have wanted their privacy and I think that fact has been misunderstood by a lot of people who seem to think they don't care.*

It's not that people think they don't care. Unfortunately, despite her true feelings about the circumstances, Alice Smith had been fooled by the media campaign. Most people felt the way she did. They understood the grief the royal family was suffering and fully appreciated their wanting to attend to the welfare of the princes in private. Later at Kensington Palace, Sasha Moyes '28, a physiotherapist', is quoted as saying:

> *She [the Queen] looked genuinely upset. She said the boys were the important thing and I think that is what everyone thinks.*

Sasha Moyes, supposedly of the generation that thinks the royal family is 'irrelevant and insensitive', is quite right. Normal feeling people of whatever generation and age agree with her about the propriety of the Queen's action in attending first to the needs of the young princes.

The Queen had spoken to Ms Moyes after she and Prince Philip had spent 15 minutes in private in the Royal Chapel at Kensington Palace where Diana's body lay. She was 'red-eyed but composed' when she emerged from her prayers. She spoke first to Fred Coltworthy, who handed her a red rose. He related the meeting in this way:

> *She asked me how long I had been waiting and said she was sorry it had taken so long ... I replied don't be sorry. I didn't think I would see her today. It was a bonus.*
>
> *I gave her the flower. I had brought it for Diana. I wanted to give it to the Queen, so she didn't think we were all against her.*

Well, Fred, most of us weren't against her but understood her anguish. It was only those with their predetermined political and commercial agenda who were against her. The headline of this report (SORRY YOU'VE HAD TO WAIT SO LONG) gave the impression that the Queen was sorry she and her feelingless family had not paid attention to the 'grieving public' sooner. Fred's words make it clear that the 'sorry' was in a totally different context. Indeed, it was not an apology for some fault. It was an expression of regret that people had to wait so long to sign the condolence book. The circumstances were such that little could be done about it — not by anybody. Another example of the easy misrepresentation the media indulges in. Such obvious falsifications are part of the job for these people.

Over the page of this edition of the *International Express* (pp. 34-5), Tobyn Andreae gives his account of the visit by Prince Charles and Princes William and Harry to Kensington Palace. The people's mood was of warmth and excitement. Much affection and sympathy were shown the three princes, especially William and Harry. All who saw and spoke with the young princes praised their courage and dignity in dealing with their mother's death. This would be a constant refrain. The princes were brave and dignified in their behaviour. Again, it was evident that most people did not agree with Murdoch's people that the princes should be *given a chance* to let it all hang out and not be subjected to the 'stiff and unbending' regime of their father and grandfather who were 'as relevant as the dodo to today's generation'. The young princes prefer the example of their father and grandfather and not that of George Costanza. Andreae's report must also be constrained by the evidence of the circumstances. Nevertheless, he still manages to throw in the following:

> *The unprecedented gesture [of the princes' visit] served as confirmation that the Royal Family have bowed to public pressure in the wake of Diana's death to adopt a more personal front to their grief.*

Yes, it is true they were forced to take action by a successful media campaign against them. The rest is based on lies and malice. The Queen appeared on TV in Britain that evening to refute the Murdoch propaganda not only by her words but by her very appearance. The appearance was of royalty, but it was also of an essentially good woman radiating essential goodness. Here's what she said:

> *Since last Sunday's dreadful news we have seen throughout Britain and around the world an overwhelming expression of sadness for Diana's death.*
> *We have all been trying, in our different ways, to cope.*
> *It is not easy to express the sense of loss.*
> *The initial shock is often succeeded by a mixture of other feelings — disbelief, incomprehension, anger, and concern for those who remain. We have all felt those emotions in these last few days.*
> *So what I say to you now, as your Queen and as a grandmother, I say from my heart.*
> *First, I want to pay tribute to Diana myself. She was an exceptional and gifted human being.*
> *In good times and bad she never lost her capacity to smile and laugh, nor to inspire others with her warmth and kindness.*
> *I admired and respected her for her energy and commitment to others, and especially for her devotion to her two boys.*
> *This week at Balmoral we have all been trying to help William and Harry come to terms with the devastating loss that they and the rest of us have suffered.*
> *No one who knew Diana will ever forget her.*
> *Millions of others who never met her but felt they knew her will remember her.*
> *I for one believe there are lessons to be drawn from her life and from the extraordinary and moving reaction to her death.*

I share in your determination to cherish her memory.

This is also an opportunity for me, on behalf of my family, and especially Prince Charles and William and Harry, to thank all of you who have brought flowers, sent messages and paid your respects in so many ways to a remarkable person.

These acts of kindness have been a huge source of help and comfort.

Our thoughts are also with Diana's family and the families of those who died with her.

I know that they, too, have drawn strength from what has happened since last weekend as they seek to heal their sorrow and then to face the future without a loved one.

I hope that tomorrow we can all, wherever we are, join in expressing our grief at Diana's loss and gratitude for her all-too-short life. It is a chance to show the whole world the British nation united in grief and respect.

May those who died rest in peace and may we, each and every one of us, thank God for the someone who made many, many people happy.

There would be few people in public life who could project such dignity and warmth in response to the malice directed at them and their family. There would be few people who could fulfil their national responsibilities as the Queen did when their closest family members had been struck down in such a tragic way. There were few who could have in the circumstances projected such an aura of statesmanship. It was a worthy prelude to the funeral that was to take place on the following day.

9

The Funeral

1. The Funeral Procession

I sat before the TV for more than three hours on Saturday evening, 6 September 1997, watching the funeral of Diana, Princess of Wales. I was away on business in sunny Queensland. As I sat that evening on the ninth floor of a beachfront apartment overlooking Burleigh Heads surf beach, I could hear the occasional rush of the surf mixing with the steady clopping of hooves on stone, the constant rattle and jangle of straps and buckles, and the faint murmur above the people watching mostly in silence. The rushing of the white water on a dark deserted beach on the other side of the world seemed to blend with the quiet progression of the funeral gun carriage pulled by six black thoroughbreds as it made its way to Westminster Abbey, shrine to all those whose mother tongue is English and who are part of the Christian tradition. But we Australians, who are first cousins to the people of the British Isles, felt particularly drawn in. You see, the force of centuries-old tradition has a deeper pull in the end than the scraps of paper waved continually in our faces by the philosophers of innovation and envy. I sat alone in that apartment in Queensland but I knew I was watching in solidarity with most of the country.

From the moment Diana's casket appeared on the TV screen draped in the Royal Standard we were locked into the solemnity of the occasion and into reflecting on our own feelings about Diana's life and the meaning of her ghastly end. On the face of it, what was there to keep our attention? A casket draped in the Royal Standard, a gun carriage drawn by six black horses flanked by soldiers from the King's

Troop and the Welsh Guards, all moving slowly from Kensington Palace? Even those who did not know the exact meaning of the colours and emblems on the Royal Standard, of the blue and gold braid of the King's Troop and of the scarlet of the Welsh Guard with their high black fur helmets, understood the significance of it all, and understood the depth of its meaning.

We accompanied that gun carriage in spirit as it slowly and solemnly made its way past places and features commemorating some of the greatest moments in the history of the people of the British Isles, and of those sharing a close cultural relationship with that history and its people. We made our way in spirit along Kensington Road, along Hyde Park, and past Constitution Hill. We collected Prince Charles, Prince Philip, Princes William and Harry, and Earl Spencer at St James's Palace. We felt the heavy heart of Prince Charles, we admired the courage and dignity of the young princes, William and Harry, walking behind the coffin containing their mother. We saw with surprise how Prince Harry walked out ahead of the royal group. We felt the deep, quiet grief of the thousands of people lining the streets. We heard the constant tolling of the bell of Westminster Abbey drawing us closer and closer. We stopped with Charles and his sons as the casket containing Diana was slowly and carefully taken from the gun carriage by the Welsh Guards and carried between the respectful silence of the dignitaries lining the aisle of Westminster Abbey. We caught the grief on the face of the Queen and saw her quickly wipe the tears away from her eyes. We saw Prince Charles with his sons standing briefly before the coffin. Prince Charles placed a wreath of flowers in front of it and made the sign of the cross before he and his sons resumed their places. Then came the Christian ceremony itself.

2. The Media Responds to the Solemn Occasion

What were the members of the media thinking at this time? Well, the last thing they were contemplating was the spiritual nature of the funeral. Their campaign was foremost in their minds and they were searching for creative ways to turn the event to their advantage. There is no Sunday edition of *The Australian*. It was left to other media instruments in Australia to take over the baton from the Murdoch people. Here is one example of the way the media pursued the week's campaign. After describing the reactions of the people as the funeral cortege made its way to Westminster Abbey, the leading report by staff reporters of *The Sunday Sun-Herald,* 7 September 1997, makes this observation:

> *The only show of genuine emotion before the Westminster Abbey service came from Earl Spencer. As the Princess's brother walked alongside Prince Harry onto Horseguard Parade, and beneath its ceremonial arch, he put his arm around Harry's shoulder then squeezed it, before returning it, limp, once more to his side. It was a brief gesture of solidarity but it spoke volumes for the difference between the Royal Family approach to public grieving and that of other people.*
>
> *Prince Charles and the Duke of Edinburgh looked straight ahead for the entire journey, neither gesturing nor acknowledging people lining the route. Nor did they openly seek to console one another.*
>
> *The Queen also looked to control her emotions as she entered Westminster Abbey before the coffin. Her stony features were a mile away from the smiling, warm face we remember of the former daughter-in-law she was about to farewell.*

This is a wonderful example of the lies, hypocrisy and intolerance the theoretic-republican media are so good at expressing. In the general reporting of the funeral it can be multiplied a thousand times by a thousand different media lackeys. *The Sun-Herald* gives a list of the staff names who contributed to the reports of the funeral. I will not include them here. They are merely the servants of the media bosses who prescribe what is to be written and the manner in which it is to be written. It seems nobody in our community is more in thrall to the systems of arbitrary authority than the humble staff reporter — who is driven from the empire if he does not toe the line. I have watched a tape of Diana's funeral several times, so I can tell the reader what actually happened when Prince Charles, Princes William and Harry, Prince Philip, and Earl Spencer walked beneath the ceremonial arch of the Horseguard Parade.

To start with, it was obvious from their actions that none of the group thought they were visible to the public. They thought they were temporarily shielded from the public gaze by the shade, the length and the relatively shallow height of the arch. They clearly did not know there was a camera fixed to the roof of the arch at their entrance end, and which swivelled to follow their every movement. Here's what happened. As the group entered under the arch Prince Charles could be seen leaning towards Harry and speaking to him. Harry seems to respond and then looks across at William. At this point, Earl Spencer's attention is drawn to Harry. In a quick gesture he gives Harry a couple of comforting taps on his left shoulder. Harry does not respond. While this is happening William appears to lean towards Prince Philip. It is not clear whether the Duke or Prince William spoke first. Prince Philip gives William a solid pat on the back and continues to talk, waving his right arm to emphasise what he is saying. As the group emerges at the other end Prince Charles is still speaking to Harry. They then resume their dignified demeanour. Try as they might, *The Sun-Herald* could not distort the actual scenario to give the propagandist contrast they were wanting. The fabrication is dependent upon the scenario being a short interlude in a long broadcast which many readers would not have seen, and those watching would not remember.

Let me also add that in the *International Express* edition of 10-16 September 1997, there is a photo of Prince Charles, Prince William and Prince Harry waiting for the funeral cortege outside the gates of St James's Palace. Prince Charles with a concerned expression has his arm around Prince Harry's shoulder. He is clearly speaking words of comfort to his sons. This was in the full view of thousands of bystanders and the worldwide audience. It is no rare gesture of affection by Charles for his sons. There is plenty of evidence of Charles's affectionate nature, particularly when it concerns his sons. There is also plenty of evidence of the young princes' love and respect for their father — a father who is far from cold and feelingless *when it matters*. I will quote a recent report about the relationship of Prince William with his father. The report is from 'Sky News' (London), 20 June 1998.

> *[When Prince Charles and his two sons arrived at Kensington Palace on the eve of Diana's funeral to inspect the floral tributes, many people were] struck by the dignity of [William] and the closeness with his father [Prince Charles], a relationship that in the last year has been nourished like never before.*

Charles Rae of *The Sun* (London) came on camera to say:

> *William has always been close to his father. It's not a publicity stunt. What we are seeing now is that closeness reflected in public.*

It is a great pity that Charles Rae of *The Sun* did not prevail upon his colleagues at the time to stop their campaign of malice when the truth about Prince Charles, his character and his relationship with his sons *was known* to be very different.[1] It was not part of the media mythology.

As for the criticism of the royal family, particularly the Queen, for not showing the 'appropriate' feelings, this is pure hypocrisy and double-dealing. In the same edition of *The Sun-Herald* there is plenty of praise for the dignity and courage shown by the young princes during the funeral. Why not for the other members of the royal family? Why condemn one group for a certain mode of behaviour and praise others for the same? Why condemn it in the royal family and not even notice it in just about everybody else who took part in the funeral ceremonies? This is malicious. Why condemn the Queen for her 'stony' expressions when she was crushed with grief for her family and was attending a solemn ceremony as the highest representative of the realm? Most of us did not want the media scriptwriters' prescription for a George Costanza mode of behaviour on that occasion. And we can only be revolted by the attempt to contrast the Queen's expression during the funeral with the expression and manner of Diana in her full glory. This is to say nothing about the 'modern', 'open', 'flexible' attitudes the media prescribe (and presumably portray) and the royal family don't. Would not a 'modern attitude' allow for different ways of expressing grief? It is no problem for the cultural relativists and moral subjectivists of the media to display a double standard. Playing the double-standard game is their specialty.

A final point in this example of media dishonesty is that the Queen did not wear a 'stony expression' during the Requiem for Diana. Her manner and expressions reflected the way most of us would act in similar circumstances. She was dignified, reflective, quietly grieving, and occasionally showing the outside world her feelings with a tear and a pained expression. Those people who applauded the Queen as she arrived at Westminster Abbey would have understood and sympathised with the Queen's personal feelings of grief and concern for her son and grandchildren. The greatest display of hard-heartedness on the occasion of Diana's funeral came from the representatives of the media, and from nobody else. And it came dressed up as mock obsequiousness, false concern and hollow hand-over-the-heart sympathy.

3. The Christian Ceremony to Honour the Passing of a Member of a Christian Royal House

The Sunday Sun-Herald's report was far from alone in carrying on the campaign of character assassination the people from Murdoch's empire are so expert in. This hateful campaign was particularly evident when it came to the actual funeral ceremony to mourn and commemorate the tragic death of Diana. Whose behaviour during that week was truly consistent with the Christian burial ritual about to take place in the thousand-year-old Westminster Abbey? The royal family's or the irreligious prescribers of religious duty among the hypocritical media? The Dean of Westminster Abbey opened up the solemn ceremony with the common Christian supplication for the repose of the soul of the departed one.

> *We are gathered here in Westminster Abbey to give thanks for the life of Diana, Princess of Wales. To commend her soul to Almighty God and to seek his comfort for all who mourn. We particularly pray for God's restoring peace and loving presence with her children, Princes William and Harry, and all her family.*

When the Queen and the royal family attended church during the week this was just what they were doing. They did not need religious guidance from the soulless media hacks in dealing with their grief. They did not need religious guidance from the liars of the media empires.

The ceremony itself was a fitting tribute to Diana. It would have tested the media's ingenuity to turn it to their advantage. Earl Spencer's funeral oration saved them from that test. Here was the occasion for the media bosses to go to work with relish. There must have been feelings of pure joy in the media citadels as they listened. There was so much in Earl Spencer's words that they could exploit for months to come.

4. Earl Spencer's Eulogy for a Beloved Sister

I will reproduce the full text of Earl Spencer's speech and highlight in bold type those parts that indicate the Earl's intent, describe Diana's essential character, and contradict the campaign the media fabricated around the speech. I will show how the media yet again on the most sensitive of occasions twisted, distorted and misrepresented an event for their political and material gain.

I stand before you today the representative of a family in grief, in a country in mourning, before a world in shock. We are all united, not only in our desire to pay our respects to Diana, but rather in our need to do so.

For such was her extraordinary appeal that the tens of millions of people taking part in this service all over the world via television and radio who never actually met her, feel that they too lost someone close to them in the early hours of Sunday morning. It is a more remarkable tribute to Diana than I can ever hope to offer her today.

Diana was the very essence of compassion, of duty, of style, of beauty. *All over the world she was a **symbol of selfless humanity.** All over the world, a standard bearer for the rights of the truly down-trodden, a very British girl who transcended nationality.* ***Someone with natural nobility, who was classless*** *and who proved in the last year that she needed no royal title to continue to generate her particular brand of magic.*

Today is our chance to say thank you for the way you brightened our lives, even though God granted you but half a life. We will all feel cheated always that you were taken from us so young and yet we must learn to be grateful that you came along at all. Only now that you are gone do we truly appreciate what we are now without and we want you to know that life without you is very, very difficult.

We have all despaired at our loss over the past week and only the strength of the message you gave us through your years of giving has afforded us the strength to move forward.

*There is a temptation to rush to canonise your memory. There is no need to do so. You stand tall enough as a **human being of unique qualities not to need to be seen as a saint.** Indeed to sanctify your memory would be to miss out on the very core of your being, your wonderfully mischievous sense of humour, with a laugh that bent you double.*

Your joy for life transmitted wherever you took your smile and the sparkle in those unforgettable eyes. Your boundless energy which you could hardly contain.

*But **your greatest gift was your intuition** and it was a gift you used wisely. This is what underpinned all your other wonderful at-*

tributes and if we look **to analyse what it was about you that had such a wide appeal we find it in your instinctive feel for what was really important in all our lives.**

Without your God-given sensitivity we would be immersed in greater ignorance at the anguish of AIDS and HIV sufferers, the plight of the homeless, the isolation of lepers, the random destruction of landmines.

Diana explained to me once that it was **her innermost feelings of suffering that made it possible for her to connect with her constituency of the rejected.**

And here we come to another truth about her. For all the status, the glamour, the applause, Diana **remained throughout a very insecure person at heart, almost childlike in her desire to do good for others so she could release herself from the deep feelings of unworthiness,** *of which her eating disorders were merely a symptom.*

The world sensed this part of her character and cherished her for her vulnerability whilst admiring her for her honesty.

The last time I saw Diana was on July 1, her birthday, in London, when typically she was not taking time to celebrate her special day with friends but was guest of honour at a special charity fundraising evening. She sparkled of course, but I would rather cherish the days I spent with her in March when she came to visit me and my children in our home in South Africa.

I am proud of the fact that, apart from when she was on display meeting President Mandela, we managed **to contrive to stop the ever-present paparazzi from getting a single picture of her** *— that* **meant a lot to her.**

These were days I will always treasure. It was as if we had been transported back to our childhood, when we spent such an enormous amount of time together — the two youngest in the family.

Fundamentally she had not changed at all from the big sister who mothered me as a baby, fought with me at school and endured those long train journeys between our parents' homes with me at weekends. It is **a tribute to her level-headedness and strength that, despite the most bizarre life imaginable after her childhood, she remained intact, true to herself.**

There is no doubt that she was looking for a new direction in her life at this time. **She talked endlessly of getting away from England, mainly because of the treatment she received at the** *hands of the newspapers.*

I don't think she ever understood why her genuinely good intentions were sneered at by the media, why there appeared to be a permanent quest on their behalf to bring her down. It is baffling.

My own and only explanation is that genuine goodness is threatening to those at the opposite end of the moral spectrum. *It is a point to remember that of all the ironies about Diana, perhaps the greatest was this — a girl given the name of the ancient goddess of hunting was, **in the end, the most hunted person of the modern age.***

She would want us today to pledge ourselves to protecting her beloved boys William and Harry from a similar fate and I do this here, Diana, on your behalf. We will not allow them to suffer the anguish that used regularly to drive you to tearful despair.

And beyond that, on behalf of your mother and sisters, I pledge that we, your blood family, will do all we can to continue the imaginative, loving way in which you were steering these two exceptional young men, so that their souls are not simply immersed by duty and tradition but can sing openly as you planned.

We fully respect the heritage into which they have both been born and will always respect and encourage them in their royal role *but we, like you, recognise the need for them to experience as many different aspects of life as possible to arm them spiritually and emotionally for the years ahead. I know you would have expected nothing less from us.*

William and Harry, we all cared desperately for you today. We are all chewed up with the sadness at the loss of a woman who was not even our mother. How great your suffering is, we cannot even imagine.

I would like to end by thanking God for the small mercies he has shown us at this dreadful time. For taking Diana at her most beautiful and radiant and when she had joy in her private life. Above all we give thanks for the life of a woman I am so proud to be able to call my sister, the unique, the complex, the extraordinary and irreplaceable Diana whose beauty, both internal and external, will never be extinguished from our minds.

This was a wonderful tribute to Diana. It is the sort of speech only a loving brother who shared some of her deeply disturbing experiences could give. Its basic structure is an analysis of her complex character, what it meant to those close to her and the world at large, the misery she suffered at the hands of the media, the causes of that suffering, and the undertakings of a brother to his dead sister. We can track the progression of Earl Spencer's thoughts.

- The world unites to mourn the death of a unique person.
- Diana's uniqueness was in her honesty of feeling.
- She put her feelings for humanity above all else.
- This unique character gave her a *natural nobility* that was accompanied by a natural appeal to people of all classes.
- Diana's life was beset nevertheless with feelings of insecurity and unworthiness. This was one cause of her suffering.
- The other causes: the abuse and misrepresentation of her feelings and intentions by a feelingless media; the unrelenting intrusion of the media into her life.
- Earl Spencer found the attitude of the media baffling. His only explanation was that the media were at the other end of the moral spectrum. They were evil.
- The suffering caused by the media was so great that Diana was contemplating leaving Britain.
- Earl Spencer undertook to prevent the William and Harry suffering the same fate.
- He had full respect for their royal background and all it entailed. But he would ensure their education followed the lines indicated by Diana.

Let's now see how the Monday, 8 September edition of *The Australian* dealt with the funeral and Earl Spencer's speech. The front-page headline immediately provides the theme for *The Australian's* coverage.

Princess at peace, families at war

Ean Higgins again has the honour of composing the edition's lead story. The front-page soapie headline is repeated to introduce his 're-port': **Queen, Earl feud over fate of princes.** The reader can now detect a certain careless thrill to Higgins's writing. He knows his star is soaring because of the week's efforts. He knows his masters are pleased. The first two paragraphs are a credit to his spirit and enthusiasm for the task.

Bitterness between the royal family and one of Britain's most eminent dynasties deepened last night as the feud over the future of princes William and Harry posed a new crisis for the British monarchy.

The Queen was said to be outraged at an extraordinary attack by Diana's brother, Charles Spencer, who used the princess's funeral to warn that her "blood family" would protect the sons from the suffocating strictures of royal tradition.

The major themes have been set for Higgins and he is now showing the flair of a senior scriptwriter for a sordid American soap opera where beautiful people with soulless expressions and trivial animosities go at each other's throats. He and his masters no longer give a damn how much their reporting wanders from the truth. He makes another appeal for support from his soul-mate, 'constitutional historian' David Starkey who, it seems, is permanently immersed in his revolutionary fantasies. Earl Spencer, according to Starkey, 'had sparked a "public tug of war" between the Spencer-Churchill clan and the House of Windsor'. The scenario becomes grander as the story progresses. Higgins then quotes the section of the speech where Earl Spencer undertook to continue Diana's education of her sons. He says that this 'visibly startled the Queen but [was] applauded by William and Harry'. Apart from showing the usual degree of malice, this latter claim is ludicrous and without any basis whatever. All the evidence of the princes' behaviour before, during and after the funeral indicates that if the young princes applauded any part of their uncle's speech it would certainly have been the part where the Earl claimed that people like Ean Higgins were 'at the other end of the moral spectrum' from their mother.

Higgins was not alone in the way he 'interpreted' Earl Spencer's speech. Just about every newspaper report and TV news bulletin I came across ran with the same line. In fact, in this present edition of *The Australian*, Cameron Forbes presents a sneering, creative version of the same 'interpretation'. Let me begin my response to Higgins's fabrication by quoting from a radio interview with Earl Spencer in South Africa. The contents of the interview were broadcast on 'Sky News', 8 November 1997.

Speaking on South African radio the Earl said he did not regret criticising the tabloids during his sister's funeral service in September.

He said the newspapers were despicable and evil ... He told the radio station in Capetown he 'was speaking from the heart when he addressed mourners at Diana's funeral'. He insisted it [his speech] had not been an attack on the royal family as some suggested at the time but he is still bitter about the British tabloid press. 'They want to destroy. They have no concept of the human soul. They are operating to increase circulation and to make their proprietors richer. If it means people committing suicide, being killed in any way or falling apart, having breakdowns or whatever, that's immaterial to them.'

These claims are consistent with the structure of Earl Spencer's speech as outlined above. The core elements of the speech were that Diana was a unique person with special gifts of intuition and feeling for the suffering of others; this unique character was hunted and tormented by a merciless media without any moral restraint whatever. A major part of the speech emphasised (if I may be permitted to use the Australian vernacular) what a pack of cruel, gutless bastards the media are collectively and how they are never constrained by a hint of moral principle in their actions. *It was from the fate suffered by Diana at the hands of the media that Earl Spencer especially undertook to protect the young princes.* This was the overwhelming commitment. All the elements of the speech were funnelled into this primary concern. If the princes were 'to sing openly', they would have to be especially protected in their royal duties from the ever-present, feelingless, amoral media. This is the most obvious meaning of Earl Spencer's words as they take their proper place in the structure of the speech. The great crowd in Hyde Park understood this and applauded spontaneously. They did *not* applaud the media distortion.

The contrast the media beat up between royal duty and singing openly is a trivial one in the circumstances, and not the main issue. Indeed, it was only a consideration by general implication. The undertaking to protect the princes from the same fate as Diana was the *negative* undertaking. The *positive* undertaking was the continuation of Diana's education of the princes. This meant to a large extent passing on the unique qualities Diana herself possessed. This positive undertaking did not entail a rejection of the character of the royal family nor a criticism of the royal state. Earl Spencer was emphatic in his respect for the princes' royal background and all that it meant ('We fully respect the heritage into which they have both been born and will always respect and encourage them in their royal role'). Further-more, the Queen and the royal family obviously do not want the princes immersed in royal duty either. Nor do they want *themselves* to be immersed in royal duty. They too want time to sing. The irony is that the manner in which they choose to 'sing' is a constant source of media criticism of the royal family. The Queen and Prince Charles before everybody else, including Earl Spencer, want the princes to have the opportunity to lead happy lives. The evidence for this is over-whelming.

On 28 June 1998, the Australian '60 minutes' program broadcast a story about Earl Spencer and his sister, Diana, which consisted of excerpts from the BBC program, 'Diana, A Birthday Tribute'. The 60 minutes presenter introduced the story with: 'He's [Earl Spencer] the man who rocked the royal family with a speech of passionate inten-sity at the funeral of his sister, Princess Diana ...' '60 minutes' highlighted the parts of the BBC program that centred on the words that, according to established media mythology, 'rocked the royal fam-ily'. The presenter, Sally Magnusson, repeating the titillating bits of the speech for the media ('blood family', 'immersed' in royal tradi-tion, and helping 'to sing openly'), said to Earl Spencer that it was surely a bit hard for Prince Charles to sit by and listen to the implicit accusation that he was incapable of bringing up his children in the proper manner. Earl Spencer replied:

Really, I was picking up on the magic of Diana. This was a tribute to Diana — a eulogy. I was not taking any swipes at anyone.

Earl Spencer's words are the accurate and sufficient reply to this charge. His reply is consistent with the structure of the eulogy and his often expressed intent of saying what he thought needed to be said. The reply was not satisfactory for the charming Scottish presenter who would have been briefed on what to ask and what to carry forward in the interview as media scripture. She showed she had learnt her les-sons well, for all the high points of the media campaign of nearly a year before were dutifully regurgitated. The dialogue proceeds in this manner (I have added emphasis):

PRESENTER: *But you can't say immersed in duty and tradition without realising it was loaded. You are a wordsmith. You understand what words mean ...*

EARL SPENCER: I don't back down from the words at all. **What I was saying was that Diana brought something to their lives that was quite different and wonderful. I was just offering in any way to her surviving family to help perpetuate that … I was just offering it to them.**

PRESENTER: By the time you stepped out of the Abbey you were being hailed on one hand as a national hero and, on the other, by some as a catalyst that might bring down the monarchy.

EARL SPENCER: Yes, right, obviously I was unaware of that.

PRESENTER: Was it a complete shock to you what was made of that speech?

EARL SPENCER: **I was pleased that I said what I said for Diana.** *And judging from the letters I kept from the public (I received 200, 000 letters) people were in agreement that it needed to be said.*

PRESENTER: You must have known it was dynamite.

EARL SPENCER: No, not at all.

PRESENTER: Well, you must be naive.

EARL SPENCER: No, I am not. I just wrote what I believed to be honestly true. **I support the Queen enormously, but individual members of the royal family I hardly know at all well.** *So although I respect their position, I genuinely do not know them. So I cannot have a strong opinion.* **The only members of the royal family I really know at any level of significance are my nephews and I am certainly not going to criticise their relatives.** *The point is they can be in no doubt that I am sincere in my wish to help them in any way they want and they'll be at an age soon when they will do what they want to do and see whoever they want to see. And if they see me as some sort of interfering uncle whom they don't want to see, I am sure they will make it very clear.*

This exchange with impromptu answers from Earl Spencer shows that he remains consistent to the end. The three pieces I have included here cohere exactly. The speech was to eulogise Diana. That was the positive aim. Intimately connected with an account of Diana's life was the torment she suffered at the hands of an evil media. But I know no matter how much evidence is produced to show the true nature of Earl Spencer's speech at Westminster Abbey, it will be simply disregarded by the media bosses. They will maintain the campaign until it can be shown that it is harmful to their material interests.

After the Earl had continually linked to Diana's misery the behaviour of people at the other end of the moral spectrum, and the crowd in Hyde Park had spontaneously showed their agreement by applauding, the media had to turn this into an attack on the royal family. Disregarded was the worldwide anger directed against the media, an anger that was constantly manifested in the streets by ordinary people during the week following Diana's death. *The Australian* reported this anger — even if it was to dismiss it as the product of emotional ignorant minds. Simon Jenkins meant to be ironic, but he was right to introduce his article with:

> *Bastards, reptiles, vultures, vermin, sewage in the gutters of the press. If I were a paparazzo, I would be keeping my head low today ... Behind the ghouls [paparazzi] lie other denizens of this underworld. The editors, picture editors, circulation managers, and bosses of the press have driven the market for the intrusive pictures ever higher.* (p.126)

The anger felt by the public towards the media found an eloquent expression in Earl Spencer's eulogy. That's why they applauded so spontaneously and warmly.

During the time of writing this book I told many people that I was examining media reports to show how the media groups were motivated by political and material interests and that no lie or distortion could be too big in attaining their goals. Everyone without exception congratulated me on the enterprise, wished me luck and said that it needed to be done. People all around the world would have warmly entered into the applause for Earl Spencer's attack on the media as people 'at the other end of the moral spectrum'. They knew who was responsible for Diana's death.

5. Higgins Completes his Propaganda Role for the Murdoch Empire

When we follow Higgins to pages 4 and 5 of the 8 September edition we are confronted with the double-page headline:

How the people stole her funeral

Under this childish notion, Higgins serves up a report headed: **Outrage translates into action**. The outrage of the people at the feelingless monarchy and the wicked Windsors translates into action to review the nature of the monarchy. Higgins calls in the academic for support:

> *Diana's death has, said London School of Economics political scientist Rodney Barker, brought out an unusual phenomenon in which Britons, collectively and individually, seem to be translating their particular sense of outrage for traditional authority into action …*
> *… many Britons believe that, somehow, Diana led them in death against an aloof and traditionalist style of monarchy they had always subconsciously opposed, but never had the courage to speak out about.*

We see how one fixed dogma of propaganda translates into further propagandist action and the creation of more dogma. We are not dealing with the strict logic of political argument here. We are dealing with the logic of human manipulation and power-broking. This is quite a different sort of logic. It is the logic of the media czars. It is the logic that has a use for the appearance of political discourse. That's why the compliant academic will be roped in to support the line. The action flowing from the 'outrage' is for the monarchy to 'modernise' and for there to be questions raised about Prince Charles's suitability as King. This theme will be taken up in the next day's edition of *The Australian*. The front-page report by Higgins for the 9 September edition is headed by: **Public turns on Charles: Long live King William**. According to Higgins public pressure was mounting to force Charles to relinquish his claim on the throne in favour of William and to introduce the sort of 'people's' monarchy Diana was establishing. This is all predictable stuff. The program is thoroughly transparent and I believe it's time for me to bring an end to my examination of one particular instrument of the Murdoch empire. I will only start repeating the same arguments with different details to demonstrate the same mentality and objectives. I will leave further and final confirmation of my arguments against Murdoch and his rapidly expanding empire to the next chapter.

6. Tony Blair Reads St Paul's Epistle on Charity

One of the highlights of the funeral ceremony for me was Prime Minister Tony Blair's reading of St Paul's discourse on charity taken from the First Epistle to the Corinthians. The Prime Minister read with feeling and eloquence. The King James's version added to the eloquence and solemnity of the thoughts. This is the idea of charity (Tony Blair substituted 'love') that applied to Diana. Diana in her best role was unselfconsciously charitable. She acted on those occasions without guile and without thought of self-advantage. This was her *true nobility*, as her brother said. It was this selfless, loving nature that the media could not fathom nor accept. The media were and remain the symbols in this context of the *anti-person*. I will finish with the passage Prime Minister Tony Blair read during the Requiem for Diana, Princess of Wales.

> *Though I speak with the tongues of men and of angels, and have not charity, I am become as sounding brass, or a tinkling cymbal.*
>
> *And though I have the gift of prophecy, and understand all mysteries, and all knowledge: and though I have all faith, so that I could remove mountains, and have not charity, I am nothing.*
>
> *And though I bestow all my goods to feed the poor, and though I give my body to be burned, and have not charity, it profiteth me nothing.*
>
> *Charity suffereth long, and is kind; charity envieth not: charity vaunteth not itself, is not puffed up.*
>
> *Doth not behave itself unseemly, seeketh not her own, is not easily provoked, thinketh no evil;*
>
> *Rejoiceth not in iniquity but rejoiceth in the truth;*
>
> *Beareth all things, believeth all things, hopeth all things, endureth all things.*
>
> *Charity never faileth; but whether there be prophecies, they shall fail; whether there be tongues, they shall cease; whether there be knowledge, it shall vanish away.*
>
> *For we know in part, and we prophecy in part.*
>
> *But when that which is perfect is come, then that which is in part shall be done away.*
>
> *When I was a child, I spake as a child, I understood as a child, I thought as a child; but when I became a man I put away childish things.*
>
> *For now we see through a glass, darkly; but then face to face; now*

I know in part; but then shall I know even as also I am known.

And now abideth faith, hope, charity, these three; but the greatest of these is charity.

I CORINTHIANS 13, 1-13

10

Royals, Reptiles and Rupert Murdoch

1. The Moral Storm of the 1960s Batters the Royal Family

During the first half of 1998, a series of three BBC programs entitled 'Royals and Reptiles', was shown on Australian TV. This was a fascinating series. It tracked the relationship between the British media (mainly the tabloids) and the British royal family. This series appeared when I was nearing the end of the first draft of this work. I was surprised and delighted to find so much confirmation of what I had written coming from the mouths of the media people themselves. The BBC had made them jump around like bumbling puppets unwittingly revealing themselves as they really are. It is well known that the chiefs of the BBC have a contempt for Rupert Murdoch and what they regard as his low vulgar activities. Was this a rare instance where the antagonism of one media organisation for another resulted in the baring of the horrible truth to the public? Whatever the case, the BBC produced a stunning documentary that let the people they were examining tell their own story. I propose to follow the course of the three programs concentrating on those parts that are especially pertinent to what I have written.

The program starts with the royal family in the 1950s. At this time there was an accepted code of behaviour for the media when it came to reporting their lives. This was to change in the 1960s. Ideas and political movements that had lived a dark subterranean existence until that point burst forth to capture the minds of the university campuses. I was there in 1964 and I have clear memories of the campus 'dialogue' and how its promoters were struggling to turn it into action. Hypocrisy and doubling dealing were cloaked in the glorious rhetoric of individual freedom. The great enemy of this 'moral' rhetoric was the traditional order with its ideas of morality and religion. In Britain, the highest family of the traditional order was the royal family. 'Royals and Reptiles' showed how the attacks on the royal family originating in satirical campus revues were successfully translated to the media at large. The royal family was advised to defend itself by making its members more accessible to the media outlets, particularly TV. A film was proposed and made about the royal family. Peregrine Worsthorne (Editor, *The Sunday Telegraph* 1986-9) criticised this course of action at the time. It would backfire. He said that the institution of the monarchy held a legitimate mystic and a semi-divine character in the minds of the people. To reduce the Queen and the royal institution to the level of mere human beings would remove this character and all that went with it. The royal family may be more popular in the short term but in the end popularity would turn into ridicule. He did not realise how prescient he was. The year of the royal media blitz was 1969.

2. Rupert Murdoch Arrives on the Scene

About the same time Rupert Murdoch bought two English newspapers: *News of the World* and *The Sun*. The viewer sees footage of a young Rupert Murdoch waltzing confidently down a London Street. Did anyone realise what sort of career path lay ahead of that man who still had an Australian passport? Harry Arnold (Royal Reporter, *The Sun* 1976-90) said Murdoch was completely outside the establishment, was not in awe of it and would not kowtow to the royal family. His instruction to his editors was to stop worshipping them. Stop treating them like gods. 'They are ordinary human beings and they will help to sell newspapers. Let's go out there and get the real stories.' The 'real' stories were whatever would help Murdoch advance his imperial ambitions. He now had two strong liege vassals who would bend to his every command.

Murdoch brought intense competition to Fleet Street. He brought the competition to the level of the reptiles that once crawled unhindered around the swamps on which the capital now stands. The tabloids dug into the private lives of the royal family and shovelled out anything that could have the appearance of dirt — especially dirt that was tainted with public funding. Big money was handed over for stories on the royal family that had the appearance of scandal. Murdoch turned *The News of the World* and *The Sun* into the highest selling newspapers in Britain.

Prince Charles found himself followed around the world by a growing bunch of photographers and journalists eagerly seeking to grab that picture and that headline to please their liege lord back in London. This group of media people was called the 'Royal Ratpack'. The speculation about who would marry Prince Charles was driven to a frenzy by their activities. No young female who came into contact with Charles was spared. Many of these young women were left bruised and humiliated by their contact with the crown prince. Prince Charles was appalled that he could not choose a wife without the intrusion of the media. Inevitably the pressure of the media activity and the royal family found Charles caught in a situation over which he had less and less control. Then Lady Diana Spencer appeared on the scene. Diana's appearance ended the first program. The second program started under the title of

UNLEASH THE GREYHOUNDS

3. The Murdoch Moral and Political Philosophy

In 1981 Rupert Murdoch bought *The Times* and *The Sunday Times*. Murdoch was asked by a reporter whether he was concerned about the evident difference in quality between the two sets of newspapers (*News of the World* and *The Sun* vs. *The Times* and *The Sunday Times*). Murdoch replied:

> *I don't consider there's any difference in quality. It's a matter of different papers for different publics.*

Murdoch's reply was highly significant. It told us about his moral vision, namely, he doesn't have one. At least not in the sense the ordinary person understands morality. A pornographic magazine would also be of the same quality. The advance of his empire was the only standard under which he would work. Murdoch told Peregrine Worsthorne that the establishment of the monarchy and the 'class system' in Britain inhibited the growth of the nation. In particular, he meant the growth of the Murdoch empire. Andrew Neill (Editor, *The Sunday Times* 1983-94) said there was no doubt where Murdoch's sympathies lay. He would 'get shot of them [the royals] tomorrow if he could'. Murdoch's sympathies lay with the Thatcher government. *The Sun* strenuously backed Thatcher and the free market, and sought to shake up class-bound Britain. Then Murdoch made another highly significant statement. This time it was about the political ethos of *The Sun*.

> *I don't think that* The Sun *is Tory at all. It is Thatcherite — which is something quite different. Tory is the conservatism, privilege and the old world; Thatcherism is change for a new world.*

Yes, change for a new order where there is a different hierarchy with its attendant class, position, privilege and power. Where Rupert Murdoch is king of the dunghill. Those of us who have read the classical political tracts and some of the modern ones recognise straightaway the distinction Murdoch has made. This is a declaration direct from the holy writ of theoretic-republicanism.

Kelvin McKenzie became editor of *The Sun* in June 1981. Murdoch did not have to oversee *The Sun* anymore. McKenzie was there to ape his every wish and every sentiment. Murdoch offered McKenzie the leashes of the hounds of hell, and they were taken with enthusiasm. McKenzie would especially let the hounds off to run before the Royal Ratpack. He sneered at the royal family as representing privilege and the old order, and kicked them around whenever he could. During the 1980s the private lives of the royal family would be sacrificed on the altars of the grubby profit motive. While all sorts of government bodies were created to syphon off public money into the hands of minority interests and protect the 'rights' of all and sundry, the members of the royal family were in the process of being reduced to the status of non-persons. McKenzie brought *The Sun* to euphoric heights of theoretic-republican bigotry and money-grubbing. The senior staff felt they could do anything. Harry Arnold comments on the spirit of the time:

> *The royals became known as the 'Germans' for obvious reasons. If we were unhappy about the way they were performing we would go out and take photos of them. We would say we have been working the Germans and giving them some more misery ...*

Roy Greenslade (Assistant Editor, *The Sun*, 1984-87), with a thoroughly amused expression for his international audience, added his recollections of this euphoric time:

> *Kelvin would adopt at a conference in the morning a mocked and shocked look and say: 'I'm afraid we have upset the palace. How can we do it today?' It was two fingers to the idea of any restraint.*

Just so.

4. Prince Charles is Pressured to Marry — and Diana is Under Seige

The pressure on Prince Charles to marry became overwhelming. He had great affection for Diana but felt driven by the media and family into a mode of behaviour and commitment over which he had little control. He committed himself in the customary way and the engagement was announced. Diana was now in a permanent state of siege. How anyone could expect a couple to make something of their marriage in these circumstances is a mystery. That did not deter the reptiles. They slithered hither and thither wiggling their slimy interests into whatever space would advance their objectives. A week before the wedding Diana reached a crisis point at a polo match where Prince Charles was playing. The attention of the hordes of media people present brought her to such a state she had to be led away in tears. Buoyed by the excitement of Diana in breakdown mode the media pressed forward like a pack of hyenas to record every moment of the occasion. Prince Charles, angry but composed, said:

> *It's not much fun watching polo when you are surrounded by people with very long lenses pointing in your direction the entire time and I think this adds up to a certain amount of strain each time and it told eventually. Hardly surprising.*

Poor Prince Charles. His efforts to remain polite and his appeals to the goodwill of the people causing the torment would have been more fruitfully directed at the worms in the ground under the polo field.

Buckingham Palace hoped that, with the wedding over, the interest in Prince Charles and Diana would die down. How tragic. How naive. Looking back it seems a mad thought that the media would back off. Diana, the media product, was able to boost circulation enormously. Murdoch would never have allowed any sacrifice of his imperial interests for the sake of Diana's and Charles's peace of mind.

At this time McKenzie and Murdoch introduced Sun Bingo in an attempt to put their competition out of business. McKenzie openly boasted of this 'business' objective. Sun Bingo and the running every day of 'stories' about the royal family were the program to advance Murdoch's imperial campaign in the British territory. Simon Jenkins (Political Editor, *The Economist*, 1979-86) comments on the nature of Diana, the media product:

> *From the moment Diana Spencer arrived on the scene you were going to get media attention devoted to her unlike anything we had seen in the world. No film star, no Pope, no Queen was going to get the sort of attention she was going to get. The only question was when she was going to crack.*

What an admission! And it's likely most of the media would not see the implications. Well, let me point out what everyone else would understand except the gentlemen of the media. This is an admission that the media attention and agenda would eventually kill Diana. Simon Jenkins is an intelligent man and a journalist of the first rank. How could he sit there calmly during that interview and make such an admission without going on to talk about the culpability of the media? It's baffling. Michael Shea, Press Officer for the Palace, said he pleaded and pleaded with the media to 'lay off' Diana. We might ask Simon Jenkins why the media would not 'lay off'.

5. The Queen Appeals to the Media

In December 1981, Michael Shea invited all Fleet Street editors to meet the Queen. The Queen wanted to appeal personally to the newspapers to get back to a reasonable coverage of the royal family. In particular, she expressed her concern for Diana and her state of mind. All the editors went except Kelvin McKenzie from *The Sun*. Roy Greenslade, McKenzie's off-sider, recalls with delight McKenzie's reaction to the invitation:

> *I do recall what Kelvin said on that famous occasion and it had something to do with needing to see Rupert Murdoch and that being*

*more important than meeting the Queen. Meeting the boss is always
more important than meeting the Queen.*

What is meant here is that the sycophantic vassal, Kelvin
McKenzie, wanted to brown-nose himself into the good graces of his
liege lord, Czar Murdoch. These words are accompanied by images
of Murdoch and McKenzie with smiling faces and holding forward a
copy of *The Sun* with the headline: **A new sun is rising today**. How
well the opposite image vividly conveys the ghastly truth sometimes.
Greenslade continued:

> *He [McKenzie] always felt that getting too close to the people who were
> his victims in his newspaper was a bad thing.*

Lloyd Turner of *The Daily Star* went on television to say that the
editors were persuaded by the Queen. Now they knew the effect the
media coverage was having on Diana they would back off. Who could
have believed it? When Diana and Charles went on holidays to the
Bahamas and a palace spokesmen told *The Daily Star* that there was
no way the media would have access to the royal couple, James
Whitaker, Royal Reporter for *The Daily Star* (1979-82) said that was
like a red rag to a bull. Lloyd Turner cried: *'Unleash the Greyhounds!
Go and Get Them!'*

6. The Hounds of Hell

It is remarkable. I found often that the images that came to mind while
I was writing this book were previously dreamt up by some member
of the media — and without any idea of the moral implications. I just
took it one step further to the real situation. It was not the greyhounds
but the hounds of hell Turner wanted unleashed. He would not let
control of these ferocious beings pass to McKenzie without a fight.
The tabloids sent their lackeys to the Bahamas to crawl through the
jungle undergrowth seeking the right moment to trap their prey. *The
Sun* came back with pictures of Diana in a bikini. The palace was outraged. Roy Greenslade said KcKenzie jumped in the air with joy at
the photos. Of course, he said, they had their usual conference about
whether it was right to publish the photos, but they all knew, said
Greenslade, they were going to publish them regardless. Prince Charles
wrote to a friend during the royal couple's trip to Australia.

*How can anyone, let alone a twenty-one year old, be expected to come
out of all this obsessed and crazed attention unscathed? It frightens
me. And I know for a fact it petrifies Diana.*

7. Charles is Comprehensively Mocked and Ridiculed

While the media subjected Diana to this crazed attention Charles was
becoming frustrated that his worthy and serious causes (e.g. his interest in architecture) were being trivialised. The tabloids began to
mock him. The mockery was extensive, cruel and without foundation.
I remember particularly the media-created caricature of Charles talking to his pot plants. This caricature was run hard in the Australian
media. It was around this time that it became crystal clear to me personally how low the honourable profession of journalism had been
brought by such people as Rupert Murdoch. It became clear that some
of the most contemptible characters I saw on the university campuses
of the 1960s had ascended to key positions in the media. I was told
by a former journalist for *The Australian* that Rupert Murdoch had a
bust of Lenin on display in his student quarters during his time at
Oxford University. I do not know whether this is true. The picture of
Lenin did not surprise me but the fact that Murdoch attended Oxford University did. What an irony!

Charles tried to enlist the broadsheets to counter the mockery. He
was advised to lie low. But Charles could not resign himself to opening factories and cutting ribbons for the rest of his life. He was right.
He had a moral duty to stand up to the ghouls of the tabloids. And it
seemed a duty of honest journalists to report the truth about Charles.
Were these honest journalists, as few as they were, so afraid of the reptiles down the road at *The Sun* and the *News of the World*?

8. The Royal Family Seek a Compromise with the Media

During the 1980s the press office of Charles and Diana tried to reach
a compromise arrangement with the media. Part of the deal was that
private holidays were out. The media were not deterred by the details
of any agreement. They followed Charles and Diana wherever they
went. On the holiday itself when the media pack became like a highly
mobile small army, Charles's staff would try to come to an arrangement that if the couple co-operated with the media for a photo session

they would be left alone. The undertaking was given and broken every time by the media people.

The members of the royal family tried to appease the media by making themselves more accessible. There were interviews during which personal details were revealed. There was that appallingly bad decision to set up a royal version of IT'S A KNOCK OUT. Peregrine Worsthorne was right. Others were saying the same thing. The attempts to appease the media would backfire. The more that was revealed to the unconscionable minds in the dark spaces of Fleet Street, the more it would be misused.

The reptiles slithered their way into the private quarters of the royal family by paying thirty pieces of silver to people on the palace staff. Max Hastings (Editor, *The Daily Telegraph* 1986-96) said that the joke at the time was whether there was anybody at the palace who was not on Murdoch's payroll. Members of the Royal Ratpack had their own (well-paid) sources within the entourage of Charles and Diana. In the end, the wonder is that the marriage was held together for so long in these circumstances. Michael Shea, palace press secretary, commented rightly that it was bad enough that the couple had marital problems, it was made a 100 or 1000 times worse with media beating it up incessantly. The antagonism between Diana and Charles grew. They then made the most tragic decision of their lives. They would try to defend themselves through the same channels that were crucifying them. The third program of the series opens with the title:

DANGEROUS LIAISONS

9. Beware of the Sirens of the Media!

For those who had heartfelt sympathy for the way events had taken control of the lives of Charles and Diana, this was painful viewing. Max Hastings (*The Daily Telegraph*) made a vital admission with regard to Diana and the media:

> *Like most editors who came in touch with her, we thoroughly enjoyed gossiping to her. We found her very human in a way the rest of the family are not and it was great fun to see her and be with her. Most of us were very susceptible but I can say that at one level and say how much I enjoyed being with her while at the same time saying if I had been advising her I wouldn't allow any of us anywhere near her.*

Why did people like Max Hastings and Simon Jenkins, who distinguish themselves from most of their colleagues by having conscience, stand on the sidelines and watch the inevitable tragedy? A better title for this program would have been:

BEWARE OF THE SIRENS OF THE MEDIA!

The royal family in following the sirens into the most treacherous liaison in modern society were going to be shipwrecked on either side of the pass. They could not, and still cannot win. We are now on the brink of a series of some of the worst judgements ever made by anybody in their relationship with the media. It was precipitated by the biography of Diana (*Diana: Her true Story*) written by tabloid journalist Andrew Morton. The biography caused a sensation. Most of us were sickened by it. Although we did not know the full story at the time we felt there was something rotten about it. Not only about the contents but also about the way it was published, the way it was serialised and the way it added to the propaganda war against the monarchy and the royal family. It stank of imprudence, nastiness and treachery. Andrew Neil, Editor of *The Sunday Times* (1983-92) serialised the book. He was taken to task for doing so. He defended his decision in debates at the time on TV. He defended it on the grounds that it was true and that the moral misdemeanours uncovered (the desecration of the 'sanctity of marriage') had enormous implications for the Constitution of Great Britain. Here was a Murdoch man in full hypocritical flight.

To his great credit Max Hastings, full of righteous anger, entered the fray to defend the royal family. He attacked Morton by saying that 'if you can't become a pianist in a brothel you become a royal reporter'. He was right to characterise Morton in this way. He continued:

Any so-called friend of the royal family who is stupid enough to talk to somebody like Andrew Morton for a book I would question whether their evidence is likely to be worth much.

10. Diana in Self-destruct Mode

Eventually the tragic truth came out. Diana had co-operated indirectly with Morton. In looking back Max Hastings regrets his action at the time. He says that he made the mistake of wishing it were not true and if it were, it should not be published. No, Max, your righteous anger was appropriate. Although it was true that Diana had co-operated, what she had done was the result of the worst inclinations of her unstable temperament. *Diana: Her True Story* was a bitter and in many respects a false account of the problems of her marriage.[1] The revelations would be used to advance the power and influence of a pernicious media empire. Max Hastings was right at the time to raise the question about the agenda of the Murdoch empire in Britain. Worst of all, the apparent collusion between the media and a member of the royal family was used as a pretext to prevent privacy laws being enacted to protect the royal family. In working with the Murdoch organisation to vindicate the product of her wild and unstable temperament, Diana had put herself into self-destruct mode. It was like the gazelle enlisting the help of the hyenas to solve the problem of their thirst for its blood. I can quote from the narration at this point:

> *During the coming months the commercial success of Morton's book would unleash another circulation war in which the tabloid press in a grim contest sought to outdo each other in sensational revelations about the royal family.*

There was much more to come. In 1992 there were rumours that tapes existed of a telephone conversation between Diana and a certain James Gilbey. It turned out that the conversation had been recorded and offered to *The Sun* by a ham radio operator in 1989. The tapes became known as the *Squidgy tapes*. This section of the program brings before the viewer various senior members of the Murdoch organisation saying that they exercised much moral restraint in suppressing tapes highly damaging to the monarchy. The order to suppress had come from Rupert Murdoch himself. When the Palace was informed of the reason for the suppression of the tapes, Charles Anson, Press Secretary to the Queen (1990-97), understandably commented: 'I am not sure whether that was a threat or whether there was something genuine in that statement.'

He was right to be doubtful. In 1989, when the tapes had been made, the press was under a threat of privacy laws. Privacy laws were something that Murdoch wanted to avoid at all costs. This was the real reason for the tapes' suppression. Murdoch's senior vassals in Britain were guilty of the hypocrisy they are famous for. Nothing done by the Murdoch men before or after the suppression of the *Squidgy tapes* would give any credibility to the apparent outbreak of a moral conscience at that time. In August 1992 transcripts of the tapes appeared (surprise, surprise) in the American tabloid, *The National Enquirer*. That same weekend quotes appeared in Britain in *The Sunday Express*. Stuart Higgins, Deputy Editor of *The Sun*, exclaimed that they had been 'scooped' on their own story. It was time to 'go for broke and publish every word of the tape'. Are we surprised? *The Sun* put the tapes on a phone line and invited readers 'to judge for themselves'. Stuart Higgins, on behalf of the Murdoch empire, had the ready answer for the charge of tastelessness and gross media intrusion. It is worth reproducing the words that thoroughly confirm the accusations I have made in previous chapters:

> *I don't consider we were intruding into anybody's privacy. The Morton book was in the public domain. It was a book I knew the Princess of Wales had co-operated in fully. Indeed, Andrew [Morton] told me to treat that book as though the Princess of Wales had signed every page, as though it was a manuscript prepared by the Princess of Wales. And that's not bad to go on. So she had opened this enormous can of worms for her own purposes. The idea we published a private conversation so enormous in its potential repercussions was great journalism.*

We see how the acceptance of one nasty and perverted tool of propaganda (the Morton book) acts as a justification for more of the same. We see how the 'you-asked-for-it' argument is used again and again by the Murdoch people to justify their unlimited intrusion into the private lives of people. We see how the powerful Murdoch organisation flouts the laws of the land with such impunity. After all, at issue was the publication of an illegally taped phone conversation. The Palace was left paralysed. They knew that invoking the laws made for their protection often backfired on them. They did not take any legal action. How untouchable those chieftains of the Murdoch organisation must have felt on that occasion. What complacency as they surveyed their domain across the roofs of the capital of Great Britain!

11. Charles's Great Error

It was now Prince Charles's turn to come under the spotlight of the media. Penny Junor, Charles's biographer, felt that he had been badly maligned and betrayed by Morton's book. She defended him publicly. Although Charles made it clear that neither he nor any of his friends should take action against the outpourings of a momentarily bitter and obsessive mind that was reflected in the Morton book, this was quietly ignored by some in sympathy with him. Out of these circumstances Charles's relationship with Camilla Parker Bowles rose into view. When we look back we should not be surprised that tapes of a highly damaging telephone conversation between Charles and Camilla Parker Bowles surfaced. It was entirely predictable. How their appearance was defended and the use they were put to was also predictable. The tapes were *illegally* made by a *Daily Mirror* reader and the *Daily Mirror* obligingly ran a series of articles about the tapes' contents. Richard Stott, Editor of the *Daily Mirror* (1991-92) said of his decision with typical hypocrisy:

> *We didn't publish the whole tape and, in fact, we never did. What we did do is to say this is the truth of what is going on and that is exactly what you should do and that is what newspapers are there for — to tell people what they don't know and to tell people things that other people want to suppress.*

What Stott did not tell the people in these comments was that the taping of private telephone calls is highly intrusive, highly illegal, that the *Daily Mirror* was complicit in an illegal act, that the *Daily Mirror* was able with impunity to flout the law, and that the only reason the *Daily Mirror* published the series is that it would boost circulation and profit for the media bosses. Nobody is fooled by this display of hypocrisy — least of all the people on staff at a tabloid newspaper.

The full transcript of the tapes in which Charles and Camilla declared their love for each other first appeared in an Australian magazine partly owned by Rupert Murdoch. In January 1993, the *Sunday Mirror* followed suit. The illegal tapes formed a wonderful basis for the media to raise questions about Charles's suitability as King of England. They went at it hard. Charles's staff and supporters responded by feeding positive messages about Charles to the media, in particular *The Sun*. Among other things they invited broadcaster Jonathan Dimbleby to make a film and write a book about Charles. Max Hastings said the plan was madness. People were only interested in the marriage, and a public relations war between Diana and Charles would backfire. During the TV program Charles made his now famous admission of adultery after his marriage had irretrievably broken down. Nobody approved of the admission in public — and certainly not the media. Jonathan Dimbleby said that an editor from one of the big tabloids had commented to an official at St James's Palace: 'You have shot our fox now.' Dimbleby replied that the speculation about this part of Charles's life was certainly at an end 'but it was naive to think the fox had been shot. *They could go on shooting it again and again.*'

12. Diana's Fatal Error

In 1993 Diana felt the pressure from the media and from Charles's staff, who she felt were out to get her. She announced her withdrawal from public life saying among other things that although she knew from the beginning she would attract the attention of the media she 'was not aware of how overwhelming that attention would become ...' If Diana thought she would be left alone she was wrong. 'Paparazzi working in teams of two connected by mobile phones trailed her 24 hours a day.' Diana's doing away with an official bodyguard so she could lead a normal life left her even more vulnerable. One paparazzo who was a witness to the despair Diana was feeling at the being hounded the whole day through took a picture of her shouting at a photographer, 'You are making my life hell.' The picture was sold to *The Sun*.

In 1994 she tried to go on a holiday to Spain with some girlfriends. She was tormented and harassed by paparazzi the whole time. The TV images of her walking through the airport terminal is a graphic example of the way the paparazzi pursued, tormented, pushed, and cornered her. The scene is like a group of cruel children chasing a rabbit around and around in an enclosed field before they corner it and stone it to death. Diana told Richard Kay of the *Daily Mirror* that 'the intrusion into her privacy was like a rape.'

Richard Kay was one of the few people in the media Diana felt she could trust to report her side of the story sensibly and fairly. On her return from the holiday in Spain she was photographed sitting in the car with him. Sitting openly in a car in a public street with a trusted friend is normally an uncontroversial action. But the photo was sold to *The Sun* who headlined it with: **TWO FACED DIANA**. *The Sun* expected Diana to lie down and have her person raped time and again by the media without being granted any opportunity at all to have her say. They were the rapist pinning the brutalised victim to the ground and saying: 'Lie still and there will be less pain for you.'

Diana continued her attempts to get on side with the media, to appeal to them as fellow human beings. She would never learn despite the miscalculations she was continually guilty of — and despite the advice from media professionals like Max Hastings. He told her in one interview to keep her head down and stay out of the public glare. While he was giving this advice the BBC film crew were preparing the cameras for *that* interview. In a judgement so appallingly bad that one can scarcely understand it now, Diana decided to reveal all in an interview with the BBC 'Panorama' team. Stuart Higgins of *The Sun* said: '... for a journalist it is a fantastic, absolutely brilliant, great, great story. Great for sales and circulation. Personally for her it was a bad decision and I think it damaged her ...' Few inside and outside the media organisations disagreed. It opened old and new wounds. If Diana was guilty of one affair (with James Hewitt), there may have been more. For the media, the admission had given complete licence to dig further. Jane Atkinson, Press Secretary to the Princess of Wales (1996) made the morally obvious comment:

I didn't see why with the Princess or with any figures in public life that just because they deal with the media on one level, it is necessarily open season on their private life.

As I have said many times in this book, this is the plain, simple answer to the 'you-asked-for-it' argument.

It was indeed open season on Diana. Her desire to be left alone was ridiculed by the media. Behind the scenes the media bosses offered handfuls of gold to those with the best trophies from the hunt. Like a wild gazelle Diana was pursued by the hyena pack until they got her in the tunnel de l'Alma in Paris during the first minutes of the new day of 31 August 1997.

11

The Accident

1. Did Henri Paul's Blood-Alcohol Level Matter?

'Diana: The Other Story' appeared on Australian television (Nine Network) in June 1998. It was produced by 3BM Television and Martyn Gregory Film Productions for Channel 4, and broadcast as an episode of the *Dispatches* program. One could not mistake the object of the program from the beginning. It was to dismiss the 'conspiracy' theories about Diana's death, to utterly discredit Mohammed Al Fayed, and to state the 'simple truth' about the accident. The 'simple truth', according to Martyn Gregory and Co., was that there was a gross security failure which resulted in a drunk driver getting behind the wheel of the car to drive 'the mother of the future king of England' to her death.

The program-makers ridicule the abundance of 'conspiracy theories' about Diana's death and in particular debunk the 'conspiracy theory' favoured by the Al Fayed camp. They pretend to cut away the overlay of paranoia and myth-making on the event and to replace it with the bare 'truth of the matter'. But in reality they dismiss any view of the accident that does not concur with their own as a 'conspiracy theory', and go on to replace a 'conspiracy theory' they do not approve of with one of their own — which is more about Mohammed Al Fayed than the accident. Secondly, they do present a 'simple' scenario of the accident, but simple in the sense of superficial and tendentious. Vital details and arguments raised and taken seriously in other reports and investigations are simply ignored or summarily dismissed. It is not difficult to summarise the main elements of their case.

Mohammed Al Fayed is painted as doing everything possible to suck up to the royal family. He particularly wanted to ingratiate himself with Diana. His plan was to 'court Diana'. He would personally welcome her whenever she turned up at Harrods. He contributed to her charities and issued a standing invitation to join him on his holidays. It is even implied that he hurried through the purchase of the A$40 million cruiser *The Jonikal* to impress her! Accompanying the verbal picture we see a series of film grabs that shows Al Fayed enthusiastically attending to the Princess, as anybody would in a similar position. The object is clearly to demonstrate the existence of some sort of Machiavellian plan to bring his son, Dodi, into contact with Diana, and to encourage a liaison which would eventually connect him with the British royal family. In this we could not have a better example of a simple-minded 'conspiracy theory'.

Martyn Gregory, the program's narrator, says unblushingly that from a recent interview with Kelly Fisher (Dodi's fiancee at the time) 'we can detail exactly how Diana now fell into the arms of the Fayed father and son.' The program-makers seem to forget at times that they are presenting a documentary and not a melodrama. Next we have an extensive account of Al Fayed's 'obsession' with his security arrangements. Among other things we learn of his bugging each of his premises so that he can keep tabs on all who drift into his web. He wanted especially to keep checks on how the 'romance' between Dodi and Diana was faring. All this is meant to show what a shabby, scheming and unsavoury pair Dodi and his father were. Now this is worth a comment.

All the supposed evidence (if we take away the dramatic music, the melodramatic tone and the hyperbole) really points to nothing more than what any person of wealth, power and position would do. Perhaps Mohammed Al Fayed displays a little more flamboyance and fussiness than his British counterparts, but the difference seems only of degree. What is said of Al Fayed here could be said fundamentally of many other 'notables'. Furthermore, there is no attempt to balance the criticism with an attempt at proposing possible reasons for Al Fayed's fussiness with security or his wanting to please his guests and friends. Perhaps this is connected with his cultural background? Here we raise a point of interest for those of us on the other side of the world reading about and seeing the Al Fayed connection for the first time.

I have already commented in previous chapters on the media's inclination to sneer about Al Fayed and his son whenever their names crop up, and that this seems strange for those of us *not in the know*. What we have seen of the father and son in film clips and interviews presents a rather sympathetic picture of both. With regard to Dodi, Sancton and MacLeod emphasise this sympathetic picture.[1] They say the media image of him as the fast, sleazy, spoilt, rich kid is false. Dodi in fact was reported by the women who were willing to talk to Sancton and MacLeod as being kind, generous and attentive. He was a good male friend for his female acquaintances. Indeed, Dodi Fayed showed similar traits to Diana. He seemed to have everything but in the end was shy and uncertain of himself. Sancton and MacLeod suggest that this was the basis for their sudden and intense relationship. They had found a soul-mate in each other.

As for Mohammed Al Fayed, what we have seen on our TV screens is a father broken by the death of his son, a father mourning for the loss of his son and his son's dear companion, and seeking to understand the reasons why. And who can blame him if he, as a father, is pointing the finger at the media? Most of us would do likewise. On the other hand, we have seen glimpses of a tough, professional businessman who gives and demands loyalty, a man with a sense of honour and ever ready to display that style of hospitality the Arabian countries are known for. Mohammed Al Fayed seems more in the mould of the gentleman of English history than many Englishmen of today. Perhaps the greatest compliment he received was the unfeigned friendship and respect of Diana, someone who did not need the wealth and position he had to offer but was taken up heart and soul into the warm family atmosphere of the first holiday with the Al Fayed family. I don't know any more about the Al Fayed connection than I have drawn from the varied information coming through the media channels and the chapter devoted to him by Sancton and MacLeod.[2] Even so, it's enough to make the object of 'Diana: The Other Story' seem unconvincing — and that is apart from the weakness of the argument and evidence actually produced. Having created this unsavoury picture, the program gets down to the real business. The narration goes on:

The car crash in Paris was a personal tragedy for Mohammed Al Fayed ... He not only lost his son but also, as he would claim, the chance of a union with royalty. Almost immediately he launched a huge

> *propaganda campaign which has continued to this day to deflect any responsibility for the crash and to promote his own closeness to Princess Diana. This campaign is based on a series of claims. We have examined some in detail.*

Mohammed Al Fayed's 'propaganda' campaign seems on the whole a reasonable attempt to put his side of the story in contradiction to those who were obviously running their own particular skewed version of events, namely the media in general. Fortunate, indeed, is he who has the resources to counter the media barons!

The examination of the claims is meant to debunk them, of course. Three of the claims are rather trivial matters in the scheme of things and do not have a big impact on the main issue of responsibility. These three claims are about Diana's last words; Al Fayed's assertion that he viewed Diana's body; and that a diamond necklace was taken from the Mercedes after the crash. We will allow that the program has been able to dismiss them although we remain conscious that their dismissal functions largely to discredit Al Fayed, and not to have any direct bearing on the question of responsibility for the accident. The fourth claim, though, is of crucial importance:

> *But Al Fayed's PR operation concentrated its greatest effort on deflecting any responsibility for the crash. The first tactic was to deflect blame away from the drunken driver Henri Paul and towards the paparazzi.*

It would seem that if it could be proven beyond doubt that Henri Paul was three to four times above the legally allowable blood-alcohol level, then surely Paul was responsible (and by implication the Ritz) for Diana's death. This is the thrust of 'Diana: The Other Story'. The program appears to make great efforts to prove Paul was drunk but all they can show is that Paul may have drunk 'something' during the afternoon or evening of 30 August, and that he had two pastis (Ricards) in the Ritz's Vendome Bar sometime between 10 p.m. and midnight. This hardly amounts to proof that Paul had drunk enough to get him up to three or four times the blood-alcohol limit for France. Sancton and MacLeod state that Paul's movements between the time he knocked off work at 7.05 p.m. and the time he arrived back at the Ritz at 10.08 p.m. remain largely a mystery. Nobody can come near to fingering him with a boozing episode.[3]

Next the program quotes the testimony of a barman who said that when Paul got up to leave the Vendome bar he bumped into a senior barman and then staggered to the exit. The amazing part of this section of the program is that we see footage from the security camera at the Ritz showing Paul walking around, conversing and descending the stairs. At one point he is even seen walking backwards as he moves away from someone he had been speaking to — all as steady as you could wish! The program-makers seem totally unperturbed about this inconsistency. One part of the narration gives the clue to the mentality behind this. Kes Wingfield and Trevor Rees-Jones, the two security guards assigned to Diana and Dodi, were sitting and talking with Henri Paul in the Vendome bar while he was having the two pastis (Ricards). Wingfield and Rees-Jones have said that Paul seemed to be drinking fruit juice. Both insist he did not appear drunk. He behaved and acted normally. But the narrator of 'Diana: The Other Story' says that Wingfield and Rees-Jones 'had no reason to believe Paul was drunk', meaning that they did not realise the 'fruit juice' was actually pastis and they could not know about Paul's blood-alcohol level at that point.

The attitude reflected here is that the knowledge of the blood-alcohol level in a person is enough to say whether or not a person is in a 'drunken' state, as the ordinary person normally understands what 'drunken' means. In fact, it is the other way around. The connection between a certain blood alcohol-level and a physical state deemed to be drunken is a scientifically proposed general connection. The actual drunken state is one that has certain manifestations: unsteadiness, slurred speech, diminishing of reflexes, confused thinking and so on. The legally stipulated blood-alcohol level for driving is a device set at the lowest common denominator to test the whole community for reasons of community security. The community accepts the stringency and a certain level of arbitrariness in order to guard against the person who reaches a state of drunkenness with relatively few drinks. Thus being legally drunk can be sometimes quite a different state than being actually drunk in the sense one understands the word 'drunk' in everyday use. The manifestations of the drunken state come first and this is ratified by a scientific test that determines a certain blood-alcohol level and its general correlation with drunkenness. The overall point that I am making here is that the makers of 'Diana: The Other Story' show the familiar inclination of the 'educated' to work only on 'theory' and paper-knowledge while ignoring the actual concrete circumstances of a given event.

It is often said of a particular person that 'they can hold their drink', meaning that there seems no alteration in their behaviour (physical and mental) when the same amount of alcohol would make someone else silly, rash and unsteady. In a recent current affairs program on Australian television (ACA Channel 9, June 1998) there was a test set up to demonstrate that women reach the legal blood-alcohol limit before men. The program did demonstrate that, but it also showed that after the same amount of alcohol different people registered different blood-alcohol levels. It showed too that after the same period of drinking some of the people were less steady than others. Finally, many years ago a medical doctor told me that some people after a moderate amount of alcohol were actually safer drivers than when cold sober, and that this for reasons of public security would never be admitted publicly. In my student days I once witnessed a severe alcoholic walk into a university bar around mid-morning. He was so strung up that he could not hold the glass of whisky brought to him by the barmaid. It had to be put on the table in front of him while he bent over to suck up the whole lot at the one time through a straw. When I and my friends returned to that bar two hours later, the alcoholic was sitting calmly eating his lunch with a knife and fork. In brief, it has been proven that some drugs have different effects depending on the physical and psychological condition of the person taking them.[4]

With this in mind let's accept the numerous official tests that Henri Paul had a blood-alcohol level of three to four times above the legal limit. It really does not seem reasonable to dispute these. I will deal firstly with the incident in the Vendome bar. The barman said that Paul got up, bumped into a senior barman and staggered to the exit. The program makers get themselves into trouble by acknowledging that a seriously drunken state would manifest itself in loss of physical control. That loss of physical control would manifest itself continually while the person was actually drunk. They have to reconcile this with Paul's behaviour as shown in the security camera footage. They also have to explain why nobody else reported Paul staggering around the Ritz and bumping into other people. They can't. It remains an embarrassing inconsistency for them. The obvious explanation is that Paul got up, did not see the senior barman and bumped into him

— which caused him to stagger. Who has never done that?

Added to the alcohol was two antidepressant drugs (Prozac and Tiapridal) in Paul's blood. These drugs, which he had been taking for two to three months, would normally multiply the effects of alcohol. Investigations also revealed that Paul was in a state of 'moderate chronic alcoholism'.[5] Paul's blood-alcohol level was not restricted to 30 August but was the result of long sustained intake of alcohol. If this is so, why didn't anybody notice it in his behaviour during the weeks (and months) before the accident? Indeed, most of the people interviewed by Sancton and MacLeod (friends, family, colleagues, etc.) said they were utterly surprised to learn that Paul was in treatment for mild alcoholism.[6] His manner and physical behaviour gave absolutely no clue. He was affable, conscientious, very careful when driving, and meticulous in his preparations for work and other formal activities. He was particularly conscientious about the annual driving tests for handling the Mercedes car.[7] At social occasions he never drank much and always remained in control of himself. Of more crucial importance was that, two days before his death, Paul underwent a physical examination for his flying licence.[8] He was judged to be in good health and he showed he had good reflexes. Philip Jacobson, in a report in *The Sun-Herald* (March 7, 1998), wrote:

> In a desk [in Paul's apartment] his pilot's log book had been immaculately maintained. It showed that Paul had reported for the obligatory annual medical only a few days before the crash and had passed the tests — urine, reflexes, hand-eye co-ordination, and mental health — without problems.

The point that I am making is that despite the scientifically established blood-alcohol level in Paul, his physical and mental state remained competent when it came to his everyday activities. He functioned as well as the next person and remained undistinguished by any abnormal behaviour.

On the night of the accident when, according to standard reckoning, his blood-alcohol level should have resulted in the typical manifestations of the actual drunken state, Paul is seen walking and talking in a normal steady manner. Those in the Ritz who claim he was 'dead drunk' have not revealed themselves (besides the barman in the Vendome bar whose testimony is not at all convincing). This is understandable, for Paul's actions simply do not support that claim. Paul drove off from the Ritz evidently with orders to evade the pursuing paparazzi. He negotiated at least five turns before he arrived at the freeway leading to the Alma tunnel all the time having to evade the swarm of paparazzi in cars and on motorbikes. He drove at high speed along the freeway flashing his lights at cars and completing passing manoeuvres. He arrived at the entrance to the Alma tunnel at a speed experts said would have made it difficult to control the car. Before the entrance the road dips and takes a slight left-hand curve. Here the car went into two skid phases.

Sancton and MacLeod commissioned a report on the accident by an expert on automobile behaviour.[9] The expert, Jean Pietri, after examining the photos of the two skid marks and considering the circumstances of the crash was amazed that Paul's reflexes were so good that he was clearly still in control of the car during the first skid phase. It was only during the second phase that he lost control. Thus all the evidence taken together shows that even if Paul's blood-alcohol level was three to four times above the legal limit it did not reduce the physical and mental competence required to drive the Mercedes in which Diana and Dodi sat. Of vital consideration is that Paul had completed annual driving tests in defence driving of the Mercedes. Whether it was a cold-sober Paul or Paul with a high blood-alcohol level, or anybody else competent to drive the Mercedes, the crash, because of the circumstances, could not have been avoided. There had to be other reasons for the crash.

This is one scenario. There is, however, a second scenario and this is canvassed seriously by royal reporter Nicholas Owen in a program by Fulcrum Productions for ITV. The program, 'Diana: Secrets Behind the Crash', appeared on Australian television (Nine Network) not long before 'Diana: The Other Story'. Nicholas Owen presents much of the detail I have included above about Paul's blood-alcohol level but adds one more rather startling claim. It has only recently come to light, he says, that tests found a high level of carbon monoxide (20 per cent) in Paul's blood.[10] This would normally indicate a state of carbon monoxide poisoning.

Owen invites carbon monoxide expert, Dr Alastair Hay, to reconcile such a high carbon monoxide level in Paul's blood with the security camera vision of Paul walking around the Ritz. He cannot. If the carbon monoxide level was 20 per cent when tested, then it would have been around 30 per cent when Paul was filmed by the security camera. That level would have left Paul in some distress: throbbing headache, unsteadiness and other physical signs of suffering. There are no such signs. Next Owen asks behavioural psychologist, Dr Martin Skinner, if he can reconcile the blood-alcohol level in Paul's blood with the security camera vision. He cannot either. Such a high blood-alcohol level would surely produce erratic, unsteady behaviour and even result in being physically sick. But, as Dr Skinner points out, Paul's manner is steady and smooth. He walks and stands straight. He chats affably with colleagues, gives orders and acknowledges people with a greeting as they walk by.

If everybody with a measurable blood-alcohol level of 1.87 g/l[11] behaved in such a manner, it would make the stipulated driving limit of 0.5 g/l laughable. This is the great point Owen wants to make. If you take the blood-alcohol level, the presence of antidepressants and carbon monoxide in Paul's blood together then you surely must have a person so affected he could not manage to walk — let alone step into a car and drive it away. This presents such an enormous inconsistency that the accusation of Paul's drunken state being responsible for the fatal accident can *never* be credible without it being resolved. It can be resolved by dismissing the findings as grossly inaccurate or by the samples being in some way polluted. But there were a number of laboratory controlled tests that came up with similar findings, and on the evidence it does not seem plausible that there was a conspiracy to manipulate the tests.

However, it can be resolved by the elements of the second scenario being absorbed by the first scenario (i.e. by Paul's apparent physical and psychological resistance to drugs). It is a difficult choice to make between the two possibilities but the weight of the evidence points to the first scenario — which does offer a resolution of all points of the inconsistency. For some unknown reason Henri Paul's body was able to accommodate the ingestion of substances that would normally affect the physical and psychological condition of most people.

2. The Most Likely Cause of the Accident that Killed Diana?

Numerous newspaper and magazine articles have been written about the accident and what witnesses saw or heard.[12] I am going to concentrate, however, on the account of the accident presented by Sancton and MacLeod. Their account, besides giving important background information on the Paris police investigation, reproduces most of the compelling evidence of the previous reports. Cutting away the unnecessary detail I will attempt to recount those features of the case that point to the most likely scenario of what happened between 12.20 a.m. and 12.30 a.m. on 31 August. Let me start by going back to the program, 'Diana: The Other Story'.

The second major claim on which this program rests to discredit Mohammed Al Fayed and all 'conspiracy theories' is the 'new' evidence provided by a hitherto mystery informant. This informant is a certain 28-year-old Frederick, a former Etoile[13] chauffeur and Ritz employee. He claims in contradiction to the Al Fayed 'PR machine' that he handed the keys of the Mercedes to Henri Paul who issued a challenge to photographers present at the back entrance to the Ritz. He then observed Paul drive off at high speed. The Al Fayed 'PR machine' had claimed that someone else had given the keys to Paul, that no photographers were present at the back entrance, and that Paul did not issue any challenge at all. We are then presented with 'Frederick' looking at the security camera footage on a TV monitor and describing in halting English what was happening. We see somebody giving the keys to Paul. Paul gets into the car and then drives off with his passengers. We do not see any photographers for they were 'out of camera range' and we do not get a clear view of the car driving off at high speed. Despite Frederick's difficulty in giving his account in English (he was asked to give an account in 'his own words') he is able to reproduce in perfectly fluent English the 'challenge' Paul threw at the photographers out of range of the camera. Paul said according to Frederick: *Don't try to follow us. You'll never catch us.*

If it is true that Paul uttered these words then it hardly constitutes a challenge to a drive-to-the-death contest. It sounds more like one of those playful throwaway comments that many people make in a similar situation. Other people had commented that Paul's manner with the paparazzi that night was playful and teasing.[14] On the other hand, the established way in which Paul conducted himself in his professional and private life is inconsistent with the claim that this was in any way serious, that he had any intention at all of entering into a race with the paparazzi. The most obvious meaning of the above sentences (if they had any serious content at all) is that Paul was confident he could drive in such a way that he would be able to evade the paparazzi. A challenge would be formulated differently, something like: 'Come on, try to catch me. You haven't got a chance.' Those wanting to label Paul as a drunk may exercise their ingenuity but they are unable to make Paul's alleged words logically entail an invitation to a race. A further point is the difficulty the program gets into by implying Paul drove off in a wild and reckless manner. Driving at high speed while negotiating difficult traffic conditions does not sit well with the claim that Paul was 'dead drunk'. It is even contradictory. The program ends with this claim:

> *Frederick's eye-witness account confirms that Henri Paul, a drunk driver, was intent on out-racing the paparazzi. Despite all the efforts of Mohammed Al Fayed and other fantasists to create myths and stoke up conspiracies, that is the sad unalterable reality of how Henri Paul, Dodi Fayed, and Princess Diana came to die.*

It confirms no such thing. Their argument and evidence is easily taken apart. Indeed, the weakness of argument and the general superficiality of the program are highlighted in their summary dismissal of a key feature of the accident taken seriously by all other investigators of the accident, including the Paris police. This concerns the Fiat Uno that appeared to be hit by the Mercedes at the entrance to the Alma tunnel. Martyn Gregory for 'Diana: The Other Story' claimed:

> *In fact there is not a shred of credible evidence to support conspiracy theorists. The one straw at which they try to clutch is forensic evidence that just before the crash the Mercedes was in collision with a white Fiat Uno which has never been found.*

Such an assertion, apart from flying in the face of the evidence, reflects the reductionist mentality that always scuttles the effort for serious discussion. The wackiest 'conspiracy theory' is made equivalent to a scenario arising out of compelling and substantial evidence. It's the mentality that cannot distinguish between a smack and a bashing. Before dealing with the evidence supporting the role of the Fiat Uno in the accident, I will go back to the point where in my view we can start to trace the events that led to the accident.

Diana's interview with the BBC Panorama program was really the beginning of the end. I have constantly compared the behaviour of the media in hunting Diana with that of a pack of hyenas. The media hunted Diana in the unrelenting and merciless manner of the hyena. They were roused by the Panorama interview in the way hyenas are alerted to an animal straying from its herd. Unwittingly Diana had put herself into open ground far from the protection that had given her some measure of safety to that point. When the photo of Diana and Dodi in an embrace opened wide the coffers of the media bosses, the hyenas suddenly smelt the blood of an animal in trouble. The hunt would not be relaxed now for a second.

The paparazzi in general plan tactics and operate in teams connected by mobile phones. But there is an even higher level of organisation in the packs that chase celebrities. Sancton and Macleod describe the elite of the paparazzi as 'stalkerazzi'. These are highly professional hunters. They do not wait around for their victim to appear and walk by. 'They are like Mafia killers; no one escapes them'.[15] A great deal of time and equipment is expended in the meticulous planning of campaigns that must catch their prey and bear a return on the investment. They stalk until they get what they want. Their prey is not a person but a thing that is the source of riches. These elites most assuredly headed up the pack that descended upon Dodi and Diana during their final days. The rewards ensured their presence.

On 30 August Diana and Dodi flew into Le Bourget Airport, Paris, after cruising around the Mediterranean. They were not only met by Ritz staff (including Henri Paul) but by the paparazzi who had been tipped off by their mates left behind in the Mediterranean. Diana and Dodi climbed into a black Mercedes and set off on the drive into Paris. Behind in a back-up Range Rover was Kes Wingfield and Henri Paul. Paul was at the wheel. As they came onto the A1 motorway they were picked up by the pack of paparazzi who buzzed the two-car convoy the whole way into Paris. Kes Wingfield reported seeing the paparazzi continually talking on their mobile phones during the drive. It leaves little to the imagination as to whom they were calling. He also reported a highly dangerous blocking manoeuvre carried out by one of the cars chasing the two-car convoy.[16] This is described in an article in *The Australian* (8 September 1997) taken from *The Sunday Times*:

> As the Mercedes carrying Diana and Fayed moved into the heavy holiday traffic and on to the motorway there was a taste of what was to come. A small black Peugeot pulled alongside and swerved in front of

the couple's car, forcing the driver to brake. As it slowed, a motorbike cut in alongside the princess's car. A photographer riding pillion took aim, his flash gun firing into the window. Within a minute, however, the driver had accelerated and lost the pursuers.

I ask the reader to keep these circumstances in mind for what follows. Diana had seen this stock tactic many times by the paparazzi to slow down the flight of their victim but evidently the manner in which it was now being executed caused some apprehension. She told Kes Wingfield later at the hotel she feared one of the motorbike riders would be hurt. Asked about Paul's handling of the Range Rover, Kes Wingfield said, 'He drove well. He was a good driver, a good guy.'[17] As this is an important episode illustrative of Paul's state of mind, physical condition and professional driving competence, let me quote from Philip Jacobson's report in *The Sun-Herald* (7 March, 1998):

With the paparazzi now in pursuit, Paul demonstrated what he had learned on 'protective driving' courses run by Mercedes, manoeuvring the Range Rover to block close-up shots of the couple; to the bodyguard travelling with him [Kes Wingfield], Paul seemed imperturbable.

Remember, this is the description of a person who is allegedly suffering chronic alcoholism and ingesting antidepressant drugs.[18] Just outside the city centre, the car driving Diana and Dodi managed to evade the paparazzi and head for the Windsor Villa in the Bois de Boulogne. Paul went on to deliver Dodi and Diana's baggage at Dodi's apartment. He joined the couple later at the Windsor Villa. After inspecting the Villa for some time the group returned to the Ritz. They arrived there at 4.35 p.m. At 7 p.m. the couple left the Ritz by the back exit to go to Dodi's apartment situated just off the Champs Elysees and near the Arc de Triomphe. Paul handed over the keys of the Range Rover to another driver and headed off home. At Dodi's apartment the group was met by a highly excited group of photographers. Kes Wingfield commented:

The paparazzi literally mobbed the couple ... That really disturbed and frightened the Princess, even though she was used to the paparazzi. These paparazzi were shouting, which made them even more frightening. I had to push them back physically.[19]

There was real anger and desperation in the situation. The paparazzi were barely controlling themselves. They were pushing, shouting and threatening consequences if they were obstructed in their actions. The hyenas were in close and biting at their victim. Wingfield tried to bring calm to the situation. Dodi was furious. At 9.30 p.m. the couple tried to drive to the restaurant Chez Benoit but the bitter close-in harassment by the paparazzi forced them to abandon the plan. They drove back to the Ritz. Dodi was furious and frustrated. At the Ritz they were met by such frenzied chaos that it was difficult for Diana to get out of the car. Wingfield had to physically protect her on the way into the hotel. Dodi steamed in the car for a few moments before following. The security cameras show the tension on the faces of Diana, Dodi and their bodyguards as they pass through the revolving doors.

Inside Diana is reported by Sancton and MacLeod as sitting down looking demoralised and close to tears. Other reports claim she sat down and burst into tears.[20] I have seen the security footage many times (at least that part that appeared on television in Australia) and it looks to me as if Diana at this point wore an expression of fatal resignation. Dodi appeared consumed with concern for her. I cannot help feeling that tragedy was written all over these last scenes of Dodi and Diana together. Henri Paul was informed of the problems. The security cameras recorded his arrival back at the Ritz. He drove up to the front of the hotel in his mini at 10.08 p.m. He drew alongside the kerb backed up once and brought the car closer to the kerbside. He got out of his car and walked towards several people with whom he spoke for a while.

It appears that the plan to fool the paparazzi by leaving from the back entrance of the Ritz was hatched and insisted upon by Dodi. Henri Paul would drive the true getaway Mercedes while the other Mercedes and the Range Rover would pretend they were leaving with Diana and Dodi from the front. The plan did not work. At 12.20 a.m. Henri Paul drove off. At the front of the Ritz an amateur video shows the sudden rush of vehicles. Amidst the hurry and squealing of tyres one can clearly hear a woman with an American accent shouting, 'They are chasing Princess Diana!'[21] The amateur video also showed previous to their departure a powerful motorbike parked in readiness. Amongst the rush of vehicles 'chasing Princess Diana' is a powerful motorbike with a pillion passenger.

The paparazzi were with the Mercedes carrying Diana and Dodi by the time it reached the Place de la Concorde. Paul was stopped by traffic lights here. Just before the lights turned green he bolted off with the pack in hot pursuit. Without any more stops the Mercedes swung right onto the Cours la Reine, the expressway that runs east-west alongside the Seine passing through a number of tunnels of which the Alma tunnel is one. After steadying the car in the direction of the west-bound lanes (on the right side of the freeway) Paul apparently put the accelerator to the floor. At this point Paul, driving from an easterly direction, was a little more than a kilometre from the Alma tunnel.

From now on the eye-witness testimony is conflicting or inconsistent about some of the details of what happened. Such inconsistencies and conflicts (however small) are a real problem for police and the justice departments. The standards of evidence are (rightly) higher for official bodies than for the ordinary person applying his reason and judgement in an everyday situation. I am going to apply the standards of everyday reasoning (inductive and deductive) to the evidence from the most important eye-witness reports. It is not uncommon to make firm and *true* decisions in everyday life based on the high probability produced by a range of sometimes conflicting information. Keeping the background of the accident in mind, I will endeavour to construct the most likely scenario and explanation for what happened in the Alma tunnel based on the eye-witness testimony that seemed in *the main*, but not always in *the detail*, consistent with or verified by other testimony.[22]

Readers will be able to follow the description of the eye-witness testimony more easily if they keep in mind that Paul was heading along the freeway in a westerly direction. As he approached from the east there were eye-witnesses in four key positions:

- Directly behind the Mercedes.
- To the right of the Alma tunnel as seen from the east.
- Directly in front of the Mercedes in the tunnel.
- On the left-hand side of the freeway heading east.

Many witnesses reported that the Mercedes flew along the Cours la Reine with motorbikes and cars closely following. The fast-moving group of vehicles looked to many like a convoy. Right to the entrance of the Alma tunnel witnesses claimed there were powerful motorbikes aggressively weaving around the Mercedes. Some of the witnesses were in cars passed by the Mercedes and the pursuing vehicles heading west. Others were standing at different positions off to the right of the freeway not far from the entrance to the Alma tunnel. These people were in critical positions. Two of these were standing on a grassy plantation on the Place de la Reine Astrid almost directly to the right of the tunnel entrance as the cars approach from the east. From this position they had a view of the approach to the tunnel but could not see the cars entering the tunnel as the road dipped behind a retaining wall. They were also looking a little up to their left across a slip road that led onto the freeway from the side street (Cours Albert Ier) parallel to the freeway. This slip road leading onto the freeway around 50 metres before the tunnel entrance is of crucial interest.

One of these witnesses on the plantation said he heard a 'whine' of a car engine and turned to see a Mercedes at high speed followed by a 'big' motorbike. Notice that his attention was drawn to a point up to the left from where he and his companion were standing. If a car had driven onto the freeway via the slip road just before his attention was caught by the Mercedes he most likely would not have seen it. Indeed, he says he saw a car in front of the Mercedes at this point. The Mercedes had to accelerate to swing around it on the left-hand side. His companion sees much the same except that he claims the car in front of the Mercedes was trying to slow the Mercedes down, forcing it to take evasive action (as in the incident after leaving Le Bourget Airport). There was a change of gears as the Mercedes accelerated to pass the obstructing car. They disappeared into the tunnel and shortly after there was the sound of a violent crash.

At the same time, about 80 metres up from the entrance to the Alma tunnel and on a grassy traffic island separating the side road from the freeway, four people were walking. They saw a Mercedes approaching at high speed and heading in the direction of the Alma tunnel. The Mercedes was followed by a motorbike carrying two people. The Mercedes passed a vehicle in the right hand lane near the entrance to the tunnel. Two of the four witnesses had the impression that there was a collision between the Mercedes and the second car.

Meanwhile two cars, one not far behind the other, were entering the Alma tunnel from the opposite eastbound direction. The people in the first car said they heard a screeching of tyres. They looked through the pillars separating the westbound and eastbound sides of the freeway and saw a large car swerving first to the left then to the right. One said that the large car had swerved to avoid another that had been blocking its route. The other person was more explicit. He heard the screeching of the tyres followed by a small impact. The car in front of the Mercedes accelerated 'brutally' when the Mercedes lost control, swerving first to the left then to the right before sliding to the left and crashing into the pillar. After crashing it swung round and came to rest facing in the opposite direction. This second person 'saw a motorcycle or a big Vespa … pass the Mercedes … The motorcycle slowed down, then accelerated and left.'[23]

The lone driver of the second car, on entering the tunnel, heard a tremendous crash. The pillars in the centre of the road blocked his view of the lead-up to the crash and the crash itself. When the Mercedes came into his line of vision on the opposite side of the freeway it had evidently just come to rest facing eastwards. At that point he saw a large motorcycle heading westwards pass around the crashed Mercedes and head off at a great speed. It seemed to him that the motorcycle only had time to slow down before it took off. He was sure he saw no other vehicle pass the Mercedes 'between the moment [he] saw the Mercedes and the moment that the motorcycle went around it.'[24]

At the moment the Mercedes entered the first screeching skid, a car carrying two people was not far in front of it. The alerted driver looked in his left-hand wing mirror (the driver's side) and saw a Mercedes crashing towards him. Reflexively he accelerated fearing the car was going to run into him. It didn't. He saw the Mercedes slide at an angle, right itself and then slam into the pillar to swing round out of the vision of his mirror. He saw no other car, which is understandable. His car was in the right-hand lane and the field of vision in the wing mirror did not take in the area other witnesses placed the second car in. His passenger who turned around to look also saw the Mercedes skid sideways and finish slamming into the pillar. She also saw 'six or seven' vehicles drive around the wrecked Mercedes. She did not see any of these cars pass her and her companion. This is backed up by a report in *Newsweek* magazine (20 October, 1997):

The photographs [taken at the scene of the accident] (most of them confiscated from paparazzi) showed that, contrary to what was at first thought, several cars — probably six — did pass the wreckage of the

Mercedes and left the tunnel before traffic was stopped ...

Not far in front of this car (about 50 metres from the Mercedes) was another car carrying two people. The driver said he heard 'two impacts ... [t]he first shock sounded like car-against-car. The second was a deeper sound, like a car ramming into a truck.'[25] Within seconds of the tremendous noise made by the crash a motorbike passed them. They did not observe any other car passing them and thought there were no other cars between them and the Mercedes. In terms of the nature of evidence given by eyewitnesses in such dramatic circumstances it is significant that the driver of this second car did not see the car which was indisputably directly in front of the crashing car and behind him.

One startling piece of eyewitness testimony came from a man named Francois Levistre. He featured as a critical witness in the program, 'Diana: Secrets Behind the Crash'. Levistre said that he entered the freeway from Cours Albert Ier along the slip road just before the entrance to the Alma tunnel. Some way into the tunnel he looked in his rear-vision mirror and saw the Mercedes with a white car in front of it. Following the Mercedes were two motorbikes. He told *Reuters* September 4:

> I saw the car in the middle of the tunnel with a motorcycle on its left, pulling ahead and then swerving to the right directly in front of the car [the Mercedes]. As the motorcycle swerved and before the car lost control, there was a flash of light. But then I was out of the tunnel and heard, but did not see, the impact.[26]

This testimony makes clear that Levistre places himself in front of the two other cars who saw the crash in their rear-vision mirrors. He does not mention seeing these cars but he told the police he saw a big motorcycle with two riders come out of the tunnel immediately after the crash.[27] Levistre repeated this in more detail to Nicholas Owen in 'Diana: Secrets Behind the Crash', and adds some significant information. When the Mercedes and the motorcycle racing beside it came over the crown of the dip to the tunnel both seemed to accelerate:

> ... at that moment the Mercedes ... the motorbike accelerates. And you can see the acceleration of the motorbike because you can see the

headlights rise up a bit. The bike is accelerating. I'm halfway through the tunnel inside when the motorbike accelerates ... cuts the Mercedes up [off]! ... At that moment there is a big white flash, a massive white light. I'm looking in the rear-view mirror and it's then at that moment I see the motorbike and I think to myself ... I think why did the motorbike cut them up [off]?

Levistre is asked if he thought the flash was a photo flash. He answers with a firm, 'No'. It was stronger. Later Nicholas Owen asks him to view two different flash sources in comparable conditions. First Levistre views the flash from a camera flash gun. Then he views the flash from an anti-personnel flash gun used by the army special forces to blind the enemy rendering them inoperable. Levistre says that the flash from the motorbike in the tunnel resembled the anti-personnel flash. Such a weapon, says Owen, is readily available in London. Owen claimed that other witnesses saw this flash. After the enormous burst of white light, Levistre says 'the Mercedes goes left, right, left' and crashes. Levistre's evidence should be treated with some reservation as his account of the accident at different times is not always consistent. I include it here to the extent that it is consistent with the other eye-witness reports.

The final testimony included here comes from a couple who shortly after 12.20 a.m. drove onto the freeway via the slip road on the westbound exit side of the Alma tunnel. They saw a 'zigzagging and backfiring' white Fiat Uno come out of the tunnel and pass them. The driver did not see them as he was busy looking in his rear-vision mirror. He nearly ran into them. Looking confused he swung suddenly to the right to park on the side of the road. The driver of the first car said that the Fiat Uno paused briefly before continuing on its way. I will make two observations about this testimony. It is not as closely connected with the sequence of events surrounding the crash as the testimony I have already cited. Secondly, the Fiat Uno could quite easily have been one of the cars that passed around the wreck. That seems consistent with a shocked witness to a car accident pausing briefly on the side of the road before continuing on his way. Or was there a distortion in the perception of the couple about this part of their testimony? After all they were continuing on their way either looking in the rear-vision mirror or turning around as they put distance between themselves and the Fiat Uno. Perhaps the Fiat swung off the freeway at the first available turn and high-tailed it out of the vicinity. We cannot know at this point — at least not on the basis of the information made public.

The Paris police carrying out the investigation of the accident have reportedly amassed thousands of pages of evidence. It may seem preposterous to offer a credible scenario on the basis of the information I have outlined above. My object, as I say, is not to build a case that can be brought before a court of law. My object is to construct a compelling scenario by calibrating the common elements of the testimony of the most important eye-witnesses in order to accommodate the apparent inconsistencies. I am going to apply the normal prudential reasoning all of us apply competently in our daily lives. In doing this, we must keep in mind that a set of dramatic circumstances will inevitably distort features of an eye-witness account. It is understandable that in a group of several key witnesses some will place objects and people slightly out of their real position or sequence. In fact, the circumstances do not have to have the pressure of a dramatic situation for us to make slight errors of perception. How many times does a family video correct our impression of what happened on a particular occasion? The mental and emotional pressures on the witnesses to Diana's accident have been enormous. On this basis, I will begin by enumerating the pre-accident sequence:

1. By the time Diana and Dodi arrived in Paris on 30 August the media were in a state of irreversible excitement and resolve to catch their prey.
2. The blocking manoeuvre executed by the paparazzi just outside Le Bourget Airport heralded what was to follow.
3. Diana was brought to a state of fear and despair by the actions of the paparazzi.
4. Dodi was angry and frustrated in his concern for Diana.
5. The most 'professional' teams of paparazzi were present. They would have their reward.
6. Dodi was driven to form a desperate plan of escape.
7. The plan failed and the paparazzi held on to the bitter end.

This brings us to the accident itself. How did it happen? In my view the following is the most likely sequence of events leading directly to the accident.

One of the professional paparazzi teams worked out a plan that would anticipate most of the moves made by the couple after they left the Ritz. It is highly probable that they had inside information about the decoy plan. They would try to execute the well-rehearsed tactic of blocking the fleeing car with one of their own cars while a photographer riding pillion on a pursuing motorbike would take pictures of the obstructed vehicle. Among other options the blocking car in this case was either ready to go onto the freeway along the Seine from the Place de la Concorde at a signal given via a mobile phone or he was situated in a position where, upon being alerted, he could join the freeway (Cours la Reine) from the slip road just before the entrance to the Alma tunnel. The layout of Cours Albert Ier, the side road providing access to the slip road, gives the driver the chance to reach a fair speed by the time he enters Cours la Reine.

I favour the second option as there is no evidence that the blocking car was following the Mercedes along the freeway. Besides, it would have to have been a high performance small car to outrun the Mercedes. Nobody would have missed such a car. The motorbike would join the pursuit from somewhere near the start. It is likely the motorbike only picked up the Mercedes when it stopped at the Place de la Concorde. That enabled the rider to join the pursuing group without exciting too much notice and without having been captured on video at the Ritz. The driver picked for this plan would have been fearless and highly skilled on a motorbike. My guess is that most of the paparazzi present that night know who he and his possible passenger are.

The powerful motorbike in question kept pace with the Mercedes and drew the constant attention of Paul (together with the other pursuing vehicles) as he drove along at speed. As they approached the Alma tunnel, the blocking car moved onto the freeway and positioned itself to execute the necessary manoeuvre. The speed of the Mercedes, the layout of the tunnel entrance and Paul's distraction by the pursuing vehicles brought him suddenly up behind the car obstructing his path. Nevertheless he started evasive action. But the small car accelerated. This was the 'whine' of a revving engine witnesses heard. It was not the Mercedes as it is a relatively quiet car. The small car also veered towards the extreme left of his lane. Paul, surprised by the aggressive action of the car in front of him, could not avoid clipping the back of the obstructing vehicle.

The motorbike in the meantime had swung around him putting himself in front of the path of the Mercedes' next evasive manoeuvre. Paul recovered from the first skid looping from the left to the right, but lost control of the second skid phase because of the combined spoiling manoeuvres of the car and the motorbike. The rear end of the Mercedes began the slide sideways as the car skidded again from right to left. It then ended up slamming into the thirteenth support pillar of the Alma tunnel. The motorbike and car, realising what they had done, immediately made good their escape. The car and the motorbike would have been destroyed immediately in an attempt to erase any connection with the powers who had a stake in the plan.

Such a scenario satisfies all the main features of the eye-witness testimony. It is also consistent with the media behaviour prior to and during the events in Paris. Most importantly it is consistent with the physical evidence gathered at the crash scene. Amongst the crash debris were found parts of the left tail-light of a Fiat Uno and fragments of white paint used in the manufacture of the Fiat Uno. Also found along the right side of the Mercedes was a horizontal line left by the scraping of rubber. It was the same kind of rubber used in the manufacture of the Fiat Uno bumper bars. The glancing collision between the two cars left this line of rubber on the Mercedes at the right height of the Fiat Uno bumper bars. There is almost no doubt that the Mercedes collided with a white Fiat Uno.

Jean Pietri, the crash expert hired by Sancton and MacLeod to write a report on the accident, provided even more compelling evidence. His analysis of the skid marks revealed that the Mercedes, after colliding with a vehicle in the right-hand lane, veered to the left glancing the kerb of the centre island. Paul was able to stabilise the car bringing it around to the right apparently heading for the right-hand lane. This manoeuvre caused the first skid. But he does not continue in that direction. Instead he swings the car to the left again and applies the brakes. He now loses control of the Mercedes and its trajectory becomes fatal. Pietri says that Paul did not head into the right-hand lane because his way was blocked by two other vehicles: the one he collided with and a second vehicle. Pietri claims that the *real* cause of the accident was the positioning of the second vehicle. He assumes the second vehicle was that of the first eye-witness in front of the Mercedes. But, considering the testimony of the driver of that car, this does not seem likely. That driver's testimony puts him too far in front of the Mercedes to force Paul to take radical evasive action. That leaves the scenario I have just outlined as the most probable sequence of events. Those directly responsible for causing the accident were the paparazzi working in co-operation with the media organisations who commissioned their activities.

3. The Conspiracy Theories

There are many conspiracy theories about the death of Diana, each one generally more outrageous than the other. There is one conspiracy theory favoured by Mohammed Al Fayed that is consistent with most of the details of the events I have outlined. The critical point of difference for Al Fayed comes with the testimony of Francois Levistre. The flash Levistre says he witnessed was meant, according to this theory, to disable the driver causing him to crash. The object was assassination. The motive apparently was to prevent the union between the British royal house and an Arab. This theory is canvassed in 'Diana: Secrets Behind the Crash'. In addition to Levistre's testimony, the supporting evidence is Paul's apparent contact with the French Secret Service, the depositing of unaccounted for amounts of cash in Paul's various bank accounts, and the testimony of James Hewitt (Diana's former lover) that he was warned away from Diana at the risk of physical harm. These pieces of evidence, as they are presented, do not hang together at all well.

I can understand Mohammed Al Fayed's concern about the circumstances of the accident but I see nothing in these details compelling enough to suggest a plan to assassinate Diana and Dodi. Much more needs to be produced to make the right connections. All this is in addition to the almost impossible task of arranging an assassination to take place in the way that Diana and Dodi died. How could anyone organise the coincidence of events as they actually took place? It seems humanly impossible. All these loose elements could be drawn together if the case can be sustained that a group of assassins had entered the chase for Diana seeking the right opportunity. But the basis and cover for such grand opportunist action were provided by the media. In such an event the action of all parties could hardly be more co-operative.

In the end this book is not an investigation of the accident itself. It is about the way the media behave collectively and how they subscribe to a 'vision' of the world that results in a particular form of behaviour. I have attempted in the previous chapters to outline the foundations and moral implications of that vision, and to demonstrate that the media's behaviour was directly connected with the death of Princess Diana. I have called that 'world vision' *theoretic-republicanism.*

THE END

[With regard to the Revolution in France we] are in a war of a *peculiar* nature. It is not with an ordinary community, which is hostile or friendly as passion or as interest may veer about; not with a State which makes war through wantonness, and abandons its through lassitude. We are at war with a system, which, by its essence, is inimical to all other Governments, and which makes peace or war, as peace and war may best contribute to their subversion. It is with an *armed doctrine*, that we are at war.

Edmund Burke, *First Letter on a Regicide Peace* (1796)

Footnotes

CHAPTER 1

1 Of course, a lot more could be said about the moral aspect of media hounding. The media collectively did not hang back in offering many refining arguments about who should bear the responsibility for Diana's death. The issue of responsibility will be an important one in the following chapters. Indeed, I intend to outline the rudiments of a philosophy of the rights and duties of 'fame'. My rhetorical question at this point is meant to indicate that most people around the world did not need any further discussion about who was to blame for the accident that killed Diana and Dodi Fayed. And still don't.

2 There have been many reports about the accident appearing in a variety of newspapers and magazines. There have also been many television programs devoted to discussing Diana, the accident and the significance of the events in Paris for the British royal family. For my purposes I am going to rely on the following book as the main reference for the accident and its background: Thomas Sancton & Scott MacLeod, *Death of a Princess: An Investigation*, Weidenfeld & Nicholson, London, 1998. The virtue of this book is that the authors have painstakingly gathered and checked their information. Most of the reliable information common to other media reports has been collected, assembled and expanded in this book. It is an example of genuine investigative journalism into the facts of the case. There are, however, many points of interpretation which I would challenge. These interpretative issues and others will be dealt with in the course of my discussion.

3 There is compelling evidence that other paparazzi who were present at the scene also fled before the police arrived. Two reported to police on 5 September. Two other paparazzi reported to the police but these claimed they did not follow the Mercedes but went straight to Dodi Fayed's apartment from the Ritz. The Paris police are still looking for the others they believe were there at the accident. *Death of a Princess*, pp.162-63.

4 Three photos were in fact printed that week. One appeared in a German tabloid newspaper on 1 September, the other two in an Italian magazine on 5 September. These photos, one of which showed 'faint images', did not present graphic images of the crash. *Death of a Princess*, p.175. The full series of graphic photos remains an irresistible temptation for the media groups.

5 I will be dealing extensively with the 3 September edition of *The Australian* in Chapter 4.

6 It is a common complaint from those expressing 'unacceptable' social and political ideas that their views are more often met with ridicule and vilification than with reasoned argument. Prime Minister John Howard is a prime example of a public figure being subjected to continuous ridicule because of his views. Paul Keating, former Prime Minister, broke his silence recently to say the following: 'John Howard has the vision of Mr Magoo without the good intentions.' This comment is typical of a man who disgraced the office of Prime Minister with his unrelenting abuse and vilification of anybody who did not agree with him. I will comment further on John Howard in Chapter 2. Professor Geoffrey Blainey, eminent historian, for years has been vilified for his opinions on immigration and its effects on Australian life. Former Governor-General, John Kerr, was so persecuted for his actions in dismissing the Labor Government in 1975 that he was more or less forced into exile. During 1997 and 1998, many ordinary citizens in our Australian liberal democracy have been abused, vilified, harassed, sometimes bashed, and at other times prevented from attending political meetings by Australia's new 'brown shirts'. These new 'brown shirts' are those who have disqualified all concerns about Australian society other than their own. The principles of 'free speech' and 'freedom of association' are evidently applicable only to those whose views are condoned by the groups responsible for the vilification and political violence. I will be dealing with these issues in Chapter 2.

7 The theorist may well ask whether anyone at all is capable of presenting 'the truth'. In Chapter 2 I will be looking further at this question and the confusion that arises from analysing such everyday expressions and the understandings they reflect.

8 Media reports over a period of time as distinct from media reports across the period of one day.

CHAPTER 2

1 As is usual, a draft copy of this book was presented to a number of reviewers. The reviewers divided into two camps with regard to their reaction to the major themes of the book. One camp agreed with the general case outlined against the media, and had differing positive views about the theoretical attack. The other camp was in strong opposition and identified with the 'theorists'. The members of this camp wrote extensive notes about the serious 'problems' they thought vitiated the object of the book — which they consider otherwise as a worthy project. For the most part I thought their criticism exemplified the general picture I had painted

of the 'theorist' group. It is not possible in the scope of this book to provide counter arguments to every objection (and its implications) raised by these reviewers. Nevertheless, as a parallel issue and further to exemplify what I have written, I will deal in the endnotes with some of the more pertinent objections. Henceforth I will refer to the critical group as CR (Critical Reviewer). One of the critical reviewers was an academic with expertise in the philosophies and the philosophic period I will be dealing with. He raised some strong objections. These I will deal with in the body of the text or in the endnotes. One of his comments was actually a warning. If I insisted, he said, on combining the various theories in the way I was doing to use as a weapon against my opponents, I might appear 'intellectually disreputable'. Without any sarcasm or irony, I thanked him for his encouragement — for he had missed the point.

2   CR found such expressions mere namecalling and insisted this weakened the argument. It was an objection he continually raised. Now this provokes a long discussion about political namecalling and abuse which I will return to shortly. In this case, the use of 'wanker' and 'bludging' is simply repeating the terms in our Australian vernacular often used to describe the members of the first group. I have heard these words used many times in the same context by people who do not have a high respect for universities and their products. The Australian vernacular has other more colourful words for the same circumstances. I have not used them here.

3   CR found this talk about jargon insulting to the reader's intelligence. According to CR all argument should be explicable in everyday terms. Nothing is beyond being explained lucidly and does not have to be couched in academic jargon — which is the prop of insecure minds. This raises many different points. Firstly, most substantial theories have developed their own terminology. One only has to think of the social sciences to understand how particular schools of thought depend on their own vocabulary. When it comes to metaphysical and epistemological issues, some theories are simply incomprehensible without an understanding of the terminology. The terminology and the theoretical background have to be known beforehand. One cannot escape it. This is just the point. When it comes to the discussion of everyday matters the incomprehensible terminology for the ordinary person does not aid or clarify discussion. Rather it confuses things. The theory and its impenetrable terminology are one and the same in the end: a body of irrelevant theory couched in its own terminology which is irreducible to the actual concrete situation the ordinary person has to deal with. CR shows that he misses the point on two accounts. Jargon is the problem of theory per se; theory is a body of thought abstracted out of the real conditions of life. This is the reason I do not want to burden the reader with the terminology specific to cer-

tain types of theory. Indeed, when it comes later to outlining the concept of classical natural law, CR showed he was not in possession of the necessary vocabulary to understand what I was talking about. CR actually gave an example of the problem of theorising. When I maintained that the media are not concerned with the 'truth' but with their material objectives, CR wanted me to consider the latest (sociological) theories about truth and subjectivity. This concerns the assertion that all reporting is subjective to greater and lesser extents. Abstractly speaking, nobody reports the 'truth'. There is always some subjective content. Well, in this case I am satisfied that the average intelligent reader fully grasps what I mean when I say that the media's main concern is their material position and not the truth of the circumstances they are reporting on. No further abstract discussion is warranted or desired. The average intelligent reader can understand the distinction between the reports of the disinterested observer and the reports made by those seeking to advance their material position without regard to the actual circumstances.

4   The metaphysical and epistemological doctrine of realism holds 'that the human intellect discovers in the particulars apprehended by sense experience an intelligible order of abstract essences and necessary relations ontologically prior to particular things and contingent events and from that order the intellect can demonstrate necessary truths concerning first causes and the being and attributes of God.' E. Moody, 'William of Ockham', *Encyclopaedia of Philosophy*, Paul Edwards, Editor-in-Chief, New York, MacMillan Inc., 1967. This is an example of specialist language. I will endeavour to explain the key points in everyday language further on.

5   CR thought that talk of the spiritual or non-material world was necessarily connected with religious belief. And did this not present a problem because belief in God is very much on the wane? In the long run belief in an immaterial world of constant laws is connected with religious belief. At least, that's the implication. But the person who recognises the non-material world and its unalterable laws need not immediately see the implications for religious belief. The essential point here is that the knowledge of God's existence and of the objective order of the world are open to all persons whatever their particular culture, nationality and spiritual beliefs. Indeed, the classical natural law is an essential proposition in Catholic teaching, and the Catholic Church recognises this element in all the great religions. It is curious to hear some people declare they are agnostics or atheists and will not have a bar of religion, but in their behaviour reflect an adherence to a set of moral principles consistent with the prescriptions of the classical natural law.

6   CR claimed that this comment was arrogant and insulting to the reader.

But again the point is missed. Immanuel Kant's major philosophical works are considered obscure and difficult by most students who study them at university level. Kant's works are an important part of the Enlightenment period which aimed at freeing the ordinary person from the tyranny of religious belief and traditional political authority. The theories of the Enlightenment, however, are even more incomprehensible in many cases than the 'superstitions' they are meant to replace. The irony is that a person must subject himself to the authority of an intellectual superior in order to arrive at even a minimal understanding of such 'freedom' theories.

7   This may not seem clear. Let me give two famous examples from the works of Scottish philosopher, David Hume, who is, in my view, the most destructive and most influential of modern philosophers — yes, even ahead of Marx. Hume said that if we see one billiard ball hit a stationary billiard ball which rolls forward, we say that the first billiard ball caused the second to move. But where do we see the 'thing' called 'cause'? It is nowhere to be found. What we see in many cases of a billiard ball hitting another is just that: one ball hitting the other after which the second moves. What we call causality is in fact merely one action constantly accompanying a second action. There is no immaterial principle of causality connected to an ordained metaphysical order of the world. There is nothing to say that the one action will not be accompanied by a different sort of action tomorrow. Many people on reading this have found it counter-intuitive. The second example is the case of somebody being bashed to death. What do we see in these actual circumstances? Merely a series of physical actions. We cannot see, whatever way we look at it, things called evil, crime, wrongness and so on. Of course, we think it is wrong and evil but that's just because we do not approve of what we see going on. There is nothing in the circumstances that is actually evil. Again, this seems outrageous and counter-intuitive to a lot of people. It is, however, a logical outcome of the overthrow of the realist vision and the adoption of the Enlightenment one. Morality and laws would come to be a result of human decision-making, an act of will expressing a particular preference.

8   CR thought that I was running close to doing this myself in a 'blanket' condemnation of universities. But an attack on universities because of a prevailing 'intellectual' vision is not the same thing as condemning those who disagree with the prevailing intellectual vision as stupid and ignorant (and sometimes corrupt). I am not attacking the notion of a university. Quite the contrary. Higher institutions of learning have a legitimate role in the life of our society, as they have always had – especially in the Middle Ages. I am attacking the regime of university life as it now exists. CR would know that I am not the first to write about a political

culture that some call 'political correctness' and which is thought to prevail in most universities.

9 CR constantly wanted to bring up the fact that the Church of Rome was hardly less famous in the past for such actions. I will leave aside the religious bigotry presupposed by the often erroneous assertions made by CR about the history of the Catholic Church. Two brief comments will suffice as relevant to the present context. Firstly, the wars that were instigated by the theoretic dogma of the Enlightenment were wholly different in nature from the wars of the past. They were far more extensive. Secondly, and this is the main point, the adherents of theoretic-republicanism have claimed that their theoretic dogma was the solution to all the evils caused by traditional social arrangements, hereditary rule and the superstition of religion. They dismissed all social structures and moral schemes that did not correspond with their theoretic dogma as illegitimate. One of my primary aims in this book is to show the great fraud theoretic-republicanism is. The last thing that the adherents of theoretic-republicanism promote is freedom and equality for all members of society. The illusion of freedom and equality is the promotional goal. Otherwise existing traditional hierarchies are to be replaced by the hierarchy of theoretic-republicanism.

10 By this I mean that the theoretic-republican elite does not form a separate administrative body with their own offices, buildings, organisations, etc. They are a group formed mainly on the basis of consensus and agreement within the existing structures of society. Their political and social discourse identifies them as belonging to their faction. Their skill in expressing and utilising the principles of theoretic-republicanism raises them to the right position of power within their hierarchy. In the end, they are recognisable by the fruits of their endeavours. Those that reject their theoretic dogma and their unabated efforts to control society can recognise them almost at first glance. They recognise the declaration of war on all elements in the political and social structure that do not fall in with their 'vision', their 'vision' being the only legitimate one.

11 By 'religion' I mean all the great religions that implicitly recognise God as the one Supreme Being whose laws are evident to human reason. This is the minimum requirement of all religions. Readers should not assume from this that I support a syncretistic position (that all religions are particular valid expressions of belief in the One God and are reducible to the one supreme religion). The issue of 'revealed' religion is too extensive to cover in this book. Traditional Christianity acknowledges the existence of classical natural law and God's divine tactic, and that this is open to human reason. Let me further comment that the claims of a

revealed religion do not in themselves affront our reason. There is no contradiction in the claim that God has revealed himself definitively.

12 CR found this reference confusing. The point I am making is that a confirmed (Marxist) communist like Bernie Taft recognised that the republicans in the Spanish civil conflict belonged ideologically to his group. The confusion evidently arises because General Franco has long been considered 'fascist', as fascist and fascism is generally understood. Rather than arguing about political tags, let me mention the key features of the conflict between the Spanish republicans and those who gathered around General Franco when he left his army base in Morocco to take up the fight to restore Spain. Not only did the republican groups continually identify themselves ideologically as implementers of key features of Enlightenment thinking as I have described them, but they accompanied their ideological discourse with the effective elimination of traditional social arrangements, the shutting down of Catholic Churches and schools, and the calculated murder of hundreds of Catholic clergy. Franco's action restored the religious and social traditions of Spain, and re-established the Spanish monarchy. When social and political stability had returned to Spain, Franco withdrew gradually from political office. The ultimate transition to a democratic form of government was comparatively smooth and peaceful. B.A. Santamaria considered that, despite the inevitable horrors of a civil war, the regime fought for by Franco and his supporters was based on social and religious principles whose philosophical background was classical natural law and its metaphysical foundations.

13 I should not have to observe that acknowledging John Howard's true moral character does not make him perfect or commit one to every policy decision he makes. For example, many people would not subscribe to economic rationalism if by that is meant the rigid implementation of an economic theory and if that is in fact truly representative of John Howard's economic beliefs.

14 It is not perfectly formed and self-sufficient. Its nature is to feed on the existing body politic. It is essentially parasitic.

15 This passage caused particular problems for our Critical Reviewer. Firstly, he thought reference to 'glories' of the past meant that there were *only* 'glories' of the past, and that there were no low points. Of course, the past did not consist only of glories. There are no perfect societies. But for all the faults and failures of some societies there are many events, peoples and achievements to be proud of. Those whose cultural heritage includes the glories of the peoples of the British Isles, and by extension, of European/Christian civilisation have much to be proud of. CR also wondered

about those Australians not of European ethnicity. How could they feel the glories of the cultural heritage represented by Prince Charles? Quite easily. Their ethnicity does not make any difference to their Australian-ness and their citizenship of Australia. Those born and bred in Australia, and who are truly immersed in their Australian-ness, will feel the same regardless of ethnicity. With this I embark on the whole issue of multiculturalism and there is not the space to pursue it any further. Let me only state an obvious conclusion from my discussion of the two different frameworks of thought: just as there are two concepts of the Constitution corresponding with the differences in the thinking of the theorist (the theoretic-republican) and the ordinary person, there are also two concepts of multiculturalism. One is healthy and legitimate; the other is destructive and illegitimate. That concept corresponding with theoretic-republicanism is the destructive concept.

16 Apart from the information gathered through the years from the frequent media reports about Charles and Diana's marriage, I will draw on a recent book about Diana by Richard Kay. The book appeared in serial form in Australia. In Melbourne it was serialised by the *Sunday Sun-Herald*. The full reference is: Richard Kay, *Diana: The Untold Story*, *Sunday Sun-Herald*, Melbourne, 1998. The great virtue of this book is that it was written by a journalist who had a genuine friendship with Diana. Richard Kay was one of the few journalists Diana could rely on to pass on her message. However, in referring to this book we must keep in mind that *Diana: The Untold Story* represents largely Diana's perception of events. The account of the way she perceived Charles, the royal family and the monarchy we can take to be true. Her perception is truly recounted. We must also keep in mind that her perception of events may not be as they really happened. Although Kay is sympathetic to Diana and her perception of things he does not hesitate to give the full picture of her insecure feelings and unstable temperament. On the other hand, Kay is keen to destroy the false image of Diana that was created by Andrew Morton's book, *Diana: Her True Story* (to which I will return). He was at pains to say that Charles and Diana, despite their many problems and the eventual breakdown of the marriage, truly loved each other in the beginning and shared some very happy times. To the last, Kay says that Diana thought the marriage could have been saved. Indeed, friends of both thought that if Charles and Diana had had the right sort of advice and assistance, the marriage would not have deteriorated the way it did. Indeed, Diana thought some time after the divorce that if she had not been so inexperienced she might have dealt with the problem of Camilla Parker Bowles, Prince Charles's 'mistress'. (pp. 6, 14, 84).

17 CR wanted to challenge whether this was a view commonly held by feminists. Anybody who has been subjected to the frequent feminist outpourings in the media and the torrent of feminist academic material over the last twenty years could hardly deny that one major theme of feminism is the inherent aggression and brutality of the state of being male. There would be few men of my acquaintance who have not been told this personally by one or other feminist colleague. Around six years ago I was attending the American Book Fair in Los Angeles. One evening I arranged to have dinner with two colleagues, one of whom brought along his professional wife. The subject arose inevitably about the unfairness and oppression that professional women had to suffer in their respective fields at the hands of their male colleagues. At a certain point to indicate the true nature of the problem, the professional wife of my business friend said that the state of being male was morally inferior to the state of being female; women were *inherently* morally superior to men. When it was suggested that that view may be sexist the professional woman replied more or less that as repugnant as it may sound to some males, it was unfortunately the reality. None of the three males present pursued this statement with any aggression or abuse. Indeed, the matter was calmly passed over with just the odd look. Such an example could be multiplied indefinitely. The affirmation of the superiority of femaleness over maleness is routine and unthinking in the media. One small example: Ray Martin, high profile compere of the top-rating *A Current Affair* on the Nine Network, is in the habit of making the following sort of casual comment to his TV audience: [When it comes to employees] 'you can't beat women for workers.' This seemingly inoffensive remark was made when he was showing his TV audience the workings of his large media office.

18 CR thought this outline of how one develops one's moral consciousness far too simple. He wanted a further sociological explanation of the processes of moral learning. But CR misses the point. This section here is a follow-on from the natural law view briefly outlined earlier, the object being to show how different moral visions have different outcomes. The opposition is between the morality of rationalistic theory and the common sense moral thinking of the ordinary person unaffected by three or four years of academic study.

19 Kay reports that some people thought that Camilla Parker Bowles (whom Diana held responsible for ruining her marriage) should have herself taken action to prevent the troubles between Diana and Charles from growing – troubles that she (Camilla) was ultimately responsible for. It was Camilla Parker Bowles's responsibility to get out of the way because Charles was too 'weak' to take action himself (*Diana: The Untold Story*, p. 10). This view, however, is premised on accepting the claim that Charles did not

take his marriage seriously and held on to his alleged affair with Bowles as his mistress into and during his marriage. Apart from Charles rejecting this claim the evidence seems to be on his side in this particular dispute. Furthermore, in such a difficult situation it is easy to accuse someone of being weak and unresponsive when they do not take the action that others prescribe for them. I remain with the claim that despite many failures and mistakes Charles shows himself on the whole to be a man of fortitude and decency.

CHAPTER 3

1　Mohammed Al Fayed maintained the family name of 'Al Fayed' while his son Dodi dropped the 'Al'. In public he introduced himself as 'Dodi Fayed'.

2　I will refer to Rupert Murdoch's corporate organisation in Australia as News Ltd.

3　CR claimed that I had no more evidence for this view than Turnbull had for hers. In an abstract sense, that may be true. The real point is the media's inclination to sneer about the royal family, the place that sneering has in the ideological mindset of the media, the absence of any supporting evidence for the sneer, and the lack of credibility conveyed by the continual sneering in similar circumstances.

4　For more information about Dodi Fayed and the Al Fayed family, the reader is referred to Chapters 5 and 6, *Death of a Princess*. A very different, sympathetic picture emerges of the Al Fayed family. The presentation of another side to Dodi and Mohammed Al Fayed shows how little balance there was in the media reports about the father and son.

5　Kay reports that Diana thought Prince Charles 'looked so sad when [he] walked up the aisle at Lord Mountbatten's funeral'. (*Diana: The Untold Story*, p. 19) I have seen no other legitimate reference that supports Herd's claim that Diana thought Charles a 'sad man'. It looks again to be more journalistic distortion. I think people would allow Charles (as Diana did) to be sad on the occasion of the funeral of a favourite uncle who had been blown apart by an IRA terrorist bomb.

6　I will come back to Charles's relationship with Camilla Parker Bowles.

7　Cf Chapter 4, Section 13 for biographical information on Diana.

8　The report centres on Diana's holiday with Mohammed Al Fayed in St

Tropez during the week ending 19 July. The 'reviled' and unsavoury Al Fayed together with Diana on his A\$40 million yacht proved an intense provocation for the British media. Diana's 'behaviour' during this week with Al Fayed prompted the British media 'to suggest the "increasingly confused" Diana was losing her grasp of reality.' Until this week, it was reported, Diana had enjoyed the sympathy of the British public — in contrast to Charles and Camilla Parker Bowles. Andrew Morton, tabloid journalist and author of the sensation-causing *Diana: Her True Story* is quoted as writing in *The Sun* (an unscrupulous and aggressive Murdoch tabloid instrument, as we shall see in Chapter 10):

These days, Diana, you are no longer the Teflon Princess. You might have the run of a stg20 million yacht but your friends and fans see a woman who is drifting on the sea of life, seriously in danger of becoming shipwrecked... To say they are disappointed by the sight of you cavorting around St Tropez like an aspiring starlet from a B movie is an understatement.

It would be hard to express the deserved contempt for Andrew Morton. Perhaps I do not need to. His record speaks for itself.

Apparently the amoral minds in the media had made a 'romantic connection' between Diana and Mohammed Al Fayed, as if it was inconceivable that Diana and Princes William and Harry could have been there on Al Fayed's yacht simply enjoying a holiday with the family of an affectionate friend. Sancton and MacLeod devote Chapter 7: St Tropez, to this week. It was particularly the family atmosphere of the holiday that pleased Diana and her children. Later events demonstrated how twisted the media mind was in jumping to their particular conclusions.

Even though the holiday had been officially cleared 'some reports asked: "Diana, how could you?" in appeals reminiscent of the shock that greeted the revelation of Jackie Kennedy's affair with Aristotle Onassis.'

It seems Diana spoke at one point during the holiday about her future plans to the hacks from the main tabloid papers (*The Sun, The Mirror* and *The Daily Mail*). What she allegedly said and what was reported by the papers was disputed by Diana's office. Well, it appears that the most shocking thing imaginable for the lying unscrupulous rags of the British Isles is to try to deceive them or take them for a ride. All tabloid hell broke loose with the indignation rising from the very depths of the sulphurous regions.

The reporters were incensed. They supported each other in their accounts of the interview. Was Diana lying? Had she gone mad? Had the St Tropez sun addled her brain? By any reckoning, Diana's claims did not add up ...

As The Guardian's Kamal Ahmed wrote: 'In the end it is a game, a battle for attention with the appearance of distress. It is a game Diana plays very well.' But this time she may have taken the game too far and lost the goodwill of its other players. As the week went on the reports about Diana and the comments by Britain's legion of columnists became increasingly cruel.

By Wednesday, we weren't reading about how fabulous Diana looked in her swimming costumes but about how much weight she had put on …

Could it be … as questions are asked about the possibility of [Charles and Camilla] marrying, Diana's game playing with the press will become increasingly extravagant?

I ask readers to keep in mind the tenor of this report and others in a similar vein at the time as they read the argument and evidence against the media in this book. Here is a good case of the media manufacturing in their inimitable way the grounds for further intrusive action.

9 This was a picture of a scene, the vision of which frequently appears on TV reports when Charles and his sons are discussed. The scene is of a father and his two sons looking relaxed and comfortable with each other. Any unease is due to the media people present.

10 Kay is very clear about Diana's attitude to the institution of the British monarchy.

At the same time, Diana was careful never to lose sight of the other main objective in her life: bringing up William and Harry to respect, understand and continue the 1,000-year tradition of the monarchy.

She would say: 'It's very important to me that my sons have a good relationship with the Queen.' Carolan Brown, the Princess's fitness trainer for five years until 1994, remembers Diana telling her: 'The boys are going to see Granny today. I'm so glad they like her.' Some people may contend that Diana destabilised the monarchy, but she was acutely conscious of its vital role in the life of the country. She did her utmost, in her own way, to promote it.

Diana was determined that her boys would grow up to be comfortable with both paupers and princes, but they would never be allowed to forget how important it was that they 'understood and respected the tradition of which they were a part' (Diana: The Untold Story, pp. 70, 75).

The only point that needs further explanation here is how Diana perceived the task of promoting the monarchy, and how faulty or otherwise that perception was. I will be dealing with this question in the course of the book.

11 CR thought that this picture was overstated, that it was a negative view, that the present-day social cohesion does not differ much from the past. This is the usual response from those supporting the ideological trends of the present day when it is pointed out that the great change in social and moral views has resulted in social devastation. The same group of

people are never finished telling us about the 'bad old days' when sexism, patriarchy, discrimination were systematic in the prevailing social structures, etc. Only a rigid ideologue would seriously attempt to claim that social conditions and moral attitudes prevailing today were no different from 30 to 40 years ago. The issue is in what way they were different. James at least has this part of his book right.

12 CR was confused about the nomination of the 1960s as the beginning of the rot. He did not know whether the rot was supposed to have started during the Enlightenment or in the 1960s. The explanation is simple. The ideas that have brought about the changes in the latter part of the 20th century were promulgated during the period of the Enlightenment. These ideas had an uneven spread internationally through the following two hundred years. In some countries they had great impact among an elite from the beginning with varying degrees of actual social success. Their influence was above all insidious. In other countries they brought about sudden catastrophic change. In Australia, the ideas worked surreptitiously among an intellectual and political elite until the early 1960s when they struck hard leaving a wake of misery and destruction through the next thirty-odd years.

13 CR claimed that in 'many traditional societies wife beating was acceptable'. Such a claim provokes a long discussion and a long defence of the true nature of tradition. Let me make a few fundamental points. I would like more details about that 'traditional society' that found wife beating acceptable. If wife beating (with all the connotations that modern feminists attach to this phrase) was acceptable I would like to know how and why it was acceptable and in what context. Secondly, a traditional society is not understood as a 'perfect' society. This is the great problem of misapprehension the rationalist ideologue has to deal with. When the social rationalist talks of social theory, he is talking about the theoretical perfectibility of society in general. Those talking about the prescriptive nature of tradition and its obligatory anchor in classical natural law are claiming not that society is perfectible through the protection of tradition but that the protection of healthy tradition is a better guarantee of social and moral stability than an abstract theory. A 'tradition' that is not healthy should be evident within the traditional social structure. If it is not, then that is a human failure within that society. 'Wife beating' cannot be a true tradition, and it can only feature in a traditional society as a social incoherence and moral failure. Its persistence would act ultimately as a warning. The failure of traditional societies to correct harmful elements in their social life would mean laying the way open by default to fundamentally inimical pressures and people to initiate change.

14 CR thought I must be joking here and reeled off a litany of feminist complaints about the inadequate work arrangements for women. I am merely pointing out here that most public and private organisations either have their own counselling facilities or can refer personnel in difficulties to the right people. I will insist that a person in a comparable position to Prince Charles in a major public or private organisation would likely have access to help and support.

15 Edmund Burke referred to the philosophers of the French Revolution in this way in many of his speeches and writings dealing with the French Revolution.

16 If 'Crawfie' was not mentioning these habits in an endearing manner, she certainly was not mentioning them as a practising psychoanalyst. If the mention of these habits had a malicious purpose then that reflects rather on 'Crawfie' than on Princess Elizabeth. In themselves the habits are no more serious than those found in most children.

17 Details of the accident and the events prior to the accident on 30 August 1997 are covered in Chapter 11.

18 Some commentators say the public are at least partly responsible. Others, as is here the case, hold the public's appetite for sensational photos entirely responsible for Diana's demise.

CHAPTER 4

1 Evidence of Prince Charles's close relationship with his sons will be given in the course of the following chapters. I will also come back to Charles and Diana's amicable agreement on the education of their sons.

2 Prince Hal of Shakespeare's *Henry V*.
The reader should keep this in mind in view of the frenzied attacks on the royal family a few days later for not wanting to change protocol. See Chapters 7-8.

3 Kay confirms this. Charles and Diana called a truce and settled among themselves how they would split the time with their children. *Diana: The Untold Story*, p. 139.

4 CR informed me that Rees-Mogg is a former editor of *The Times*.

5 See *Diana: The Untold Story*, pp. 70, 75.

6   In an authorised biography of Prince Charles by Jonathan Dimbleby, *The Prince of Wales: An Intimate Portrait*, Charles himself gives an account of his relationship with Camilla Parker Bowles. He described that relationship as 'the most intimate friendship of his life'. The Prince was introduced to then Camilla Shand in 1970. By 1972 he thought she would be the one woman for him. The relationship ended when Camilla Shand married a friend of Charles's to become Mrs Parker Bowles. The relationship resumed in the late 1970s and continued until just before Charles's engagement to Diana. Dimbleby goes on:

> *He [Charles] met Mrs Parker Bowles on only one other occasion before the wedding, when he handed her a farewell gift of a bracelet inscribed GF, for Girl Friday ...*
>
> *The Prince told Princess Diana before the wedding that he and Mrs Parker Bowles had enjoyed a close relationship, but that it was over and there would be no other woman in his life, though Princess Diana never accepted this.*
> (Serialised in the *Herald Sun*, Melbourne, 24 October 1994, p. 2.)

Prince Charles insists the third period of their relationship started in 1986 when his marriage had irretrievably broken down.

7   CR vigorously disputed this 'unreal' scenario. He thought feminists would laugh it to scorn. Undoubtedly, this brief description of a certain code of behaviour does not match the voluminous writings of feminists on gender relations. The object, however, is to give a brief account of a code of behaviour between men and women that was anchored in classical natural law thinking and which endured with varying degrees of social success through the centuries. Some of literature's greatest love stories rest on the assumptions of the traditional relationship between men and women.

8   'Pruriently' in this context does not make sense. I assume that 'prurient' is meant to describe the interest of the people in the market for photos of people like Diana.

9   CR was not aware that I am criticising one particular analysis of human rights. He thought I was denying the existence of human rights. Well, as I have said many times this mentality does not recognise an analysis of rights that deviates from theirs. In fact, it's the classical natural law analysis of rights that I am basing my arguments on.

CHAPTER 5

1   See Chapter 11 for more details of the accident.

2   Ms Hope seems to be talking about the first visit the Queen made after her coronation.

3   This is the most accurate media description of the conflict in Northern Ireland.

CHAPTER 6

1   *Death of a Princess*, Chapter 10: The Driver, pp. 139-57.

2   The word 'apology' is one of the most effective ideological weapons used by the theoretic-republican class. To force an opponent to make a public apology is to win an ideological victory at the highest level. You see, a public apology in theoretic-republican terms is not just an expression of regret that an undesirable or harmful event took place, it's not just the assuming of responsibility for past events and the undertaking to remedy the problems so that reconciliation in the community can be genuinely achieved. A public apology forced out of the theoretic-republican opponent is taken as an admission that not only was the undesirable event to be regretted but that the whole moral and social vision of the person offering the apology is forever wrong and pernicious, and that such a person adhering to that particular vision is forever outcast in the theoretic-republican realm. An apology from Prince Charles in Holden's terms (Holden is one of the bitterest opponents of the royal family) would be an act of harakiri. Indeed, Holden's talk of an apology is full of ideological presumption. There's no question in the mind of such people as Holden that Prince Charles was responsible for the break-up of the marriage. The bare facts contradict the bigoted ideas of a so-called royal reporter like Anthony Holden.

CHAPTER 7

1   **Where is our Queen? Where is her flag?** *The Sun*; **Show us you care,** *The Express. The Sun* has been one of the most virulent anti-royal family newspaper in Britain. See also Chapter 10.

CHAPTER 8

1   Edmund Burke, *Reflections on the Revolution in France*, 1790.

2   The character from the most popular American sitcom of the 1990s, 'Seinfeld'. As the characters of 'Seinfeld' often indicate themselves, George Costanza is the very paradigm of the weak-willed, self-indulgent, deceptive, cowardly male of our present time.

3   This was not an isolated event. 'Penny Junor, who wrote a biography of
the Prince [Charles] and has become a friend, recalled how Prince Harry
at a dinner party smothered his father with kisses until "in mock embarrassment, Charles begged for mercy".' *International Express*, 10-16
September 1997. Richard Kay also recounts the same occasion, *Diana: The
Untold Story*, p. 78.

CHAPTER 9

1   This is particularly damning when one considers the role Murdoch's *The
Sun* played in the unrelenting and cowardly attacks on Prince Charles and
the royal family. The following chapter will unfold the low levels of
behaviour Murdoch's minions are capable of reaching down to.

CHAPTER 10

1   Richard Kay wrote:
*But to really know Diana was to discover a woman of much greater depth and
complexity than the bitter bulimic portrayed by biographer Andrew Morton. That
is why I believe the time has come to put the record straight and correct many of
the false and destructive impressions still in circulation ten months after her death.*
Diana: The Untold Story, p. 3.

  *'If only Diana had sought proper advice about her marriage from the right
people instead of turning to that dreadful man Andrew Morton, things might
have been different,' says Nanny Clarke, talking as never before about the Princess. 'Morton got her at her most vulnerable and has tried to fossilise her in that
bleak period when she was unimaginably unhappy. She told me she bitterly regretted helping with that book. She said she wasn't her true self then but a
desperate woman searching for a way out.'* Diana: The Untold Story, p. 14.

CHAPTER 11

1   Although there are many references to Dodi Fayed by Sancton and
MacLeod in their book, *Death of a Princess*, the full sympathetic picture
of Dodi Fayed is produced in Chapter 5: Dodi, pp. 56-74.

2   *Death of a Princess*, Chapter 6: The Pharaoh of Knightsbridge, pp. 75-93.

3   *Death of a Princess*, pp. 134-5.

4   CR objected that anecdotal evidence is not proof. Again, CR unwittingly
touched on a major theme of this book: the *uncritical* acceptance that all
data and assertions, in brief, all experience, should pass a particular paradigm of theoretical and scientific scrutiny before being ratified as genuine

knowledge. Apart from creating a new 'clerical' class of supervisors in society (sociologists and the like), this view disqualifies the trustworthy product of everyday human reasoning. We continually make true and reliable decisions based on non-scientific evidence. For one thing, we do not have the time to do otherwise. I do not reject the necessity for rigorous scientific reasoning in some circumstances, but I reject the proposition that 'scientific' knowledge is the only sure and reliable form of knowledge. In this present case, the medical doctor's opinion was based on 'research' that he was familiar with. That was his point at the time. The anecdote of the alcoholic in the university bar is not meant to be conclusive. It is meant to be illustrative of the claim based on scientific evidence that drugs can affect people differently depending on their physical and psychological condition. Finally, the argument here is meant to reconcile Paul's behaviour with his *scientifically* established blood-alcohol level. The inconsistency of the Paul's behaviour with his blood-alcohol level must be resolved if the police investigation is to be brought to a satisfactory conclusion.

5 *Death of a Princess*, p. 141.

6 Sancton and MacLeod report that some staff at the Ritz knew Paul was drunk, had seen him drunk on other occasions and said that he 'appeared' to have an inclination to drink. None of these assertions are supported by names or by hard facts about Paul's *public* behaviour. It seems to be the sort of ridicule or put-down that resentful subordinates direct at their managers. On the other hand, people who identify themselves and claim to have known Paul in his various capacities give a completely different picture. Those that want to sustain the picture of Paul in public as an indulgent and indiscreet drunk have to present more concrete evidence. *Death of a Princess*, Chapter 10: The Driver, pp. 139-57.

7 *Death of a Princess*, pp. 151-2.

8 The certificate issued by the French doctor is headed: 'CERTIFICAT D'APTITUDE PHYSIQUE ET MENTALE' (Certificate of Physical and Mental Aptitude). 'Diana: Secrets Behind the Crash'.

9 *Death of a Princess*, Chapter 14: Skid Marks and Debris, pp. 210-27. The report is referenced as: D. Jean Pietri, *Accident du Passage Souterrain de l'Alma. Paris, Dimanche 31 Aout 1997, 0h25. Proposition d'Analyse Scientifique et Technique. Synthese et Conclusions.* Report commissioned by the authors, December 1997.

10 Sancton and MacLeod cover this 'troubling fact, which now defies expla-

nation', pp. 238-9. Also, no carbon monoxide was found in Dodi's blood sample ('Diana: Secrets Behind the Crash').

11 *Death of a Princess*, p. 137.

12 I have a number of important reports from *The Times, The Sunday Times* and *The Australian, Time* magazine and *Newsweek*. I also have a particularly interesting report from a Dutch magazine, *Panorama*, that draws on reports appearing in German, English and American newspapers and magazines. Most of the important information in these reports and articles is included in Sancton and MacLeod's book, plus more. Where I go outside the information provided by Sanction and MacLeod I will name the source.

13 'Etoile' is the limousine company that provides limousines for the Ritz.

14 Nobody claimed that Paul's teasing manner was that of a drunk.

15 *Death of a Princess*, p. 167. This sentence is quoted from the book, *Paparazzi*, by Rostain and Mouron, 1988.

16 'Diana: Secrets Behind the Crash' claims there were two dangerous incidents caused by the blocking tactics of the pursuing paparazzi.

17 *Death of a Princess*, p. 130.

18 It may be objected that the antidepressant drugs helped to keep Paul calm and positive. But this would support my assertion that Paul's control of the Mercedes was not affected by the cocktail of drugs discovered by the laboratory tests on his blood after the accident.

19 *Death of a Princess*, p. 132.

20 According to 'Diana: Secrets Behind the Crash' one of the bodyguards in the Ritz reported this.

21 From the TV program, 'Diana: Secrets Behind the Crash'.

22 The main points will still be drawn from the summarising account of Sancton and MacLeod.

23 *Death of a Princess*, pp. 9 & 186.

24 *Death of a Princess*, p.192.

25 *Death of a Princess*, p.187.

26 *Death of a Princess*, p.191.

27 *Death of a Princess*, p.191.

Bibliography

The most important references for Diana, Prince Charles and the royal family in
The Media of the Republic are:

Kay, Richard, *Diana: The Untold Story*, Melbourne, serialised in Sunday Sun
Herald, 1998.

Sancton, Thomas and MacLeod, Scott, *Death of a Princess: An Investigation*,
London, Weidenfeld and Nicholson, 1998.

Dimbleby, Jonathan, *The Prince of Wales: An Intimate Portrait*, Melbourne, serialised
Herald Sun, 1994.

The following books will provide the reader with an introduction to the key
philosophical ideas of the Enlightenment and the problems of rationalism:

Oakeshott, Michael. *Rationalism in politics and other essays*. London, Methuen & Co.
Ltd., 1962.

Sabine, George H., & Thorson, Thomas L., *A history of political theory* 4/E.
Hindsdale, Dryden Press, 1973.

Scruton, Roger. *A short history of modern philosophy*. London, Routledge & Kegan
Paul plc., 1981.

The most important features of classical realism and classical natural law dealt with
in *The Media of the Republic* can be found in the following original texts and
commentaries:

Aquinas, St. Thomas. *St. Thomas Aquinas politics and ethics*, trans. and ed. by Paul
Sigmund. New York, W.W. Norton & Co. Inc.,1988.

Aquinas, St. Thomas. *The political ideas of St Thomas Aquinas*, ed. by Dino
Bigongiari. New York, MacMillan Publishing Co., Inc., 1953.

Aquinas, St. Thomas. *Summa contra gentiles, books 1-4*. trans. Charles J. O'Neil.
Notre Dame, Notre Dame Press, 1975.

Augustine St. *City of God*, Trans. by Henry Bettenson. Harmondsworth, Penguin, 1972.

Augustine St. *Confessions*, trans. by R.S. Pine-Coffin. Harmondsworth, Penguin, 1961.

Copleston, SJ. Frederick C., *Aquinas*. Harmondsworth, Penguin, 1955.

Copleston, SJ. Frederick C., *A history of philosophy* vols. i-ix. New York, Doubleday, 1962/3.

Haakonssen, K. 'From natural law to the rights of man: A European perspective on American debates', Chapter 1. In K. Haakonssen and M.J. Lacey, eds. *A culture of rights: the bill of rights in philosophy, politics and law - 1791 AND 1991*. Cambridge, Cambridge University Press, 1991, pp.20-61.

Haakonssen, K. 'Natural law'. In Lawrence C. Becker, ed. & Charlotte B. Becker, assoc.ed. *Encyclopedia of ethics*. New York, Garland Publishing, Inc., 1992, pp.884-90.

Hooker, Richard. *Ecclesiastical polity: selections*. Edited with an Introduction by Arthur Pollard. Manchester, Carcanet Press, 1990.

Sigmund, Paul E. *Natural law in political thought*. Massachusetts, Winthrop Publishers Inc., 1971.

There are many references to the thoughts of Edmund Burke throughout *The Media of the Republic*. These can be found found in the following collections and commentaries on Burke's political philosophy

Burke, Edmund. *Edmund Burke on revolution*, ed. by Robert A. Smith. New York, Harper and Row, 1968.

Burke, Edmund. *The political philosophy of Edmund Burke*. Iain Hampsher-Monk ed. New York, Longman Inc., 1987.

Burke, Edmund. *Reflections on the revolution in France and on the proceedings in certain societies in London relative to that event.* edited with an introduction by Conor Cruise O'Brien. London, Penguin Books, 1968.

Burke, Edmund. *The writings and speeches of Edmund Burke, vol.viii, The French revolution, 1790-1794*, L.G. Mitchell ed. Oxford, Clarendon Press, 1989.

Burke, Edmund. *The writings and speeches of Edmund Burke, vol.ix, I: The revolutionary war, 1794-1797. II: Ireland*, R.B. McDowell ed. Oxford, Clarendon Press, 1991.

Canavan SJ, Francis P. *The political reason of Edmund Burke*. Durham, Duke University Press, 1960.

Canavan SJ, Francis P. *Edmund Burke's conception of the role of reason in politics*, The Journal of Politics, XXI (Feb. 1959), 60-79.

Macpherson, C.B. *Burke*. Oxford, Oxford University Press, 1980.

O'Brien, C.C. *The great melody*, London, Mandarin Paperbacks an imprint of Reed Consumer Books, 1993.

Stanlis, Peter. *Edmund Burke and the natural law*. Ann Arbor, 1958.

Stanlis, Peter. *Edmund Burke: the Enlightenment and revolution*. New Brunswick, Transaction Publishers, 1991.

Key ideas from the Enlightenment discussed in *The Media of the Republic* can be found in the following texts:

Descartes. *Descartes' philosophical writings*, trans. and ed. by Elizabeth Anscombe & Peter Thomas Geach. London, Thomas Nelson and Sons Ltd., 1954.

Hobbes, Thomas. *Leviathan*, Harmondsworth, Penguin Books, 1968.

Hume, David. *A treatise of human nature*. Oxford, Clarendon Press, 1978.

Locke, John. *An essay concerning human understanding*, London, William Collins & Sons and Co., Ltd., 1964.

Locke, John. *Two treatises of government*. Cambridge, Cambridge University Press, 1960.

Rousseau, Jean-Jacques. *The social contract and discourses*, trans. by G. Cole. London, J.M. Dent & Sons Ltd., 1973.